NURTURING
THE **NATIONS**

NURTURING
THE **NATIONS**

Reclaiming the Dignity of Women in
Building Healthy Cultures

Darrow L. Miller
with Stan Guthrie

Paternoster:
thinking faith

COLORADO SPRINGS • MILTON KEYNES • HYDERABAD

Paternoster Publishing
We welcome your questions and comments.

USA   1820 Jet Stream Drive, Colorado Springs, CO 80921 www.authenticbooks.com
UK   9 Holdom Avenue, Bletchley, Milton Keynes, Bucks, MK1 1QR
        www.authenticmedia.co.uk
India   Logos Bhavan, Medchal Road, Jeedimetla Village, Secunderabad 500 055, A.P.

Nurturing the Nations
ISBN-13: 978-1-934068-09-0
ISBN-10: 1-934068-09-8

Library of Congress In-Publication-Data

Miller, Darrow L.
  Nurturing the nations : reclaiming the dignity of women in building healthy cultures /
Darrow L. Miller, with Stan Guthrie.
    p. cm.
  Includes index.
  ISBN 978-1-934068-09-0
  1. Women's rights. 2. Sex discrimination against women. 3. Women--Religious aspects. 4.
Women--Social conditions--Cross-cultural studies. I. Guthrie, Stan. II. Title.
  HQ1236.M45 2007
  270.08209172'4--dc22
                                    2007041664

Cover and interior design: projectluz.com
Editorial team: Andrew Sloan, Dan Johnson

Printed in the United States of America

Dedication

This book is dedicated, with gratitude, to "Esther," Geeta, and other women of courage who stand, not with clenched fists but with broken hearts, calling the world to recognize the intrinsic worth and dignity of women. Thank you! Your passionate stories have compelled me to write this book.

Other Books by Darrow L. Miller

Discipling Nations, with Stan Guthrie (YWAM Publishing, 1998; second edition, 2001)

God's Remarkable Plan for the Nations, with Scott Allen and Bob Moffitt (YWAM Publishing, 2005)

God's Unshakable Kingdom, with Scott Allen and Bob Moffitt (YWAM Publishing, 2005)

The Worldview of the Kingdom of God, with Scott Allen and Bob Moffitt (YWAM Publishing, 2005)

Against All Hope: Hope for Africa, with Scott Allen and the African Working Group of Samaritan Strategy Africa (Disciple Nations Alliance, 2005)

The Forest in the Seed, with Scott Allen (Disciple Nations Alliance, 2006)

Contents

Acknowledgments ix

Introduction 1

PART 1: THE WAR AGAINST WOMEN

Chapter 1: Waking Up to the Pain 7

Chapter 2: A World of Abused Women 19

PART 2: THE LIE: THE ROOT OF THE PROBLEM

Chapter 3: The Framework for Examining the Issue 39

Chapter 4: The Crushing of Women 49

Chapter 5: The Disappearance of Women 69

PART 3: THE BIBLICAL FOUNDATIONS

Chapter 6: Worldview and God's Word 87

Chapter 7: The Trinity as a Model 93

Chapter 8: The Two "S" Words 105

Chapter 9: The Transcendence of Sexuality 123

Chapter 10: God's Motherly Love 139

PART 4: THE TRANSFORMING STORY

Chapter 11: The Big Story 161

Chapter 12: The Creation and the Fall 171

Chapter 13: The Dark Years and the Coming Dawn 189

Chapter 14: The Coming of the Bridegroom 205

Chapter 15: The Bride of Christ 219

Chapter 16: The Wedding of the Lamb 235

Chapter 17: God's Design for Women: Nurturers of Nations 241

Glossary	263
Subject Index	269
Biblical Reference Index	273
About the Authors	276
About Disciple Nations Alliance	277

Acknowledgments

Many people have contributed to this book—in fact, too many to name. With fear and trembling on behalf of those I may fail to honor, I want to acknowledge the following nonetheless:

Thank you, Cindy Benn, Mandie Miller, Amy Carson, Lindsay Lavery, Stephanie Shumate, Laura Robertson, and Sarah Gammill, for your day-to-day help on this project. It never would have come to the light of day without your efforts.

Stan Guthrie, thank you for your heart for the things that God has put on my heart and for your rich gift with words. You have taken my rough musings and extensive notes and turned them into a book worth reading.

To my editor, Andrew Sloan, thank you for your keen mind and questions and for helping to fine-tune our final product.

Many women have inspired me with their lives, told me their stories, engaged me in dialogue, critiqued my work, and given me their input. They have encouraged me to put my thoughts into a book. Thank you, Geeta, Soohwan Park, Elizabeth Youmans, Ana Santos, Irene Tongoi, Beatrice Langa, Anna Ho, Joanna Kim, Anu Dongardive, Wendy Davidson, Belaynesh Tadesse, Kristina Avanesyan, Heather Hicks, Jewell-Anita Hendrix, Rosaura Mesones, Patricia Cuba, Eli Oliveria, Kate Marsden, Karla Tesch, Ruth Mangalwadi,

Luki Ortiz, Beth Kanda, and Midori Yanagisawa. Thank you all for speaking into my life.

A special thanks to Yarley Nino and her team at Youth with a Mission in Puerto Rico. The work that your "kids"—Discipling Nations through the Arts (DNA)—do has inspired me, as you challenge machismo culture in Puerto Rico.

To two of my best friends, Bob Moffitt and Scott Allen, thank you for walking with me all these years. Thanks for challenging me and being a small band of brothers who love to wrestle with ideas.

I owe a dept of thanks to two friends who have been the CEOs of the organization in which I have worked since 1981. In their administrations, Randy Hoag and Greg Vestri have created a space for me to write the things that God has put on my heart. Thank you both.

To Volney James and Angela Lewis: Thank you for your willingness to publish this book. As you know, this is a book that has been on my heart for many years. Without your support, it would have limited circulation. Thanks for taking a risk with me.

A special thanks to Marilyn, the bride of my youth, my best friend, and my best critic. You have defined nurturing in the care of our children and grandchildren; through your love, compassion, and sense of humor you have nurtured your circle of friends. In your words and life, you have introduced me to the maternal heart of God. ILY!

Above all, I am in debt to the One who is both *Ish* and the Bridegroom. His creation and character help us to know the glory of female!

While many have helped, encouraged, and inspired me, any limitations and errors are mine alone.

Introduction

A number of years ago a young Korean woman stood up in a public set-ting and, with a broken heart, challenged the men and women present to consider the plight and dignity of women. Her words touched a chord within me; I was intrigued. At my suggestion we met for coffee the next day, and she asked, as is the custom in Korea, for me to suggest an "English" name for her. I immediately recommended the name Esther. Like the Esther of biblical fame, this woman had stood up for her people. After explaining this to her, I said that I wanted to be a Mordecai—to stand *with* her and *for* women.

I began asking myself the question, *What can I do to stand up for women?* In my international travels I began speaking out for the dignity of women. As people heard me speak, they encouraged me to write a book. *Nurturing the Nations* is the result. My hope and prayer is that this book will raise up legions of "Esthers" and "Mordecais" to stand with women and for their dignity.

The subtitle, *Reclaiming the Dignity of Women in Building Healthy Cultures*, responds to the lie that men are superior to women. Women are made in the image of God and therefore have intrinsic dignity and worth. This dignity is not given by men, but by God. However, women and society need to reclaim that dignity. Our world is filled with nations that are unhealthy largely because half of their people are disenfranchised. The woman's divine role of nurturing nations needs to be restored.

This is not just a book about women; it is also a book about poverty. It is a book that deals with the intersection of three seemingly very different subjects: women, poverty, and worldview. This is expressed in the following theme: One of the greatest causes of poverty in the world is based on a lie—the lie that men are superior to women.

Working since 1981 for an international relief and development organization, I have been confronted by more poverty than one could imagine. Some of the most heartbreaking poverty I have seen has been in the eyes and lives of women. In culture after culture around the world, girls, wives, sisters, mothers, and lovers suffer at the hands of those closest to them. The emotional, spiritual, and physical poverty this causes is immense. You will weep at some of the things you read. Some pages will make you angry. Others will bring you hope that something can be done to reduce the cruelty and suffering of women and to begin to restore their God-given dignity.

My immediate hope for this book is that it will prick the consciences of both men and women and that a generation of "Mordecais" and "Esthers" would be raised up to defend the dignity of women. Are you willing to be one of them?

The larger goal is to see cultural stories transformed from the demeaning of women to the honoring of women, so that through women's divine work healthy nations will be built and nurtured.

This book has four major segments:

In part 1, "The War against Women," I will share my personal awakening to the pain of women's suffering; then we will take a view, from 40,000 feet, of the abuse of women around the world, examining the fruit of misogyny.

In part 2, "The Lie: The Root of the Problem," we will focus on the root of misogyny by examining the framework for analyzing the problem. We will establish this framework by looking at three visions for what humankind is, which in turn influence a proponent's view of women. Since framework is established in the power of our cultural stories, we will then look at how sexism crushes women and how radical feminism calls for women's disappearance.

In part 3, "The Biblical Foundations," we will examine five broad biblical themes that will help to frame our response to the lie. First, we will study the principles of biblical interpretation that will guide our examination. Second, we will explore how the unity/diversity of the Trinity proves the model for our social theory that women are not inferior to men. Next, we will examine two concepts that the world sees as vices but that the kingdom of God identifies as virtues: service and submission. Fourth, we will consider our sexuality—discovering that it is more than mere plumbing, but rather is a reflection of our transcendent nature. Lastly, we will see that the very structure of the female body reveals the *maternal* heart of God.

In part 4, "The Transforming Story," we will examine the metanarrative, or "big story," of the Bible that casts a vision of women born in the mind of God and hallowing the halls of eternity as the bride of Christ. We will see that the Scriptures begin and end with *the nuptial*. Starting at creation, we will see that humankind, male and female, was created in a Trinitarian pattern of unity and diversity. Our in-depth look at the Fall will reveal the distortion of male-female relationships leading to the depreciation and degradation of women. We will then visit the depths of sin in the Hebrew nation to see the rise of sexism in the spirit of Baal. Turning to the New Testament, we will discover that Jesus was the first feminist. He challenged both his Jewish culture's and the larger Greco-Roman culture's understanding of women. Next, we will follow the birth of the church, and the faint shadow of the coming glorious bride of Christ. As we come to the end of the book, we will study the image of the wedding of the Lamb as the nuptial that consumes all of human history. The book ends with the profound reality that "the hand that rocks the cradle is the hand that rules the world"!

Because of the unusual scope of the book, I am writing to a number of groups. One group is composed of Christians who work among the poor. These may include missionaries, relief and development workers, social workers, volunteers, church and organizational leaders, and other spiritual leaders. My hope is that they may find, in these pages, biblical foundations for ministering to and building communities that respect women.

A second group would include anyone who may have a professional interest in women's issues and needs. This may include Christian and non-Christian social workers, medical workers, therapists, counselors, educators, clergy, and mentors.

A third group is made up of all Christians who need to be awakened to the neglect and injustice toward women around the world, sometimes even in the name of Christianity. The church is God's primary instrument for social transformation, and thus the church needs to be awakened to the abuse of women both inside and outside its walls so that it can be used of God to bring healing to this most personal form of brokenness.

A fourth group consists of non-Christians interested in poor and abused women. These readers can learn about a biblical view of women, gaining new insights and perhaps redeeming their opinions about abuses of women in Christianity. They can also learn of God's love for all women, inside and outside the church.

The final group is composed of women in general who are interested in studying their role in society. These women can learn about their biblical roles and develop personal responses to them.

We are in the midst of a great struggle for language and ultimately for the very fabric of what it means to be human, to be a family, to be married, and, ultimately, to build a godly nation. Friends may differ in this debate, but in the end the disagreement must be handled with civility and clarity. Civility means that we must never demean another person or position; we must treat each other with respect as fellow human beings and as brothers and sisters in Christ. Clarity means that we must seek clear meaning and distinctions, not blurring the issues for the sake of unity. It is with this tone that I have sought to write this book.

We are all in process. Since God broke my heart and opened my eyes to the pervasiveness of this lie, I have been on a journey to be a Mordecai, to stand with and stand up for my sisters. I invite you to join me on this journey by keeping your mind open to the working of the Holy Spirit as you read. I hope that by the end of this book you will be as fired up with righteous anger over the mistreatment of women as I am and will move into the world with a mission to right this wrong.

PART 1

THE WAR
AGAINST WOMEN

CHAPTER 1

Waking Up to the Pain

This book is about the dignity of women. Though I have been happily married since 1966 to a strong and intelligent woman, my professional and personal sensitization to this issue began in 1980 while driving down the main street in Flagstaff, Arizona, where I lived. A radio preacher was talking about Christian marriage, pondering the meaning of Genesis 2:24: "And they will become one flesh." The preacher asked, "How can the *two* become *one?*" After a moment, he answered his own question: "Only if the woman becomes a *zero. One* plus *zero* equals *one!*"

A feeling of revulsion whelmed up from the core of my being. How could any Christian so diminish the wonder of a woman made in the image of God?

This diminution of women is not just an American problem, of course. A few years later, I began traveling to South Korea to train volunteers about worldview issues at the Korea Food for the Hungry International office in Seoul. (Food for the Hungry is an international relief and development organization.) During my second visit, a young woman who had been in the first training program came to me for counseling. She said she was in love with a young Korean man who had asked her to marry him. But rather than bringing her a sense of joy and anticipation, the proposal had brought a sense of dread.

She explained how Korean men change after they get married. She described a Confucian concept known as *namjon yobi*, which is variously translated as "men high, women low" or "men are honored, women are despised." Then this woman went on to tell me how Korean men treat their wives. Her father had demeaned her mother for so many years that it drove the poor woman to suicide.

Then the young woman asked me plaintively, "What should I do? I love my boyfriend, but I am so afraid of what he will become because he is a Korean man!"

My heart was broken for this young woman, and inside I wept for her dilemma. As I continued to travel overseas, I heard more and more stories like this. They emerged from demeaning attitudes and abusive actions toward women, from both Christians and non-Christians.

In January 1997 I was flying to Korea to help my good friend Moses Kim facilitate a conference for more than six hundred students and young people. On the flight, an article in the *New York Times* caught my attention. The piece, by Sheryl WuDunn, bylined Seoul, was titled "Korean Women Still Feel Demands to Bear a Son."[1] It told the story of a young Korean woman, Lee Young Sun. Young Sun and her husband already had one child, a daughter, when she found that she was pregnant for a second time. She secretly visited her doctor to confirm the pregnancy and to discover the sex of her second child. The doctor said that she would bear another daughter.

Young Sun talked with her husband, who told her, in no uncertain terms, that if she were to deliver another child, it had to be a boy. Getting the message, Mrs. Lee aborted her unborn baby girl.

My eyes filled with tears. I thought, *O Lord, how can this be? If female babies are so despised in Korean society that they are killed, how must this young mother feel as a woman? What must life be like for Young Sun in a society that so hates females?*

Through my tears, I continued to read. WuDunn noted that misogyny is common across Asia. "South Korea has 30,000 fewer girls born each year than would be the case if there were no such abortions," WuDunn said. "That compares with 330,000 born each year, suggesting that about one female fetus[2] in twelve is aborted because of sex. China, India, and other countries are also discovering that expectant mothers are aborting female fetuses, resulting in shortages of women and girls in society."

For years I had personally seen profound mistreatment of women. But in these moments alone on the plane I grasped the profoundly shocking truth that there is nothing less than a worldwide holocaust of females going on: the killing of preborn baby girls, of born baby girls, and the abuse and murder of women. If it can occur in South Korea, where a third of the population claims to follow the teachings of Christ, then it can and does happen everywhere.

Feeling brokenhearted, I landed in South Korea. Later that week, I was invited by the staff of the organization that was hosting the conference to a question-and-answer time. There were perhaps forty of us sitting in a large circle on the floor of a basement meeting room. A woman in her late twenties spoke first, saying, "I hate being a woman in Korea." Her words rang in my ears and stung my soul; I did not even hear her question. As she sat down, I asked her why she felt that way.

Thus began a most remarkable and painful experience. As she told her story, she began to weep. Within a few minutes, the other women were quietly weeping. After she finished, another woman spoke, then another. Their broken hearts were exposed and the deep-seated pain in their lives was revealed. The men in the room began to hang their heads in shame. They were hearing, many for the first time, the brokenness that their words and deeds had wrought on their sisters. After forty-five minutes, the wounded spirit was fully manifested in the room. But there seemed to be no spirit of contrition on the part of the men—only, perhaps, a certain sadness.

More weeping and brokenness emerged from the women as we prayed. Then one of the men prayed, "Lord, let women be released into leadership." I could hear nothing else after these words, as anger flooded over me. These men believed all would be solved if only the women were given something "important" to do. These Christian men were mostly blind to what they had done to hurt their sisters in the Lord. They also were blind to the biblical truth that a woman has worth in her *being*, in her very existence, in her personhood. They also apparently did not appreciate all the tasks these women were already doing. They thought that only by doing one particular thing—"leading"—does a person have value.

My mind whirled. *Where is the prayer of repentance, the repentance of the men for their attitudes and depreciation of women? Where is the prayer of thanksgiving to God for the most precious gift of women? Where is the prayer of wonder for the female counterpart, for their simply being women? Where is the prayer of gratitude for a woman's doing?*

After Moses and I returned to our accommodations, we read through the questions submitted by the students at the conference. The first reinforced for me that God was doing something we hadn't planned. From a young man, it read: "Do you think that men and women are equal? Exactly equal? Genesis 3:16 says that your husband will govern you. I have a girlfriend. I love my girlfriend. What does this mean? Are we equal? Am I going to govern her?"

The second question was from a young woman. A long one, it read:

> I have a question about the women's role and station in the family, in the church, and in society. You said that ideas produce consequences. I would like to tell you some consequences about women, especially their work. Let me tell you about their work in a family. In our country [in the past], women did all the housework, washing the dishes, cooking, cleaning, washing the clothes, and carrying all the babies. And also they did farming. In the morning, the women got up early to prepare the breakfast. After all the family ate it, she cleaned the house and went out to farm. She would work all day in the farm and then she would come home, fix the dinner, put the children to bed, clean all the dishes, clean the house.
>
> Things are changing in Korea. Now women don't go to the farm, they go to the office. But they do everything before they go to the office and after they come home from the office. I want to know how God thinks about this problem and the poor woman. And I also have a confidence that it's not a personal problem, but a social, structural, and historical problem.

Moses and I sensed that God wanted us to set aside our agenda. So on Thursday morning we announced that we were going to deal with male-female relationships. God met with us. It was one of the most profound days of my life. The animated small-group discussion, the confession, the repentance and forgiveness, and, finally, the worship all contributed to this day being one I will never forget.

I began to call the young woman who had made the opening statement at the Q&A time by the English name Esther (many Korean Christians adopt biblical names), because of her courage, like that of the biblical Esther, to stand up for "her people"—other women. I could only pray that God would make me a Mordecai, an advocate and encourager of women.

The Theme

This is not just a book about women. It is a book about ideas. The ideas we harbor in the deep recesses of our souls have influence that goes far beyond our individual lives and families. They can create either healthy societies or impoverished ones. They can build or destroy nations. This book seeks to address a deceitful idea that, to one extent or another, has infected every culture, with disastrous consequences for all of us: *Men are superior to women.*

In my previous book, *Discipling Nations: The Power of Truth to Transform Cultures*,[3] Stan Guthrie and I made the case that of the planet's three major worldviews—theism, animism, and secularism—only the first provides the intellectual and spiritual capital for healthy societies and human development. And yet, as the examples in this introduction sadly demonstrate, too often Christians have bought into the lie.

Of course, the early church, heeding Christ's revolutionary example,[4] became a bastion of hope for women. Knowing they would be treated with respect as women, they fled the misogynistic paganism of ancient Rome, seeking the respect proffered by the body of Christ, in which "there is neither. . . male nor female" (Galatians 3:28). Throughout history, as Christians have followed the words and life of Jesus Christ, their obedience has brought freedom to women. To take just one example, William Carey, the late-eighteenth- to early nineteenth-century British missionary to India, was instrumental in bringing to an end the brutal Hindu practice of widow burning.

But the church, sadly, has not always heeded Christ in its treatment of women. Too often the church has supported—and still supports—the status quo of sexist culture, justifying and participating in the inhuman treatment of women. Seeing the injustice, a growing percentage of Christian women's advocates have sought, inadvertently, to side with the male values of sexism.

While they affirm the dignity and worth of women, they have ended up calling for women *to become like men*. This is the call of radical feminism. (We will examine this flawed approach in more detail later.)

This book, however, seeks a middle way, rejecting sexism in all its forms as well as the pseudosolution of feminism. Are we to waste our lives by simply acceding to the norms of our culture? Or will we make trouble in our world? Will we live lives worthy of the trust and grace that God has invested in us?

We will examine how women and families are viewed from the perspective of three fundamental paradigms and two compromising paradigms. These each create distinct visions of what it means to be a woman.

Three Fundamental Paradigms

- The first paradigm, *atomism*, believes in *absolute diversity*, with no unity. Atomism values maleness and is expressed in all forms of *sexism*. Sexism, in turn, leads to the *crushing* of women.
- The second paradigm, *monism*, believes in *absolute unity*, with no diversity. The Hindu belief that "all reality is one" perfectly captures this paradigm. It exalts androgyny. This paradigm is expressed in *radical feminism*. In practice, this approach leads to the *disappearance* of women.
- The third paradigm, *Trinitarianism*, believes in a middle way—*community*—reflecting the unity and diversity of the Godhead. This paradigm, grounded in orthodox Christian theology, values both female and male and finds its expression in *complementarianism*. Trinitarianism, when rightly understood, leads to the *dignity* of women.

Two Compromising Paradigms

Of course, people—including Christians—do not always perfectly live out their paradigms. Nor do they always follow such clear, textbook definitions. In the real world, people sometimes pick and choose their philosophies or even combine them according to their desires or needs. In this book we will look at two compromises to the three fundamental paradigms individuals employ in their attitudes and treatment of women.

The first, *chauvinism*, attempts to find a compromise between atomism and Trinitarianism. Like atomism, chauvinism, as the name implies, leads to the *crushing* of women.

The second, *egalitarianism*, is an attempted compromise between monism and Trinitarianism. Unfortunately, like monism, egalitarianism leads to the *disappearance* of women.

The Challenge

If all the antiwoman paradigms and compromises are based on the deep-seated but false idea that men are superior to women, then clearly the solution must also reach down to the level of worldview. All the money in the world will not stop the violence against women and the breakdown of the family. New laws, without transformed lives, will only lead to more police and more prisons. The root of the problem is in the lie, in a counterfeit metanarrative. We need to change societies' perceptions of women and families.

We need a new metanarrative. We need God's story. When told and believed, this idea will create a new backdrop for people's lives, a backdrop that will bring the dignity of and respect for women for which they have been made.

Overview

This book has four major segments: "The War against Women" (which will examine the fruit of misogyny), "The Lie" (which will examine the root of misogyny), "The Biblical Foundations" (which will examine the metanarrative of the Bible), and "The Transforming Story" (which will examine God's design for women).

My primary audience is people—both women and men—who have been called to work among the poor as missionaries, relief and development workers, social workers, pastors, and church leaders. My secondary audience is feminists, including *first-wave feminists* (maternal feminists who long to understand their calling as homemakers and mothers), *second-wave feminists* (modern feminists who have gnawing doubts that perhaps they have bought a bill of goods in believing that motherhood is bad and a woman's worth is found in the marketplace), and *third-wave feminists* (postmodern feminists who have accepted androgyny's illusion of neutered sexuality and who are longing for reality).

Language

These are obviously sensitive, and often hotly contested, issues. The words one uses—words like *mankind* and *brothers*, for example—can spark a debate by themselves. That's not surprising. We are in the midst of a great struggle for language. But the struggle is really about much more, including such basic issues as what it means to be a human being, to be a family, to be married, and to build a godly nation.

Venturing into this superheated atmosphere is not for the faint-hearted. I seek to speak as a friend to friends—or at least to potential friends. Friends may disagree in this debate, but our disagreement must be characterized by civility and clarity: the former because we are fellow human beings and the latter because precision and understanding are vital if we are to move the discussion forward.

In that spirit, what words are appropriate for this book? Do we say *man* and *mankind* or the more neutral *humankind?* Do we use *he* when we mean *he or she?* What about *they* or *them* instead of *he/she* or *him/her?*

Sensitivity to the dignity and intrinsic worth of women is important, and I don't want to raise red flags unnecessarily. But we also must understand that language is a reflection of a culture's worldview. Language is not neutral. One sociological maxim states: "Before you change a society, you must first change the language of the society." Whether we know it or not, the war for the heart and soul of nations begins with language. We have certainly seen linguistic evidence of such a war in the West.

Missionary hero Elisabeth Elliot notes: "Words like *manhood* and *masculinity* have been expunged from our vocabulary, and we have been told in no uncertain terms that we ought to forget about such things, which amount to nothing more than biology, and concentrate on what it means to be 'persons.'"[5]

Keith Windschuttle shows how language has shifted from the word *sex*, which has biological (male and female) and transcendent (masculine and feminine) distinctives, to the word *gender*, which became a malleable, fluid term that allows for gender reassignment and interchangeability of sexual roles and functions. "*Gender* is a term that reeks of the sexual politics of the Seventies. It made its first appearance when gay activists began to demand that homosexuality be not merely tolerated but given equal standing with heterosexuality in all things. It was reinforced by feminists who wanted to eliminate the differences between men and women."[6]

This change in language reflects a change of worldview. Not only that, it has become concretized in the laws of a society. Windschuttle writes, "What this means is that the word *gender*, which until recent years was little more than a politically fashionable substitute for *sex*, has now been enshrined in legislation."[7]

Until the twentieth century, the word *man* meant *imago Dei* (the "image of God," a biblical concept) and was understood to include both female and male. Unfortunately, this understanding is eroding as many people see this kind of language as a throwback to primitive, patriarchal times. But I contend that this language usage comes not from male chauvinists, but from God. As such, we have no right to jettison it. Instead, we have the responsibility to understand and follow it.

As maternal feminist and author Mary A. Kassian writes, "It is God's right to name Himself, the world and the people He has created. . . . It is from *Him*—not psychology, sociology, anthropology or any other human science—that we gain a proper framework for understanding ourselves, our world, and God Himself."[8]

So let's briefly examine the record. Genesis 1:26–27 states: "Then God said, 'Let us make *man* in *our image*, in our likeness, and let them rule over the fish of the sea and the birds of the air, over the livestock, over all the earth, and over all the creatures that move along the ground.' So God created man in his own image, in the image of God he created him; *male* and *female* he created them" (emphasis added).

The Hebrew word *adam* makes clear that *man* is a generic term covering both the male and the female of the human species. The term does not mean male only. It means "human being" or "humankind." The word *man* reflects the unity of all human beings. "Male and female" reflect the diversity of humankind. *Man* means all of the human family, female or male, child or adult, young or old, healthy or infirm, wealthy or poor, black or white.

"Our image" demonstrates the unity of all human beings. Every human being, both male and female, is made in the image of God.

The text also shows us that while male and female are equal in their humanity, they are also diverse in their sexual identity. The word for male in Hebrew is *zakar*; the word for female in Hebrew is *neqebath*. Note that the words for *male* and *female* do not have the same root, thus reflecting the diversity of humankind.

We understand that the male *procreates*—"to beget, to generate and produce, and to engender"—while the female *conceives*—"to receive into the womb." These are basic differences that reflect the roots of our sexuality. These differences are not merely physical, but reflect differences in our transcendent natures.

Yet male and female are neither merely equal nor merely diverse. They are *complementary*. In Genesis 2, God reveals his eternal purpose to create families. Two new words are introduced in verse 23: *man* (Hebrew *ish*) and *woman* (Hebrew *ishshah*). Note that the word for woman here is derived from the word for man—not from *adam,* the generic word for man, or humankind. This reveals the common source and complementary nature of woman and man.

Figure 1: Hebrew to English Translations

Generic Term	"Man" - *imago Dei* - Humankind	
Transcendent Nature	Masculine	Feminine
Sexual Nature	*zakar* - Male	*neqebath* - Female
"Complementary Nature" Man/Husband and Woman/Wife	*ish* - Male	*ishshah* - Female

In English, according to the 1828 Webster's Dictionary,[9] *woman* is a compound of "womb" and "man." The idea is that a woman is the female of the human race, grown to adult years. A woman is a "man with a womb." Thus, there are two types of human beings:

- men with a womb
- men without a womb

God has designated both male and female to be *imago Dei.* Both male and female are "man." Because God has the right to do this, I will use the following terms interchangeably: humankind, *imago Dei,* man, and mankind.

Now, in the spirit of civility and clarity, let's move ahead.

Notes

1. Sheryl WuDunn, "Korean Women Still Feel Demands to Bear a Son," *New York Times,* January 1, 1997.

2. Here WuDunn uses a technically correct word to describe what a woman carries in her womb. However, the more accurate word is *baby.* For generations what a woman has carried in her womb has been referred to as a *baby.* Modern sensibilities have led us to use the term *fetus,* thus softening the language and making it easier to abort babies—and, in the case of this story, for Koreans to abort 30,000 precious baby girls each year. As human beings we should weep for the loss of the lives of these baby girls—as well as for their mothers, in particular, and the women of these societies, in general, in which being female is so despised.

3. Darrow L. Miller, *Discipling Nations: The Power of Truth to Transform Cultures* (Seattle: YWAM Publishing, 1998; second edition, 2001).

4. Christ's revolutionary example will be developed in chapter 14.

5. Elisabeth Elliot, "The Essence of Femininity: A Personal Perspective," in *Recovering Biblical Manhood and Womanhood: A Response to Evangelical Feminism,* John Piper and Wayne Grudem, eds. (Wheaton: Crossway, 1991), 394.

6. Keith Windschuttle, "Language Wars," *Quadrant* (May 2004); http://www.sydneyline.com/Language%20Wars.htm.

7. Ibid.

8. Mary A. Kassian, *The Feminist Gospel: The Movement to Unite Feminism With the Church* (Wheaton: Crossway, 1992), 242–43 (italics in the original).

9. The reason that I so often use the 1828 Webster's Dictionary is that, unlike many modern dictionaries, it was consciously written from a biblical worldview.

CHAPTER 2
A World of Abused Women

At a conference in Rwanda about men's attitudes toward women, one of the participants proclaimed, without shame, that in his culture "real men beat their wives!" When I later shared his proclamation in Kenya with a group of African relief and development workers, laughter rippled through the room. I asked the men why they were laughing. They acknowledged, "This is true in Kenya, as well!"

Apparently it is true in many areas of the world. A Korean proverb says, "Dried fish and women are both better after they are beaten." *New York Times* columnist Nicholas D. Kristof tells an all-too-typical story in his article "Do Korean Men Still Beat Their Wives? Definitely":

> Asked if he had beaten his wife, Lee Un Kee straightened himself in indignation and the warm sparkle suddenly left his eyes, leaving them as chilly and harsh as the wind gusting through this farming village.
>
> "I was married at 28, and I'm 52 now," Mr. Lee declared icily. "How could I have been married all these years and not beaten my wife?"
>
> He paused, looked down the dirt road that cuts through this little hamlet of tile-roofed homes 30 miles northwest of Seoul, and added that it is sometimes unhealthy to suppress the urge.

"I would hit her, and she would grab on to me, and then I would go out and drink and calm down," said Mr. Lee, who farms a rice paddy beside the village.

"For me, it's better to release that anger and get it over with," Mr. Lee said. "Otherwise, I just get sick inside."[1]

This is going to be a depressing chapter, but a necessary one. All across the world, men—and women—believe the lie that men are superior to women. Because ideas have consequences and because we live in a fallen world, the outworking of this lie is a world of abused and mistreated women. Let us stare this evil in the face.

Every Culture

In 1990, Harvard economist and Nobel Prize laureate Amartya Sen shocked the world with his claim that there were 100 million "missing women." They weren't really *missing*, of course. They were *dead*. Prejudice against females had killed them. Sen wrote: "In view of the enormity of the problems of women's survival in large parts of Asia and Africa, it is surprising that these disadvantages have received such inadequate attention. The numbers of 'missing women' in relation to the numbers that could be expected if men and women received similar care in health, medicine, and nutrition, are remarkably large. A great many *more than a hundred million women are simply not there* because women are neglected compared with men."[2]

While the West generally treats women better than the rest of the world, it is safe to say that there is no culture that treats women with the same integrity as men. For the most part, life in every culture is lived out against the backdrop of the supposed superiority of maleness. In areas where sexism reigns, this attitude leads to the *crushing* of women.

The female child is often unwanted before birth and aborted. If she survives her mother's womb, she faces neglect and malnourishment. Frequently denied an education and health care, she often becomes a child laborer. She may be molested, raped, sold into prostitution, or married at an unconscionably young age. Malnourishment is common, even while she is pregnant. Overworked and underappreciated, she may be beaten or humiliated by her husband or other men, even to the point of murder. If not, she could be abandoned as a widow, forced to scratch out a living on the outskirts of society, with no family or social safety net to provide for her.

The justice system often turns its back. In some places there are no laws to protect women.

Other times the abusers simply walk away, unpunished. The church, which should be the first institution to defend women, is too often apathetic, even complicit, in the war against women.

Domestic Violence

Domestic violence is a universal phenomenon. It transcends racial and ethnic boundaries, education and economic levels, and religion. Mostly perpetrated by men, it is a means to exercise power and control.

Worldwide, an estimated 25–50 percent of adult women have been victims of domestic violence.[3] In Pakistan, an estimated 70–90 percent of women have been abused by their husbands.[4] Half of all females murdered in Bangladesh were killed at home.[5] Some 30 percent of all women killed in the United States were murdered by their boyfriend, husband, or ex-husband.[6] Domestic violence is the number one health risk for American women between the ages of fifteen and forty-five.[7] In Brazil, 80 percent of the murders of women and 70 percent of rapes are done by husbands, relatives, or "friends."[8] A survey of a hundred women in one Cairo suburb found that 30 percent were beaten every day and that 34 percent were beaten once a week.[9]

In parts of South Asia, women's faces are cut or disfigured by acid as punishment and to make them undesirable to other men. In Bangladesh, acid attacks disfigure 2,200 women every year.[10]

Sexual Violence

In some cases, physical violence turns to sexual violence. Rape is not merely an assault on a woman's body. It is an attack on her soul, her personhood, her dignity, and her identity. The impact of rape on her inside will last longer than the scars on the outside. Depression, an inability to risk giving herself wholly to another person, loss of trust in men, and other psychological problems can result.

Worldwide, according to the United Nations Children's Fund, between one in five and one in seven women will be raped in their lifetime.[11] The situations in which rape can occur are horrifyingly numerous.

Rape is often used as a weapon of war, particularly in situations of ethnic cleansing. Many of the wars in sub-Saharan Africa are marked by wanton rape of girls and young women. This not only terrorizes the population into submission, but it is a means to ethnically "cleanse" a tribe by producing a generation of babies from the dominating group. While rape as an act of war has happened throughout history, in recent years it has been documented in seven countries, not all of them African.[12]

Bintu lived the normal life of a nine-year-old child in Sierra Leone until civil war broke out in her country. Raiding her village, a rebel commander nicknamed "Bullet" took Bintu as his "wife." She was forced to travel with the rebels for several years. When Bullet died, his bodyguard, "Forty Barrel," became Bintu's "husband." This man raped her repeatedly, even using foreign objects. The abuse eventually caused Bintu to develop a fistula—"a hole from her vagina to her bladder and rectum. As a result, Bintu constantly leaked urine and feces."[13]

Besides the other horrors associated with rape, this brutality also furthers the spread of the AIDS pandemic in Africa. "During the genocide of 1994, Hutu militia groups and the Rwandan military regularly used rape and other sexual violence as weapons in their genocidal campaign against the Tutsi community," *Human Rights Watch* reports. "Although the exact number of rapes that occurred in Rwanda may never be known, testimonies in [a] 104-page report confirm that rape was extremely widespread and that women were individually raped, gang-raped, raped with objects such as sharpened sticks or gun barrels, held in sexual slavery or sexually mutilated."[14]

In South Africa, a widespread rumor holds that a man who has sex with a virgin will be protected from AIDS. Needless to say, this folktale has brought devastation to the lives of young girls. The world's militaries can be a source of devastation to women, as well. During World War II, Japan used Korean women as "comfort women" to improve the morale of their soldiers. Even today, South Korea has so-called rest and relaxation centers where Philippine and Russian women serve and "entertain" U.S. troops. While some of this may be a "simple business transaction," for many it is forced prostitution.[15]

Pornography

The multibillion-dollar pornography business is another pernicious source of exploitation. In much of the world, sexuality has been divorced from its moral and spiritual moorings. With the rise of secularism in the West, sex has become recreational and a spectator sport. With the rise of the Internet, pornography has been mainstreamed and easily accessible and is often seen as a legitimate entertainment option.

While Hollywood produces four hundred feature films per year, the porn studios produce eleven thousand a year.[16] America's pornography industry, which rakes in $10 billion to $14 billion a year, has become one of the most flush and fast growing in the country, one journalist comments. "It outpaces the combined revenues of all the professional football, baseball, and basketball franchises—and it outruns the take at all the nation's movie box offices."[17]

Rather than being a harmless pastime and an example of free speech in action, pornography ultimately dehumanizes women and the men who lust after them. It also creates a fantasy world that no real woman can match. This leads to the destruction of marriage.

With the rise of the Internet, access to pornography has skyrocketed, with approximately 28,258 Internet users viewing Internet pornography every second, choosing from over 4.2 million possible pornographic websites.[18] They are referred to in the literature as "cybersex compulsive." This private compulsion has ugly results in society. Many experts believe that it destroys marriages and leads to sex crimes, sex trafficking, and violence against women.

James Dobson of Focus on the Family interviewed Ted Bundy, one of America's most brutal serial killers. Bundy stated that the "most damaging kinds of pornography are those that involve violence and sexual violence. Because the wedding of those two forces, as I know only too well, brings about behavior that is just too terrible to describe."[19]

Prostitution

Pornography fuels prostitution, the sex trade, child prostitution, and sex tourism. Martin Dawes, the South Asia regional spokesman for UNICEF, has stated that from Bangladesh about 300,000 women and children have been trafficked to India and about 200,000 to Pakistan. In addition between 100,000 and 200,000 Nepali women and girls are said to be working in India's sex industry.[20] Even in North America, an estimated 300,000 children were involved in prostitution ten years ago.[21]

Prostitution, whatever popular culture may say, is violence against women. The Coalition Against Trafficking in Women says that "prostitution victimizes all women, justifies the sale of any woman, and reduces all women to sex."[22]

Unbelievably, the United Nations Convention on the Elimination of All Forms of Discrimination against Women calls for all signatory nations to recognize that prostitution is a "career choice."[23] Senator Hillary Clinton, supposedly a strong advocate for women, wants "sex workers" to be recognized as part of a legitimate profession.[24] Thankfully, not everyone thinks that way.

The Hudson Institute's Michael Horowitz notes, "The real fight today is between those who believe that prostitution inherently victimizes women and those who believe that the answer is some combination of ergonomic standards for mattresses and minimum wages."[25]

Sex Trafficking

Sex trafficking is another name for slavery. Worldwide, approximately 2.5 million females a year are forced into this bondage.[26] Even in the United States, between fifty thousand and seventy thousand girls and women are sex slaves.[27] It costs traffickers $16,000 to place each Asian woman in American brothels.[28]

Most victims are very young. The average age ranges from preteen to early teen. Doctors Without Borders states, "In Cambodia, 5 year olds are forced to perform oral sex on clients; girls as young as 10 are penetrated."[29] As many as ten thousand children between the ages of six and fourteen are enslaved in brothels in Sri Lanka.[30]

Bride Trafficking

In China, because of the one-child policy and because of a cultural preference for boys, there are now 111 million men who will not be able to find a wife.[31] The problem is so acute that a thriving slave trade in brides has developed. "The thirst for women is so acute that the slave trader gangs are even reaching outside of China to find merchandise. There are regular reports of women being abducted in such places as northern Vietnam to feed the demand in China."[32]

In Afghanistan, fathers sell their young daughters as brides so they can feed their starving families.[33]

Sex Tourism

This form of abuse involves men, from such places as the United States, Japan, and Europe, traveling to another country (usually in Asia, Latin America, or Eastern Europe) to have sex with young women and children.

Unscrupulous companies, enticing buyers via the Internet and other media, put together packaged tours covering airfare, ground transportation, accommodations at a nice hotel, and the buyer's choice of a "companion." Such activities appeal to older men who are looking for sexual companionship and who are willing to travel to places where they are not known. Sex tours allow them to escape the social constraints they might find at home with prostitutes or in having sex with young girls.

Many men falsely believe that sexually transmitted diseases are less likely when having sex with a younger girl. However, the Office of the United Nations High Commissioner for Human Rights states that "children in prostitution are at greater risk of contracting the virus than adults," and thus the idea that that having sex with younger partners is safer is a myth.[34]

Forced Sterilization

Women in poor areas of the world also face sterilization at the insistence of bureaucrats seeking to eliminate societal problems such as poverty and poor education.

Margaret Sanger, a leader of the American eugenics movement and founder of the American Birth Control League (which eventually became Planned Parenthood), provided the rationale for forced sterilizations in her book, *The Pivot of Civilization*. She argued that poverty and sexual relations are linked. Sanger talked of the poor as "of the inferior classes"[35] and "choking human undergrowth."[36] Such ideas have taken hold, even if the vocabulary hasn't.

When a government team held a "ligation festival" to register women for sterilization in La Legua, Peru, Celai Durand resisted.

> According to Mrs. Durand's now-widowed husband, Jaime, the 31-year-old mother of three was appalled at pressure tactics government health workers used to induce women to have tubal ligations. Not only did they go house-to-house to round up candi-dates, but they paid repeated visits to those who refused to comply. Mr. Durand says they reassured his wife that the operation was "simple and quick," adding that she could "go dancing" the same night.
>
> Even though Mrs. Durand knew that the local health station was equipped with little more than an examination table, pressure from government health workers finally wore her down. On July 4, 1997, she reluctantly underwent surgery. Two weeks later, she died from complications.[37]

Unfortunately, such incidents are far from uncommon in developing countries. Consider these facts:

- In Vietnam, more than 31,000 women underwent quinacrine sterilizations between 1989 and 1993.[38]
- The Peruvian government began a public health sterilization program in 1995. By 1997, about 110,000 women were sterilized.[39]
- Between 1965 and 1971, approximately 1 million women in Brazil were sterilized.[40]
- "Lee Brightman, United Native Americans President, estimates that of the Native population of 800,000 (in the US), as

many as 42 percent of the women of childbearing age and 10 percent of the men . . . have been sterilized. . . . The first official inquiry into the sterilization of Native women . . . by Dr. Connie Uri . . . reported that 25,000 Indian women had been permanently sterilized within Indian Health Services facilities alone through 1975."[41]

Abortion

Since 1973, when *Roe v. Wade* legalized abortion on demand, abortion has been a perennial political issue in the United States. Abortion-rights supporters frame the debate in terms of a woman's "right to choose," asserting that denying a woman this freedom is tantamount to denying her humanity. Many people have succumbed to this argument. There have been over 40 million abortions since 1973, or about 4,000 a day.[42]

The toll from abortion, which is the deliberate killing of developing human life in the womb, is far higher in other parts of the world. Globally, about 46 million abortions take place per year (126,000 a day), 78 percent of which occur in developing countries. Incredibly, 20 million of those abortions occur in countries where abortion is illegal or restricted. The worldwide lifetime average is about one abortion per woman.[43]

God designed a woman's womb to be the safest place in the world. Sadly, this place of compassion has become one of the most dangerous places in the world. Pro-life feminist Frederica Mathewes-Green writes: "In a culture that treats pregnancy and childbearing as impediments, it [abortion] surgically adapts the woman to fit in. If women are an oppressed group, they are the only such group to require surgery in order to be equal. In Greek mythology, Procrustes was an exacting host: if you were the wrong size for his bed, he would stretch or chop you to fit. The abortion table is modern feminism's Procrustean bed, one that, in a hideous twist, its victims actually march in the streets to demand."[44]

Abortion, which promises women freedom, is simply another tool of male domination. Here the unity of masculine values over feminine values forces women to be like men. Abortion reflects a value system that respects women only when they can compete with men within the workplace. An empty womb allows a woman to do that.

Because men do not have to be pregnant, abortion-rights supporters believe it is unfair for women to be "forced" to carry a baby to term. Becoming un-pregnant, however, carries a heavy price, not only for the unborn in the womb but also for the woman who makes this deadly "choice." Abortion denies the most fundamental part of her nature. Mathewes-Green notes that the modern feminist's slogan, "a woman's right to choose," should be amended to "a woman's right to capitulate."[45]

Female Mutilation

Female genital mutilation (sometimes called by the more polite term "female circumcision") involves cutting the clitoris of women for various religious or cultural reasons. The practice predates Christianity and Islam. Evidence of the practice has been found on some Egyptian mummies dating back several thousand years.

Unlike the practice of male circumcision, there are no medical reasons for engaging in female genital mutilation. Also unlike male circumcision, female genital mutilation harms a person's ability to enjoy sexual intercourse. Depending on the culture in which this rite is practiced, female genital mutilation is seen as a way to ensure a woman's virginity or to control her sexuality. In some places, you are not considered a woman if you are not circumcised.

Two million girls each year (just under 6,000 a day) are genitally mutilated.[46] Some 130 million girls have undergone genital mutilation.[47] Most common in the Middle East and Africa, it is practiced in more than forty countries, including in immigrant communities in the United States.[48]

The World Health Organization recognizes four types:

- Circumcision: "Excision of the prepuce, with or without excision of part or all of the clitoris." This is analogous to male circumcision.
- Excision: "Excision of the clitoris with partial or total excision of the labia minora."

- Infibulation: "Excision of part or all of the external genitalia and stitching/narrowing of the vaginal opening."
- Type 4: All other types.[49]

Female genital mutilation usually happens to girls between the ages of two and fifteen and is often done in primitive, unsterile conditions with common cutting instruments, including kitchen knives, sharp rocks, pieces of glass, razor blades, or household scissors.

Hannah Koroma, a young woman from Sierra Leone, tells her story:

> I was genitally mutilated at the age of ten. When the operation began, I put up a big fight. The pain was terrible and unbearable. . . . I was badly cut and lost blood. . . . I was genitally mutilated with a blunt penknife. After the operation, no one was allowed to aid me to walk. . . . Sometimes I had to force myself not to urinate for fear of the terrible pain. I was not given any anesthetic in the operation to reduce my pain, nor any antibiotics to fight against infection. Afterwards, I hemorrhaged and became anemic. This was attributed to witchcraft. I suffered for a long time from acute vaginal infections.[50]

Feticide and Infanticide

Female feticide, the murder of female babies before they are born, is a chronic problem in much of the developing world. Amniocentesis, ultrasounds, and abortion technology have helped parents identify and kill huge numbers of unwanted baby girls in their mothers' wombs.

In China, female feticide has increased since the Chinese government decided in 1979 to institute the infamous one-child policy. Families with more than one child saw their wages reduced and, in some cases, their homes destroyed. Mandatory abortions became law. In a country where boys are more highly valued, it's no surprise that female babies became targets for abortion.

A national census in China reveals that there are more than 116 male births for every 100 female births.[51] Additionally, between 2 million and 5 million female babies are aborted each year in India.[52] In India, abortion clinics advertise that it is "better to spend $38 now to terminate a female fetus than $3,800 later on her dowry."[53]

Because female feticide is so widespread, we shouldn't be surprised at the presence of female infanticide, which is the murder of girl babies after they are born, usually by their own mothers. There are many factors:

- In India, where the average civil servant earns the equivalent of $3,500 per year and dowry and wedding expenses often add up to more than $35,000, the decision to commit female infanticide is often an economic one. "Given these figures, combined with the low status of women, it seems not so illogical that the poorer Indian families would want only male children."[54]

- In China, where baby girls are often known as "maggots in the rice,"[55] about 1 million baby girls are abandoned at birth every year, simply because they are girls.[56] State-run orphanages sometimes have "dying rooms" where the weakest or sickest children, mostly baby girls, are left without food, water, or human touch.

Honor Killing

In parts of the world, especially in Muslim areas,[57] about five thousand women and girls are killed each year to restore a warped sense of family honor.[58] Women may be shot, stoned, poisoned, beheaded, stabbed, or strangled. Considered a family matter, this crime often goes unreported. Many times the victim's body ends up in an unmarked grave, as if the woman never existed.

While precise figures are unavailable, some estimate that 25 percent of all homicides in Jordan are honor killings.[59] In Pakistan, an estimated three women die for reasons of honor every day.[60]

Norma Khouri, in her book *Honor Lost*, says the root of honor killing is in the Qur'an.[61]

Family honor is one of the prime values in Arab societies. Young girls are taught to remain virgins until marriage and to cover their bodies so as not to dishonor their fathers, brothers, or husbands. Khouri recounts what her mother and aunts drilled into her as a young girl: "A woman is like a cup; if someone drinks from it, no one will want it. . . . A woman is like a sheet of glass; once it is broken it can never be fixed."[62]

In Islam, a woman is often seen as a man's possession, as a commodity. Thus, her behavior is a reflection on his honor. If her behavior (assumed adultery, premarital sex, even flirting, or as a victim of rape) brings dishonor on the family—a husband, father, or brother—he or another relative may kill the woman to restore that honor.

Often the young girl's brothers are more guards than brothers. As one woman put it, "For most of us, our brothers are like big, barking dogs who feel that their whole purpose in life is to guard our bodies. It's a kind of oppression for them, too, that they have to go through their lives feeling responsibility and worrying that at any moment we will snatch their honor away."[63]

Dowry Deaths

In many cultures, primarily on the Indian subcontinent, the families of brides are required to provide a dowry—some combination of food, money, and goods—to the families of grooms. This can be a crushing burden. It can also be an occasion to punish the bride who enters a marriage with an inadequate dowry.

Baskar, a fifteen-year-old bride from Firozpur Namak, India, will never forget her first day of marriage. "As is tradition in India, the family provided a dowry, sending a refrigerator, furniture and other household goods. They could not, however, afford one item the groom had demanded—a motorcycle. On her wedding night, Baskar says, her drunken new husband and his three friends beat her and took turns raping her. They forced her to crouch on all fours while they taunted her. They said, 'Let's make her a motorcycle.'"[64]

Baskar was one of the fortunate ones. More than fifteen thousand women are killed every year in India over inadequate dowries.[65] Besides direct murder, the husband or his family may drive the wife to commit suicide. Or they may arrange a fatal "kitchen accident." A "stove death" may occur, in which the husband and his mother set the woman on fire. Even where dowry deaths are illegal, the authorities rarely prosecute.

Other Aspects of Abuse

Women are also least likely to get an education, on the theory that girls are only going to get pregnant, have babies, and take care of the household. About 60 percent of the children worldwide who are kept out of school are girls.[66] Some 66 percent of the world's 880 million illiterate adults are women.[67]

Maternal mortality rates are also extremely high in much of the world. An estimated 600,000 women die each year worldwide related to pregnancy and childbirth.[68]

According to one observer, "For every woman who dies, 30 more incur injuries, infections, and disabilities. That equals 15 million women each year. . . . Over a generation, the cumulative total is conservatively estimated at 300 million, more than a quarter of the adult women now alive in the developing world."[69]

Women also face inordinate degrees of homelessness,[70] suffering as refugees,[71] in poverty,[72] and in poor health due to malnutrition.[73]

Metaphysical War

Because ideas have consequences, the war against women has produced 100 million fewer women and the untold suffering of a billion more. This war is the result of faulty metastories, the cultural stories that explain all of life in a culture. Because of these stories, women are often unseen and unrecognized. Assumed to be inferiors, they are often only seen as the backdrop for a man's life. Those values lead to behavior that has dire consequences for women.

Underdevelopment or poverty does not cause women to be crushed. Rather it is the lie—*men are better than women*—that wreaks its horrifying havoc, leading to the abuse of women worldwide.

Notes
1. Nicholas D. Kristof, "Do Korean Men Still Beat Their Wives? Definitely," *New York Times*, December 5, 1996.
2. Amartya Sen, "More Than 100 Million Women Are Missing," *The New York Review of Books*, vol. 37, no. 20, December 20, 1990, http://www.nybooks.com/articles/3408 (italics added).

3. Robert Selle, "A World That Seems to Hate Women," *Washington Times National Weekly Edition*, July 2001.

4. Ibid.

5. "The Condition of Women in South Asia: Violence in the Life-Cycle," *The Hunger Project Online Briefing Program*, Unit 4, June–August 2000, http://www.thp.org/sac/unit4/cycle.htm.

6. Chuck Colson, "Domestic Violence: In the Mayor's Mansion?" *BreakPoint Commentary*, March 5, 2001, http://www.breakpoint.org/listingarticle.asp?ID=5013.

7. Ibid.

8. "Beating Women Isn't a Crime in Many Places, Report Finds," *International Herald Tribune [France]*, August 14–15, 1999.

9. Ibid.

10. Ellen Goodman, "How Long Before We Take the Honor Out of Killing?" *Washington Post*, in *The Guardian Weekly [Manchester]*, April 6–12, 2000, in "Case Study: 'Honour' Killings and Blood Feuds," Gendercide Watch website, http://www.gendercide.org/case_honour.html.

11. Charlotte Bunch, "The Intimate Enemy," *Women Commentary*, http://www.unicef.org/pon97/women1a.htm.

12. Charlotte Bunch, "The Intolerable Status Quo: Violence against Women and Girls," *Women Commentary*, http://www.unicef.org/pon97/women1.htm.

13. Lydia Reynolds, "Unforgettable Bintu," *Mercy Ships Outreach* (November 2001–March 2002): 42–43.

14. "Rwanda: HR Abuses against Women," *Human Rights Watch*, September 24, 1996, http://www.africaaction.org/docs96/rwan9609.htm.

15. "Topics in Sex Trafficking: Types of Sex Trafficking," http://www.humantrafficking.com/humantrafficking/trafficking_ht3/topic_types.htm.

16. Adult Video News, in "Pornography and Divorce Statistics," http://www.divorcewizards.com/divorcestats_porn.html.

17. Robert Selle, "Violated by Porn," *Washington Times National Weekly Edition*, July 2001.

18. Jason Rovou, "'Porn & Pancakes' Fights X-rated Addictions," CNN.com, April 6, 2007, http://www.cnn.com/2007/US/04/04/porn.addiction/index.html.

19. Kerby Anderson, "The Pornography Plague," Probe Ministries website, http://www.leaderu.com/orgs/probe/docs/pornplag.html.

20. Martin Dawes, "Children in South Asia Deserve Better Protection from Sex Abusers and Traffickers," UNICEF Press Release, Colombo, Sri Lanka, October 1, 2004.

21. Sheryl Watkins, "Five Barriers Facing Women in the Developing World: Overcoming the Obstacles," *World Vision Today* (April–May 1997).

22. Jo Doezema, "Loose Women or Lost Women?" *Gender Issues* 18, no. 1 (Winter 2000): 23–50; available at http://www.walnet.org/csis/papers/doezema-loose.html.

23. Chuck Colson, "A Job No Woman Would Choose: Hillary and Her 'Sex Workers,'" *BreakPoint Commentary*, December 13, 2002, http://www.breakpoint.org/listingarticle.asp?ID=5443.

24. Ibid.

25. "Sex and Slavery: Hillary Clinton Backs 'Voluntary' Prostitution," *Wall Street Journal Editorial Page*, November 15, 2002.

26. Selle, "Violated by Porn."

27. Ibid.

28. "Sex Slavery: The Growing Trade," CNN.com/World, March 8, 2001, http://archives. cnn.com/2001/WORLD/europe/03/08/women.trafficking/.

29. Anne Morse, "The Abolitionist," *World Magazine*, March 1, 2003, 20.

30. "Sex Slavery: The Growing Trade," CNN.com.

31. Jonathan Manthorpe, "China Battles Slave Trading in Women: Female Infanticide Fuels a Brisk Trade in Wives," *Vancouver Sun*, January 11, 1999, in Adam Jones, "Case Study: Female Infanticide," Gendercide Watch website, http://www.gendercide.org/case_infanticide. html.

32. Ibid.

33. Marc Kaufman, "Amid Poverty, Afghan Families Sell Young Daughters as Brides," *Wall Street Journal Europe [Brussels]*, February 24, 2003.

34. "HIV/AIDS and the Sale of Children, Child Prostitution and Child Pornography," Office of the United Nations High Commissioner for Human Rights, http://www.ohchr. org/english/issues/children/rapporteur/hiv.htm.

35. Margaret Sanger, *The Pivot of Civilization* (reprint edition, Amherst, NY: Humanity Books, 2003), 64.

36. Ibid., 247.

37. Steven W. Mosher, "In Peru, Women Lose the Right to Choose More Children," *Wall Street Journal*, February 27, 1998.

38. Mohan Rao, "Neo-Eugenics: The Quinacrine Sterilization of Women in India," *Woman's Link*, July–September 1997, http://www.globalhealth.harvard.edu/hcpds/wpweb/ george1001.html.

39. Anthony Failoa, "Peru Is Accused of Coercing Poor Women to Be Sterilized," *International Herald Tribune [France]*, February 13, 1998.

40. Bonnie Mass, *The Political Economy of Population Control in Latin America*, Editions Latin America, Montreal, 1972, in "500 Years of Indigenous Resistance," *Oh-Toh-Kin*, vol. 1, no. 1 (Winter–Spring 1992); available at LibertadLatina website, http://www.libertadlatina. org/Americas_500_Years_of_Indigenous_Resistance_1992.htm.

41. "Growing Fight against Sterilization of Native Women," *Akwesasne Notes*, vol. 11, no. 1 (Winter 1979): 29; quoted in "500 Years of Indigenous Resistance."

42. "Abortion Statistics," AbortionTV website, http://www.abortiontv.com/Misc/Abortion-Statistics.htm#United%20States.

43. Ibid.

44. Frederica Mathewes-Green, "Abortion: Women's Rights . . . and Wrongs," Feminists for Life, 1996, http://www.members.tripod.com/~danewe/fem.html.

45. Frederica Mathewes-Green, "The Bitter Price of 'Choice,'" Feminists for Life, 1996, http://www.members.tripod.com/~danewe/choice.html.

46. Bunch, "The Intolerable Status Quo: Violence against Women and Girls."

47. Nicholas D. Kristof, "Guest Commentary: Bush vs. Women," *Naples Daily News/Perspective*, August 16, 2002.

48. Robin M. Maher, "Female Genital Mutilation: The Modern Day Struggle to Eradicate a Torturous Rite of Passage," *Human Rights*, vol. 23, no. 4 (Fall 1996): 12–15; available at http://www.abanet.org/irr/hr/fall96/fgm.html.

49. "Frequently Asked Questions on Female Genital Mutilation/Cutting," United Nations Population Fund website, http://www.unfpa.org/gender/practices2.htm.

50. Amnesty International, "Female Genital Mutilation: A Fact Sheet," http://www.amnesty-usa.org/Violence/Womens_Human_Rights/page.do?id=1108439&n1=3&n2=39&n3=739.

51. John Gittings, "Growing Sex Imbalance Shocks China," *The Guardian*, May 13, 2002, in Adam Jones, "Case Study: Female Infanticide," Gendercide Watch website, http://www.gendercide.org/case_infanticide.html.

52. Robert Selle, "Gendercide: Killing Female Infants and Fetuses," *Washington Times National Weekly Edition*, July 2001.

53. "The Condition of Women in South Asia: Violence in the Life-Cycle," *The Hunger Project Online Briefing Program*, http://www.thp.org/sac/unit4/cycle.htm.

54. Marina Porras, "Female Infanticide and Foeticide," in Adam Jones, "Case Study: Female Infanticide," Gendercide Watch website, http://www.gendercide.org/case_infanticide.html.

55. Brian Woods, "The Dying Rooms Trust," in Adam Jones, "Case Study: Female Infanticide," Gendercide Watch website, http://www.gendercide.org/case_infanticide.html.

56. Ibid.

57. Norma Khouri, *Honor Lost* (New York: Atria Books, 2003), 196.

58. "Honor Killings," Voice of America, The United States International Broadcasting Bureau Editorial #0-09399, August 25, 2001, www.ibb.gov/editorials/09399.htm.

59. Ibid.

60. Hillary Mayell, "Thousands of Women Killed for Family 'Honor,'" *National Geographic News*, February 12, 2002, http://news.nationalgeographic.com/news/2002/02/0212_020212_honorkilling.html.

61. Khouri, *Honor Lost*, 59.

62. Ibid.

63. Geraldine Brooks, *Nine Parts of Desire* (New York: Anchor Books, 1995), 51.

64. Hema Shukla, "Rape Case Exposes Position of Women in India," SouthCoastToday.com, August 2, 1997, http://archive.southcoasttoday.com/daily/08-97/08-02-97/a11wn073.htm.

65. "Making Violence against Women Count—Facts and Figures," Amnesty International Media Briefing, March 5, 2004, http://web.amnesty.org/library/Index/ENGACT770362004?open&of=ENG-373.

66. Kristof, "Guest Commentary: Bush vs. Women."

67. "The State of World Population 2000: Lives Together, Worlds Apart; Men and Women in a Time of Change," United Nations Population Fund, http://www.unfpa.org/swp/2000/pdf/english/chapter1.pdf.

68. Watkins, "Women: Five Barriers Facing Women in the Developing World."

69. Ibid.

70. Ibid.

71. Justin D. Long, "Female Circumcision," *Monday Morning Reality Check*, no. 7, March 1998.

72. Ibid.

73. Watkins, "Women: Five Barriers Facing Women in the Developing World."

PART 2

THE LIE:
THE ROOT
OF THE PROBLEM

CHAPTER 3

The Framework for Examining the Issue

Monument Valley, near where Arizona, Utah, Colorado, and New Mexico meet, entrances me. Rising from the desert floor, a series of monoliths reaches hundreds of feet into the air. As awe inspiring as they are, you have to be careful when standing atop these pinnacles, because, unlike a cliff, you can fall off of more than one side. Experienced climbers know not to back too far away from any one side because of the danger of pitching headlong off another.

Seeking the truth is a little like that. Over dinner, the late Francis Schaeffer, my mentor, pointed out to me that most people see truth as a pinpoint on a line. If you are on one side of the pinpoint, you are right; if you're on the other side, you are wrong.

Figure 2: View *Only* Right or *Only* Wrong

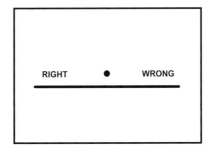

But the Bible presents truth as balanced between errors. For example, the truth of the three-in-one God of Scripture is poised between polytheism (many gods) on one hand and atheism (no god) on the other.

Figure 3: Truth Balanced between Errors

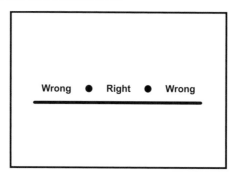

Truth is the radical middle. Schaeffer said truth is like a finely balanced child's mobile. As long as all the pieces are in place, the mobile works. But if you remove just one piece (even from a twelve-piece mobile), the contraption will become unbalanced and static.

The Pendulum

Too often, when we look at women's issues, the philosophical pendulum swings from one extreme to another, bypassing the middle. Reacting to the one extreme of *sexism*, which states that women are inherently inferior to men, *radical feminism* goes to another extreme and states that men and women are the same. Both these ideologies miss the radical middle, which holds that men and women are *equal* in being and *different* in function. This balanced position is often called *complementarianism*.

The Trinitarian faith reveals that God is one and many, having individuality within community. Not surprisingly, we find this pattern in men and women, who together are made in the image of God (*imago Dei*). As Christians, we must not allow our culture to pull us either to sexism or to radical feminism.

We must fight *from* and *for* the middle ground of Trinitarian faith. Schaeffer said this is a perennial challenge for the church: "In this fallen world, things constantly swing like a pendulum, from being wrong in one extreme way to being wrong in another extreme. The devil never gives us the luxury of fighting on only one front, and this will always be the case."[1]

Three Visions

From the animism of the Amazonian jungle to the highly developed religious systems of Zen Buddhism, from the chanting of brightly clad devotees of Krishna to the numerous reflections of a Christian on a spiritual pilgrimage, it's easy to see that humanity is incurably religious. From cave paintings to cathedrals, the evidence of our search for meaning and the divine is impossible to deny. Scholars have counted thousands of religions in the world, and more are being formed every day.

And yet, when you get right down to it, there are really only three main visions for what humankind is, derived from three very different philosophical/theological expressions. We will examine these positions in this chapter, remaining aware of the danger of standing on a monolith in Monument Valley. The only safety is in the radical middle.

Keep in mind that I am speaking in generalities, using broad brushstrokes. I acknowledge that people and cultures are very complex and may hold, consciously or unconsciously, more than one vision or a combination drawn from different belief systems.

• All is diverse—Atomism

First, let's look at what the philosophers call atomism. This worldview holds that "all is diverse," that reality is a series of indivisible and indestructible *particles*. Atomism has several notable religious expressions, including Unitarianism,[2] Islam, modern Judaism, Jehovah's Witnesses, deism, and polytheism[3] (animism, shamanism, and Mormonism[4] included). In this worldview, God (Islam's Allah) or the gods (polytheism) are known for their power, harshness, and capriciousness. In this "unitarian" system, "God" is absolutely *other*. He is transcendent, not immanent. A main proponent of this philosophy was Aristotle.

- **All is one—Monism**

Second is monism, which holds that "all is one," that reality is a *unified*, undifferentiated whole. This worldview is expressed religiously in Hinduism, Buddhism, New Age, and other forms of pantheism. To the monist, "all is God." In this worldview, "God" is the pantheist's Mother Earth or the Hindu's or New Ager's one indivisible spirit. A main proponent of this philosophy was Plato.

As I have referred to Aristotle and Plato as classical proponents of atomism and monism, respectively, it would be good to offer a few clarifications. Plato was the classic definer of a dualistic view of the world. For Plato, reality is composed of physical and spiritual realms. But for Plato the spiritual realm was the higher of the two. The physical realm is the shadow of the Ideal. It is in the spiritual realm that everything collapses into monism. Plato began with reason and moved toward Idealism. His pursuit was the transcendent nature of truth. For Plato, Goodness, Truth, and Beauty were beyond "this world."

Aristotle, Plato's contemporary and student, rejected his mentor's Idealism in favor of Realism. Aristotle began, not with reason, but with his five senses. His focus was on the solidness and practicalness of the material world. He wanted to pursue truth through empirical examination. His methodology later became foundational to modern, naturalistic science.

The Italian painter Raphael (1483–1520) captures the essence of the dispute in his *The School of Athens*. In this painting we find Plato standing with his right hand pointed toward the heavens, reflecting that Truth, Beauty, and Goodness are transcendent ideals. His "rebellious" student, Aristotle, is standing next to him with his right hand extended horizontally toward the earth. His five fingers are stretched out, reflecting the five senses exploring the real world.

Beginning as they have with man, not God, Aristotle and Plato are unable to find an integration point of the one and the many. As we shall see, there are dire social consequences for this failure. But there is hope. A third alternative to monism and atomism begins with God's self-revelation as Trinity.

- **Unity and diversity—Trinitarianism**

The third vision is Trinitarianism, which holds the principles of unity and diversity in biblical tension. The person who holds this worldview knows that reality is both the one and the many. Trinitarianism is expressed only in biblical theism, which is found in orthodox Christianity and in Judaism before the philosopher Maimonides.[5] In Trinitarianism, the one God is a divine community of Father, Son, and Holy Spirit. Moses and Jesus, of course, were proponents.[6]

Practical Effects

These three approaches have practical effects on how women are treated. Atomism, which postulates absolute, hierarchical distinctions in being, holds that there are clear gulfs between God, man, and creation. This focus on differences reinforces the belief in male superiority. In human relations, atomism can lead to patriarchal tyranny. The female is crushed by the male value system, leading to the perversion of sex via rape, forced prostitution, sex slavery, female genital mutilation, violence, and sadomasochism—in short, a war against women.

Monism, which recognizes no ultimate distinctions in being, posits that God, man, and creation are one. This focus on equality leads to the belief that male and female are fundamentally the same. In human relations, monism produces no hierarchy between man and woman, because there are no differences that matter. When consistently lived out, monism produces radical feminism, in which the female disappears into an androgynous set of values. In this system of sexual sameness or interchangeability, sex is too often perverted into homosexuality, lesbianism, bisexuality, and transsexuality.

Trinitarianism recognizes that while there is no distinction in *being*, there is a hierarchical distinction in *function*. The Father has authority over the Son, and the Father and the Son have authority over the Holy Spirit. (In the modern world, the word *authority* is a dirty word; later in the book we will examine this issue in detail.) In human relations, men and women are designed uniquely for distinct purposes, and female and male are valued equally as the *imago Dei*. In practice, this leads to complementarianism, modeled on the biblical picture of Christ and his bride.

In relation to creation, God is at the same time both transcendent and immanent. Concerning God's *infinite* nature, there is a chasm between God, man, and creation: man is a creature under God's authority. Concerning God's *personal* nature, the gulf is between man and creation: humankind is the *imago Dei* and rules over creation in God's stead. Male and female are to have dominion over creation. In human relations, servant-leadership is the paradoxical rule.

Here is a comparison of the three approaches:

Figure 4: Three Distinct Visions

Categories	Absolute Unity	Unity and Diversity	Absolute Diversity
Philosophic Expression	Monism	Trinitarianism	Atomism
Religous Expression	Hinduism Buddhism New Age	Judeo-Christian Theism	Unitarianism Islam Polytheism
Nature of God	One Undivided Spirit	Divine Community: Father, Son, and Holy Spirit	Power Harshness Capriciousness
Historic Proponents	Plato	Moses Jesus	Aristotle
Hierarchical Expressions	No Hierachy in Being	No Hierachy in Being Hierachy in Function	Hierachy in Being
Values	Maleness	Female and Male	Maleness
Sexual Expression	Radical Feminism	Complementarianism	Sexism
Reliance	Absolute Female Independence	Interdependence	Absolute Female Dependence

Compromising Christians

Facing these three options, many Christians often add their own cultural understandings to biblical teachings rather than doing the hard work of

maintaining the radical balance of Scripture. Being uncritical about one's own culture is natural, of course. But the apostle Paul calls us not to be conformed to this world (Romans 12:2).

There are two main compromising approaches:

- When socialized into a sexist society, Christians sometimes end up with a patronizing brand of *chauvinism*. In this case, the belief in diversity overpowers unity.

- Other Christians have a conscious desire to stand against sexism by embracing its opposite, radical feminism. Here feminism is "tempered" by Scripture into the *egalitarianism* held by some evangelicals. In this case, the belief in unity trumps diversity.

Figure 5: Compromising Approaches

		Professing Christians		
Syncretism with Monism		Transformed (Romans 12:2)	Syncretism with Atomism	
Monoism ←		Trinitarianism	→ Atomism	
Unity	Unity / Diversity	Unity and Diversity	Diversity / Unity	Diversity
Feminism	Egalitarianism	Complementarianism	Chauvinism	Sexism
The **Disappearance** of Women		The **Dignity** of Women	The **Crushing** of Women	

The Demise of Female

Because of their erroneous worldviews, males disrespect the feminine enough to make war against women. Women, facing this disrespect and abuse, hate their feminine natures enough to want to be like men. This is bad news for women, because they often have difficulty competing with men in ways valued by sexist cultures. A sense of male superiority pervades these societies because men are, generally, physically stronger and more aggressive than women. When this warrior mentality becomes a virtue, women are made second-class citizens.

Writing in 1833 in her *Letters to Young Ladies*, Lydia H. Sigourney, an early feminist, says that in these cultures a woman can only be appreciated when she acts like a man: "But still, wherever the brute force of the warrior is counted godlike, woman is appreciated only as she approximates to sterner natures."[7] Similarly, Ivy George of Gordon College writes, "When women's work of caring is rendered invisible by societal arrangements and structures, a kind of social *femicide* is in process."[8]

This is the sad story of so many cultures: only men are presumed god-like. But into this world the Bible maintains the balance between unity and diversity, rooted in the Trinity, to proclaim that women are like God—made in the *imago Dei*. Sadly, because sexism begins with absolute diversity and feminism begins with absolute unity, both camps fail to distinguish between *being* and *function* among humankind.

Sexism fails to recognize both the equality of being between men and women and the intrinsic value of what makes a woman a woman. Feminism equally fails, by equating equality in being with *sameness*. This requires the woman to cease to exist as a woman and become just like a man. Despite their obvious differences, both ends of the spectrum are lived out against the backdrop of cultures that primarily value the masculine. So on the one side, the woman is *crushed*. On the other, she *disappears*.

But in Trinitarian faith—the radical middle—there is harmony. There is harmony in the Godhead, which has both unity and diversity. The three persons are equal in being but diverse in function. Human beings, made in God's image as male and female, also are equal in being but have different functions. Christian families are to live out their professed Trinitarian faith by treating women as joint heirs with men of God's blessings, honoring God-given male and female virtues.

Of course, Christians are not automatically immune to the cultural poison of sexism and feminism. You can be a Christian and say that men and women are made in the *imago Dei* and still try to live as though males are superior. But the backdrop against which we live should not be either male values or female values. The backdrop is the recognition that we are *all* made in the *imago Dei*, males and females. Being female is good. Being male is good. The diversity of male and female is the *imago Dei*.

Testing the Virtues

In complementarian cultures, women's virtues are honored; in sexist cultures, these virtues are despised; and in feminist cultures, they turn to vices. Let's take a look:

- Complementarian cultures celebrate the expressed differences in virtue between men and women:

Figure 6

Male	Female
Stronger	Finer
Rational	Intuitive
"Hunt the deer"	"Cook the deer"
Roam	Nest
Protect	Nurture

- Sexist cultures judge women by male virtues:

Figure 7

Good	Bad
Stronger	Finer
Rational	Intuitive
Hunt	Cook
Roam	Nest
Protect	Nurture

- Feminist cultures say (mainly by their actions) there is only one virtue—male:

Figure 8

Only Virtues
Stronger
Rational
Hunt
Roam
Protect

In the next chapter, we will explore the development of these values. They did not spring up out of thin air. Instead, they are the logical consequence of the worldviews that produced them. But a worldview is not a set of dry propositions to most people. It is communicated in story. We will examine the powerful, often unconscious, influences of story in how we view and treat women.

Notes

1. Francis Schaeffer, in Mary A. Kassian, *The Feminist Gospel: The Movement to Unite Feminism with the Church* (Wheaton: Crossway, 1992), 241.

2. Unitarianism, in contrast to polytheism, is a monotheistic religion that believes there is only one God. But in contrast to the unity and diversity of in the Godhead of Trinitarianism, Unitarians believe that the infinite God is a single, undivided person.

3. Polytheists, like monotheists, believe in "personal" as apposed to "impersonal" deities. But in contrast to monotheists, polytheists believe in many finite, personal gods.

4. While Mormonism has historically come more from a Judeo-Christian framework more than any other, philosophically it is more polytheistic than monotheistic. Mormonism teaches that the "Godhead" consists of three separate and distinct beings who are one in purpose.

5. Please see the discussion of this claim in chapter 7, "The Trinity as a Model."

6. In the sense that neither Jesus nor Moses ever used the word *Trinity* (the word did not exist at the time of their lives), they were not proponents. But to the extent that both Jesus and Moses (see Genesis 1:1–2,26; 3:22; 11:7) articulated the plurality of the Godhead, this makes them, in my mind, proponents of Trinitarian faith.

7. Lydia Huntley Sigourney, *Letters to Young Ladies*, 4th ed. (New York: Harper & Brothers, 1837), 14; available at http://www.openlibrary.org/details/letterstoladies00sigouoft.

8. Ivy George, "The Past Interrupted," *Sojourners Magazine,* June 2004 (italics added); available at http://www.sojo.net/index.cfm?action=magazine.article&issue=soj0406&article=040 621.

CHAPTER 4
The Crushing of Women

Every kid in America has probably heard the saying "Sticks and stones will break my bones, but words will never hurt me." Parents use it to comfort their children when they are verbally abused. The reasoning seems to be that words don't matter, that ideas don't have consequences. That reasoning is dead wrong, and we have 100 million females dead or missing to prove it.

Cultures and nations have fundamental ideas, and they can be either genuine or counterfeit. The apostle Paul identifies the counterfeit building blocks as *stoicheion*, as "the basic principles of the world"—first principles as satanic tools of enslavement (Galatians 4:3–10; Colossians 2:2–8). One of the worst of these counterfeit principles ever told by Satan is that men are superior to women.

The greatest cause of the abuse against women that we saw in chapter 1 is a lie. The lie, spoken or unspoken, is this: "Men are superior to women." This lie is entrenched in cultures around the world, rooted in people's sacred belief systems, and repeated in their sacred stories. When we believe that male is superior to female, then we deny all those attributes of God that are manifest most fully in women, and we deprive ourselves. This lie has impoverished individuals—both male and female—families, and nations.

All the money in the world will not end the poverty or stop the resulting abuse. The only answer is to root out the lie and replace it with the truth.

What we need is another story, a transforming story. And fortunately, we have such a story. It is found in the Bible and is thus transcultural. This story reveals that women have dignity. We will explore the stereotype-busting implications of this story throughout this book. In this chapter, we will look at its broad contours.

The Big Story

Every culture already has a story that reveals its worldview. Called a metanarrative, this story answers the basic questions of life.[1]

- *Epistemological questions* address the nature, limits, and validity of knowledge. Is there truth? What is true? Can I know?
- *Metaphysical questions* address the fundamental nature of reality and being. Does God exist? What is real? Where did life come from? What is my purpose?
- *Moral questions* address values, ethics, and morals. Is there right and wrong? What is good? Where did evil come from? What is beautiful?

Questions concerning the nature of women belong in the metaphysical realm. These questions include:

- Is a woman a human being? Is she made in the *imago Dei*?
- Is a man superior to a woman? Is a woman inferior to a man?
- Is *female* a sociological construct, or does it fundamentally reflect a transcendent feminine essence? Are men and women equal? Are they different? Are they the same?

In the realm of morals, what is good and beautiful, we encounter a different set of questions:

- Are women's roles seen as good or bad?
- Is feminine beautiful? Or is only masculinity attractive?

The way we answer these kinds of questions depends on our culture's metanarrative, or "big story." That story, in turn, establishes the philosophical *stoicheion*, which, for our purposes, usually boil down to three overarching approaches to reality: monism, atomism, and Trinitarianism. Each offers very different answers, and we will look at these approaches in more depth later.

The metanarrative determines if a person or culture values or despises women. It will determine the place of women in society and their relationship to men and show if womanhood has intrinsic worth. These next two chapters will examine the role of metanarrative and culture in establishing *maleness* as the backdrop against which people live their lives.

Femininicide

We have seen that there are 100 million missing—dead—women. These are missing daughters, sisters, wives, and mothers. We will further reflect on this *crushing of women* in this chapter. Some people have called this murder of women *gendercide*. That it is! Women die through murder and societal neglect.

However, *gendercide* is not the best term for what is happening to women. That term focuses exclusively on those women who have been physically killed. It does not take into account the hundreds of millions of women who live but who suffer emotional, sexual, physical, and spiritual violence every day, simply because they are female. Neither does *gendercide* take into account the hundreds of millions of women who are seeking to disappear. These are women who have consciously or unconsciously accepted the sexist mantra that male is superior to female. They are seeking to be equal with men by becoming like men. *Gendercide* does not reflect this phenomenon.

Underlying the crushing of women and the disappearance of women is a metaphysic that denies transcendent sexuality; it denies that there is a transcendent male quality known as *masculine* and a transcendent female quality identified as *feminine*. The crushing and disappearance of women stem from *femininicide*—the death of the transcendent feminine. Because the metaphysic of feminine is "killed," there is a worldwide war against women.

In the next two chapters we will witness the consequences of femininicide, the war against women. In this chapter we will look at how sexist, male-dominant metanarratives in many cultures crush women, if not physically, then emotionally and spiritually. In the following chapter we will see how the despising of the feminine by the radical feminist movement leads to the disappearance of women. It is only by uncovering the roots of the problem that we can begin to see it at its source: in the realm of ideas.

Let's take a look now at several key cultural expressions of sexism.

Machismo

The Spanish and Portuguese conquistadors who conquered the Americas did not take their wives and families with them. This gave them the opportunity to exploit slaves and indigenous Indian women to satisfy their sexual appetites, and many did so. They viewed these women as inferior and treated them thusly. This was the beginning of the so-called *macho* culture in the New World.

Macho simply means male. But the culture of *machismo* is a distorted culture of virility, about men having power over women. It values a man's ability to procreate, but it doesn't care about his ability to husband or father. The exaggeration of male virtues leads to domestic abuse and other sins. According to two contemporary observers, "Being macho is considered synonymous with being a wife-beater, a philanderer, a drunk, a 'bien gallo'—a fighter, like a rooster."[2]

While macho cultures value strong (and often violent) men, they do not value strength in women, except the strength of enduring suffering. The female counterpart to *machismo* is *marianismo*. As you might guess, this ideal springs from Roman Catholicism, which venerates the Virgin Mary as the "Mother of God." In this scheme, a simple Jewish peasant girl becomes the "Queen of Heaven." While you might assume that this view exalts women, in practice it tends to diminish them. How so? As Mary is transformed into a celestial figure, her humanity and womanhood are denied. As Lilian Calles Barger writes, she becomes the *perpetual* virgin: "As the Virgin Mother, Mary of church tradition remains a virgin forever, untouched by the passion of sex. . . . This symbol of *perpetual* virginity points to the dangers of female sexuality. . . . The *perpetual* Virgin Mother of church tradition denies the reality of women's entire embodied life as good and spiritually significant."[3]

This led to the idea that a woman's virginity is ideal, that sex in and of itself is bad, and that sex is something "done to a woman."

Barger describes three types of women in her native Argentina:

- *Las buenas mujeres:* "good women," who, like her mother and aunt, spent their days in the kitchen.
- *Mujeres renegades:* "embittered women," such as the Catholic nuns who supposedly denied their womanhood and who were "foreboding figures who walked down the streets in pairs wearing long black robes."
- *Mujeres pintadas:* "painted women," who had questionable reputations.[4]

This dichotomy has other effects in Latin culture. *Marianismo* leads to an ideal of the woman who, like Mary, accepts her "fate," whatever that might be, including unfaithfulness and abuse. Like the perpetual virgin, she is seen as morally and spiritually superior. She demonstrates this by enduring the pain and suffering created by the machismo male. It is worth pointing out that *machismo* cannot exist without *marianismo*. If women did not accept their alleged "fate," machismo would collapse.

A young Brazilian told me of what I hope was an extreme case. She said that after her own macho father sired eight children, he abandoned the family. Then he began impregnating a series of girls her age and younger. Whenever they became pregnant, this man abandoned them for another conquest. It doesn't take a genius to see the cycle of poverty that such behavior perpetuates.

Where is the glory and wonder of being a woman? Not in machismo.

African Animism (Folk Religion)

Unlike the major religions of the world—Hinduism, Buddhism, Islam, and Judeo-Christianity—African traditional religions are largely tribal in nature. There are 3,500 ethnic groups and 2,000 languages on the continent. The cultural stories are similarly numerous. Many of them say that God made the woman first. According to John Mbiti:

Some myths speak about an original Mother of mankind, from whom all people originated. For example, the Akposso (of Togo) tell that when Uwolowu (God) made men, He first made a woman on the earth and bore with her the first child, the first human being. The Ibibio (of Nigeria) say that human beings came from the divinity Obumo, which was the son of the mother-divinity Eka-Abassi. It is told in eastern Africa about a virgin woman Ekao, who fell on earth from the sky and bore a son; the son got married to another woman and founded human society. . . . The main idea here is to link human life directly with God through the woman. She is created by God, and in turn becomes the instrument of human life."[5]

Many African tribes have stories that explain the miserable condition of humankind. Much like the Book of Genesis, they say that God put a test before the world's original inhabitants, who failed the test. Mbiti writes: "There are, however, considerable myths which put the blame on the women."[6]

Perhaps as a reflection of this, Africans value having many wives, like they value having many cattle. Viewed as property, wives are a sign of a man's wealth and stature in the community. Widespread polygamy is no surprise in such cultures. A proverb from East Africa describes the relationship between men and women: "The man is an axe; he can cut as many trees as he wants." The name for *women* in the language of one ethnic group is the same as the word used for a tool.

You can guess how such values are translated into behavior. Married and unmarried men "graze" freely in many parts of Africa. Not surprisingly, this leads to extreme vulnerability for women. While there are some indications this may be changing in some parts of the continent, men's sexual behavior is one of the main causes of the AIDS pandemic in Africa.

A friend of mine, Susan Bolman, MD, had an eye-opening conversation with her translator at a health project in Mozambique. Calling his story an "extreme, but not isolated example," Bolman says he told her, "Here in the *campo* [village or bush], men don't work. They marry, and their wives work the *machamba* [small field]. The more wives, the more *machambas*, and the more profits. There is one man in our community who has 29 wives. He is now 74 years old and used to be the administrator."[7]

Where is the glory and wonder of being a woman? Not in most of the traditional religions of Africa.

Hinduism

Reincarnation, the belief that "life is on the wheel," is one of the major tenets of Hinduism. Reincarnation posits that life consists of endless cycles of birth and rebirth, in which the individual soul may inhabit lower or higher life forms, depending on his or her karma. If people have done evil, they will come back in a lower form; if they have done good, they will come back in a higher one.

The range starts with lowly insects and progresses to the highest *male* form of *homo sapiens*. According to Hinduism, a woman is a man who committed great sin in a previous life. Women who hope to come back as a man in the next life must suffer as a woman in this one. If women ever hope to be one with their "gods" (a key goal in the religion), they must first become men. Not surprisingly, this belief system has led to perhaps the most horrible and inhumane treatment of women in the world.

Motivated by the dowry death of a younger sister, Sita Agarwal has written a challenging book entitled *Genocide of Women in Hinduism*. Agarwal says the root of the war on women in India comes from Brahmanism, or *astika* Hinduism. "These religions clearly and unambiguously justify and prescribe the crushing of women to the status of sub-humans. Rather than being due to some kind of 'corruption,' the ghastly practices of sati [a widow's act of cremating herself on her husband's funeral pyre], female infanticide, dowry and related acts are actually enforced by Vedic and Hindu scriptures. . . . These religions, and nothing else, are the main culprits behind the most anti-woman system the world has ever seen. . . . Indeed, Brahmanism is nothing but the legitimized genocide of women."[8]

Compared with Hinduism's crushing of women, Agarwal describes the coming of Islam to India as the "liberation of women." She writes, "Contrary to Brahmin fanatic propaganda, Islam acted as a liberating force for women. The custom of seclusion of women in Islam was far milder than that practiced by pre-Islamic Hindus."[9]

An Indian proverb says, "Bringing up a daughter is like watering a plant in another's courtyard." Raised in a Hindu family, Grace (not her real name) was told that being a girl was like being the sixth finger on a hand. It is lifeless, something to be removed and discarded. Grace wrote a poem that conveys how a young Indian woman feels responding to such attitudes.

Sixth Finger

I hang there,
Limp,
Shriveled,
Not Needed.
An embarrassment to the owner,
An object of ridicule for others.

A lump of flesh,
A deformity,
Ugly,
"Cut it off!"

How helpless,
And yet . . .
How true.

Do you want to meet me?
I am the sixth finger![10]

Al-Ash'Ari, an Indian scholar, writes of the dehumanizing demands of Brahmin culture on women: "Here, on the one hand, the woman is made to worship the man who becomes her master and lord: she has to subserve her father as a maid in childhood, become a chattel of the husband in youth and submit humbly to her children in widowhood. She is required to sacrifice herself over the burning bier of her husband."[11]

A good friend born in a Hindu family told me that if she could have one prayer answered, it would have been that she had been "born a man." While lecturing in India, I was approached by a young Nepalese. He said that weddings in his community in Nepal called for brides to wash the bridegroom's feet and then drink the water. One of Hinduism's sacred texts, the Puranas, sanctions such degradation: "Let a woman who wishes to perform sacred oblations wash the feet of her lord and drink the water, for her husband is her lord, her priest, her religion. Wherefore abandoning all else she ought to chiefly worship her husband."[12]

Such attitudes, based on sacred religious texts,[13] lead to the widely documented outrages of female feticide, female infanticide, malnutrition and starvation of female infants leading to a high female infant mortality rate, child marriage, and widow burning.

Prabhat Jha of Saint Michael's Hospital at the University of Toronto in Canada and Rajesh Kumar of the Post Graduate Institute of Medical Education and Research in Chandigarh, India, write: "We conservatively estimate that prenatal sex determination and selective abortions account for 0.5 million missing girls yearly. If this practice has been common for most of the past two decades . . . then a figure of 10 million missing female births would not be unreasonable."[14]

The Australian Broadcasting Corporation recently reported how a man in southern India buried his new granddaughter alive because he did not want the responsibility of another female. The article goes on to note, "The Indian Government says around 10 million girls have been killed by their parents either before or immediately after birth over the past 20 years."[15] In 1996 the World Bank estimated that approximately 35 million girls and women had apparently died as a result of the past and present discriminatory treatment girls and women received compared to boys and men.[16]

On a more personal note, I contacted a good friend in India to help me find statistics for this section. As part of her heartfelt response, she wrote, "I myself have lost four nieces to female feticide; it is an issue close to my heart."[17]

Where is the celebration of the glory and wonder of being female? Not in Hinduism.

Buddhism

Buddhism, prevalent in India, Nepal, Sri Lanka, Myanmar, Japan, Korea, Thailand, and Tibet, began as a nonreligious response to the excesses of Hinduism. Philosophically, it is one of the most benign religions in how it views women. The founder, Siddhartha Gautama, taught that "salvation," emancipation from this world, comes through *merit*—good works—and that men and women were on the same footing. He established an order for monks (Bhikkhus) and for nuns (Bhikkhunis). In contrast with other major religions in Asia, Buddhism has allowed women to achieve what L. S. Dewaraja of Sri Lanka describes as "near equality" to men. She states, "We could say that the secular nature of the marriage contract, the facility to divorce, the right to remarry, the desegregation of the sexes and above all else the right to inherit, own and dispose of property without let or hindrance from the husband, have all contributed to the alleviation of the lot of women in Buddhist societies."[18]

However, "near equality" is not the same as equally valued in both their being and their function. Buddhism, like so many other non-Christian systems, in fact assumes the innate inferiority of women. Siddhartha's teaching concerning women displayed a basic distrust of, and disdain for, women. From *The Collection of Jewels*, a king visits the Buddha to learn why "women are evil." Part of his response:

> You should know that when men have close relationships with women, they have close relationships with evil ways. . . .
> Fools lust for women
> Like dogs in heat. . . .
> Women can ruin
> The precepts of purity.
> They can also ignore
> Honor and virtue.
> Causing one to go to hell
> They prevent rebirth in heaven.
> Why should the wise delight in them?[19]

In *The Shadow of the Dalai Lama*, Victor and Victoria Trimondi note, "During his lifetime, the historical Buddha was plagued by a chronic misogyny; of this, in the face of numerous documents, there can not be slightest doubt."[20] Siddhartha's teachings reinforced male superiority, and that bias continues to this day in Buddhist-majority lands. A Burmese saying holds that "males are much nobler than females. . . [so much so that] a male dog is nobler than a female human."[21] A popular Thai saying states, "Males are elephant's front legs; females are elephant's posterior legs"—which "leads to the belief that the husband should be the leader, and [the] wife should be subordinate, or a follower."[22]

Along these lines, Buddhism sees women's bodies as unclean and worldly. Monks who have taken vows of celibacy are taught to hate women's bodies. Similar to Hinduism, if a man has bad karma, he will be reborn as a woman. For women to reach Nirvana, they must first become men.

Asanga, one of the founders of Mahayana Buddhism, speaks of the moral and physical inferiority of women: "The female's defects—greed, hate, and delusion, and other defilements—are greater than the male's."[23] Buddhism regards the womb as a "foul place."[24] A devout Buddhist woman's prayer asks "that I may be reborn as a male in a future existence."[25]

This contempt for women that pervades much of Buddhism has provided fertile ground for Thailand's despicable sex trade. Out of a population of 60 million people, 600,000 Thai women are known to be prostitutes. Forty percent of them were forced into it. This "industry" brings in as much as $15 billion a year.[26] As one worker with the International Justice Mission observed, "The leap for a woman from being an inferior, contaminating, lust-inducing Other to that of a prostitute is not a large one."[27]

Where is the glory and wonder of being a woman? Not in Buddhism.

Islam

What about Islam? Do women fare any better under the teachings of Muhammad? Sadly, no. Ibn Warraq's essay "Islam's Shame" states, "Islam is deeply anti-woman." The piece continues: "Islam has always considered women as creatures as inferior in every way: physically, intellectually, and morally. This negative vision is divinely sanctioned in the Koran, corroborated by the hadiths [all that is narrated from the prophet], and perpetuated by the commentaries of the theologians, the custodians of Muslim dogma and ignorance."[28]

Islam's prophet, Muhammad, had a low view of women, saying, "The woman is a toy, whoever takes her let him care for her."[29] After the Qur'an, one of Islam's most influential books is Muhammad ibn Ismail al-Bukhari's *Al-Jami al-sahih*. Al-Bukhari, a scholar, compiled the sayings of Muhammad into this book. A conversation recorded between one of Allah's apostles and a group of women portrays women as inferior:

> "I have not seen anyone more deficient in intelligence and religion than you. A cautious sensible man could be led astray by some of you." The women asked, "O Allah's Apostle! What is deficient in our intelligence and religion?" He said, "Is not the evidence of two women equal to the witness of one man?" They replied in the affirmative. He said, "This is the deficiency in her intelligence. Isn't it true that a woman can neither pray nor fast during her menses?" The women replied in the affirmative. He said, "This is the deficiency in her religion."[30]

The Qur'an explicitly sanctions domestic violence against women. "Men are in charge of women, because Allah hath made the one of them to excel the other, and because they spend of their property," it notes. "So good women are the obedient, guarding in secret that which Allah hath guarded. As for those from whom ye fear rebellion, admonish them and brandish them to beds apart, and scourge them."[31]

In some Islamic countries, the community commonly celebrates when a baby boy is born. The birth of a baby girl, however, prompts mourning and tears. Princess Sultana of the Royal House of Saud describes the stress of the childbearing years: "Certainly, desire for male children is common in much of the world, but no place can compare with Arab lands, where every woman must endure boiling tension throughout her childbearing years, waiting for the birth of a son. Sons are the sole reason for marriage, the key to satisfaction for the husband."[32]

She adds that in Saudi Arabia only male births and deaths are recorded in public records.[33] When her own mother died, Sultana mourned not only her death but that she would not be recognized as a human being even in death. She speaks wistfully of that moment: "We were leaving Mother behind in the empty vastness of the desert, yet I knew it no longer mattered that there was no stone placed to mark her presence there, or that no religious services were held to speak of the simple woman who had been a flame of love during her lifetime."[34]

Nawal El Saadawi, an Egyptian physician and a director of public health, says female education in Arab countries reduces the girl into a compliant woman who will accept being the property or plaything of a man:

> The education that a female child receives in Arab society is a series of continuous warnings about things that are supposed to be harmful, forbidden, shameful or outlawed by religion. The child therefore is trained to suppress her own desires, to empty herself of authentic, original wants and wishes linked to her own self, and to fill the vacuum that results with the desires of others. Education of female children is therefore transformed into a slow process of annihilation, a gradual throttling of her personality and mind, leaving intact only the outside shell, the body, a lifeless mould of muscle and bone and blood that moves like a wound up rubber doll.
>
> A girl who has lost her personality, her capacity to think in-dependently and to use her own mind, will do what others have told her and will become a toy in their hands and a victim of their decisions.[35]

While it is not popular to say so, the Qur'an permits a man to marry four wives and to copulate with slave girls as well. "If ye fear that ye shall not be able to deal justly with the orphans, marry women of your choice, two or three or four; but if ye fear that ye shall not be able to deal justly (with them), then only one, or (a captive) that your right hand possess, that will be more suitable, to prevent you from doing injustice."[36]

Al-Ghazali (AD 1058–1111) has been recognized as one of the most influential Islamic thinkers. In his work *The Revival of the Religious Sciences*, he defines a woman's role:

> She should stay at home and get on with her spinning, she should not go out often, she must not be well-informed, nor must she be communicative with her neighbours and only visit them when ab-solutely necessary; she should take care of her husband and respect him in his presence and his absence and seek to satisfy him in eve-

rything; she must not cheat on him nor exert money from him; she must not leave her house without his permission and if [he] gives his permission she must not leave surreptitiously. She should put on old clothes and take deserted streets and alleys, avoid markets, and make sure that a stranger does not hear her voice or recognise her; she must not speak to a friend of her husband even in need. . . . Her sole worry should be her virtue, her home as well as her prayers and her fast. If a friend of her husband calls when the latter is absent she must not open the door nor reply to him in order to safeguard her and her husband's honour. She should accept what her husband gives her as sufficient sexual needs at any moment. . . . She should be clean and ready to satisfy her husband's sexual needs at any moment."[37]

Ghazali warns men to be on guard against the guile and immorality of women, saying, "It is a fact that all the trials, misfortunes and woes which befall men come from women."[38]

Sultana, a direct descendant of King Abdul of the House of Saud, tells of the authority of a Saudi male: "The authority of a Saudi male is unlimited; his wife and children survive only if he desires. In our homes, he is the state. This complex situation begins with the rearing of young boys. From an early age, the male child is taught that the women are of little value. They exist only for his comfort and convenience. . . . Taught only the role of master to slave, it is little wonder that by the time he is old enough to take a mate, he considers her his chattel, not his partner."[39]

Islam, like the Pharisees of old and some Christian fundamentalists, seeks to apply moral constraints from the *outside*. Instead of telling men to avert their eyes, Islam demands that women stay indoors or cover themselves. This kind of external morality leads ultimately to tyranny, especially toward women.

Where is the glory and wonder of being a woman? Not in Islam.

Confucianism

Confucianism has dominated much of Asia for 2,500 years. Confucius (551–479 BC) taught more of a moral and political philosophy than a religion.

His main goal was to bring order to society. Confucianism establishes a social hierarchy, beginning with the family and permeating all of society.

In this hierarchy, men are superior to women. All Korean children, for example, learn the phrase *namjon yobi*, which is variously translated "men high, women low" or "men are honored, women are despised." Confucianism inculcates in women the Three Tenets of Obedience (*samjong*): (1) obedience to her father before she is married, (2) obedience to her husband in marriage, and (3) obedience to her husband after his death. There are also Seven Evils for Expelling (divorcing) a Wife (*chilgo*): (1) disobedience to in-laws, (2) not being able to bear a male heir, (3) adultery, (4) jealousy, (5) having an incurable disease, (6) talkativeness, and (7) stealing.

In China, to keep women close to home (and also because small feet were considered a symbol of gentility and wealth), the painful custom of foot binding was practiced from the tenth to the twentieth century: "First her foot was washed in hot water and massaged. Then the child's toes were turned under and pressed against the bottom of her foot. The arches were broken as the foot was pulled straight with the leg, and a long narrow cotton bandage would be tightly wound around the foot from the toes to the ankle to hold the toes in place."[40] When unbandaged, the feet were about three inches long and were called "lotus feet."

The antifemale bias persists in China. In 2002, for every hundred girls born, 117 boys were born. Such social attitudes lead to real-world consequences. By the year 2020 there will be 40 million more men in China than women.[41] Because of the famine in North Korea, starving families are selling their daughters to Chinese men.

Where can we find a culture that honors female? Not in Confucianism.

Accommodating the Culture

Unless the church consciously examines its own culture and seeks to understand and apply kingdom culture, it, too, will end up crushing women. It is a fallen human tendency. The church often has degraded women, at times committing unimaginable offenses. Instead of calling the world to repentance, we have too often stood against reform.

Establishing a culture that has lead to the abuse of women has a long and disturbing lineage in church history. Instead of heeding Christ, too often Christians have been "conformed to this world." Among the church fathers who condoned or justified sexism:

- Tertullian (ca. AD 160–225) wrote that women "are the devil's gateway; you are the unsealer of that [forbidden] tree: you are the first deserter of the divine law: you are she who persuaded him whom the devil was not valiant enough to attack. You destroyed so easily God's image, man."[42]

- Origen (185–254) wrote of the essentially fleshly and thus evil nature of women: "What is seen with the eyes of the creator is masculine, and not feminine, for God does not stoop to look upon what is feminine and of the flesh."[43]

- Epiphanius (ca. 315–403) wrote: "For the female sex is easily seduced, weak, and without much understanding. The devil seeks to vomit out this disorder through women. . . . We wish to apply masculine reasoning and destroy the folly of these women."[44]

- Ambrose (ca. 339–397) wrote: "Whoever does not believe is a woman, and she is still addressed with her physical sexual designation; for the woman who believes is elevated to male completeness and to a measure of the stature of the fullness of Christ."[45]

- Jerome (ca. 342–420) wrote: "As long as woman is for birth and children, she is different from man as body from soul. But when she wishes to serve Christ more than the world, then she will cease to be a woman and will be called man."[46]

- John Chrysostom (ca. 347–407) warned: "Should you reflect about what is contained in beautiful eyes, in a straight nose, in a mouth, in cheeks, you will see that bodily beauty is only a whitewashed tombstone, for inside it is full of filth."[47]

- Augustine (354–430), considered perhaps the greatest Christian theologian of all time, said (erroneously) that only males are made in the image of God: ". . . when I was treating of the nature of the human mind, that the woman, together with her own husband, is the image of God, to that the whole substance may be one image, but when she is referred to separately in her quality as a helpmeet, which regards the woman alone, then she is not the image of God, but as regards the man alone, he is the image of God as fully and completely as when the woman too is joined with him in one."[48]

Too often the modern church has reverted to the justification of the church fathers in maintaining sexist treatment of women. There is a refusal to recognize either the dignity of a woman's being or the glory of her unique function. Too often men who profess Christ use Scripture to justify the beating and subjugation of their wives. Too often "Christian men" treat women as sex objects. Philip Yancey notes that 70 percent of evangelical Christians in the United States engage in premarital sex.[49]

For these and many other sins, we need to repent.

Notes

1. For more on this subject and how worldviews contribute to poverty and prosperity, see my book *Discipling Nations: The Power of Truth to Transform Cultures* (Seattle: YWAM Publishing, 1998; second edition, 2001).

2. Roberto Rodriguez and Patrisia Gonzales, "Deconstructing Machismo," *Chronicle Features*, San Francisco, June 20, 1997; available at Azteca website, http://www.azteca.net/aztec/literat/macho.html.

3. Lilian Calles Barger, *Eve's Revenge* (Grand Rapids: Brazos Press, 2003), 148–49.

4. Ibid., 144.

5. John Mbiti, "The Role of Women in African Traditional Religion," *Cahiers des Religions Africaines* 22 (1988): 69–82; available at http://www.afrikaworld.net/afrel/atr-women.htm.

6. Ibid.

7. From personal e-mail correspondence with Dr. Susan Bolman from Beira, Mozambique; July 26, 2000.

8. Sita Agarwal, *Genocide of Women in Hinduism* (Jabalpur, India: Sudrastan Books, 1999), http://www.geocities.com/realitywithbite/hindu.htm.

9. Ibid.

10. "Grace," November 27, 1988; sent in personal correspondence August 17, 2002.

11. Al-Ash'Ari, *Purdah and the Status of Women in Islam* (New Delhi: Mohit Publications, 1999), 17.

12. Edna Gerstner, "The Woman as Wife," in *Family Practice: God's Prescription for a Healthy Home*, R. C. Sproul Jr., ed. (Phillipsburg, NJ: Presbyterian & Reformed Publishing, 2001), 50.

13. Atharva Veda, 6.2.3: "Let a female child be born somewhere else; here, let a male child be born"; Taittirya Sambita VI.5.10.3: "Hence they [Aryans] reject a female child when born, and take up a male"; Manu.IX.94: "A man, aged thirty years, shall marry a maiden of twelve who pleases him, or a man of twenty-four a girl of eight years of age; if (the performance of) his duties would otherwise be impeded, he must marry sooner"; Garuda.Purana.II.4.91–100 states that if a woman does not perform sati, she will be continually reborn in the "lowly body of a woman" until she does. In contrast, Daksa Smrti IV.18–19 states that a woman who performs sati on her husband's funeral pyre will have eternal bliss in heaven. All references from Agarwal, *Genocide of Women in Hinduism.*

14. "India Lost Ten Million Females Due to Abortion," *The New Jain,* April 2006, http://www.yjponline.org/TNJ-April06/TNJ_06-2_files/page0008.htm.

15. "Granddad Buries Newborn Alive," Reuters, Australian Broadcasting Corporation, July 6, 2007, http://www.abc.net.au/news/stories/2007/07/06/1971505.htm.

16. Victorian A. Velkoff and Arjun Adlakha, "Women of the World: Women's Health in India," U.S. Census Bureau, December 1998, 6–7, http://www.census.gov/ipc/prod/wid-9803.pdf.

17. Personal e-mail correspondence, July 15, 2007.

18. Dr. L. S. Dewaraja, "The Position of Women in Buddhism," The Wheel Publication No. 280 (Kandy, Sri Lanka: Buddhist Publication Society, 1981); available at http://www.urband-harma.org/udharma/positionofwomen.html.

19. Speech of the Buddha to King Udayana, from the *Mahratnakuta,* in Diana Y. Paul, *Women in Buddhism: Images of the Feminine in the Mahayana Tradition* (Berkeley: University of California Press, 1985), 30–31.

20. Victor and Victoria Trimondi, *The Shadow of the Dalai Lama: Sexuality, Magic, and Politics in Tibetan Buddhism* (Düsseldorf and Zurich: Patmos Group, 1999); available at http://www.trimondi.de/SDLE/Part-1-01.htm.

21. Melford E. Spiro, *Buddhism and Society: A Great Tradition and Its Burmese Vicissitudes* (New York: Harper & Row, 1972), 432.

22. Angkana Boonsit, Ron Claassen, and Suwatchara Piemyat, "Restorative Justice and Domestic Violence Resolution in Thailand," *VOMA Connections* no. 17 (Summer 2004): 10, http://www.voma.org/docs/connect17.pdf.

23. Quoted in Rita M. Gross, *Buddhism after Patriarchy: A Feminist History, Analysis, and Reconstruction of Buddhism* (New York: State University of New York Press, 1993), 63.

24. Ibid., 83.

25. Melford E. Spiro, *Kinship and Marriage in Burma: A Cultural and Psychodynamic Analysis* (Berkeley: University of California Press, 1977), 260, in Dewaraja, "The Position of Women in Buddhism."

26. Monique Beadle, "The Sangha and the Thai Sex Industry," Institute for Global Engagement, August 26, 2003.

27. Ibid.

28. Ibn Warraq, "Islam's Shame: Lifting the Veil of Tears," Secular Islam Summit; available on the Committee to Defend Women's Rights in the Middle East website, http://www.middleastwomen.org/.

29. Tuffaha, Ahmad Zaky, Al-Mar'ah wal-Islam [The Woman and Islam], Dar al-Kitab al-Lubnani, Beirut, first edition, 1985, 180, in Saleem Almahdy, "The Treatment of Women In Islam," *The Voice of the Martyrs,* April 1998, 8.

30. Muhammad ibn Ismail al-Bukhari, vol. 1, book 6, no. 301, in Almahdy, "The Treatment of Women in Islam," 8.

31. Qur'an 4:34.

32. Jean Sasson, *Princess: A True Story of Life behind the Veil in Saudi Arabia* (Atlanta: Windsor-Brooke Books, 2001), 151–52.

33. Ibid., 23.

34. Ibid., 85.

35. Nawal El Saadawi, *The Hidden Face of Eve: Women in the Arab World* (London: Zed Books Ltd., 1980), 13.

36. Qur'an 4:3.

37. Al-Ghazali, "The Revival of the Religious Sciences," in Azam Kamguian, "Islam and Women's Rights," Committee to Defend Women's Rights in the Middle East, http://www.middleastwomen.org/html/islamwomen.htm.

38. Ibid.

39. Sasson, *Princess*, 22.

40. "Bound Feet," *Golden Legacy Curriculum* (Sunnyvale, CA: Chinese Historical and Cultural Project, 1994), http://www.eduref.org/cgi-bin/printlessons.cgi/Virtual/Lessons/Social_Studies/Anthropology/ANT0201.html.

41. Yan Yai, "Shortage of Females in China Grows Grave," *Washington Times National Weekly Edition*, March 15–21, 2004, 24.

42. Tertullian, "*De cultu feminarum,*" 1.1, *The Fathers of the Church*, vol. 40, 117ff., in Leonard J. Swidler, *Biblical Affirmations of Woman* (Philadelphia: Westminster Press, 1979), 346.

43. Origen, "*Selecta in Exodus* XVIII," 17, Mingne, *Patrologia Graeca*, vol. 12, cols. 296ff., in Swidler, *Biblical Affirmations of Woman*, 342.

44. Epiphanius, "Adversus Collyridianos," Migne, *Patrologia Graeca*, vol. 42, cols. 740ff., in Swidler, *Biblical Affirmations of Woman*, 343.

45. Ambrose, "*Expositio evangelii secundum Lucam,*" liber X, n. 161, Migne, *Patrologia Latina*, vol. 15, col. 1844, in Swidler, *Biblical Affirmations of Woman,* 346.

46. Jerome, "*Comm. in epist. ad Ephes,*" III.5 Migne, *Patrologia Latina*, vol. 26, col. 567, in Swidler, *Biblical Affirmations of Woman*, 345.

47. John Chrysostom, "Letter to Theodora," chap. 14, *Sources chretiennes*, vol. 117, 167, in Swidler, *Biblical Affirmations of Woman,* 343.

48. Augustine, "*De Trinitate,*" 7.7, 10, in Swidler, *Biblical Affirmations of Woman*, 349.

49. Philip Yancey, *Rumors of Another World* (Grand Rapids: Zondervan, 2003), 79.

CHAPTER 5
The Disappearance of Women

Sexism, at its root, is hatred of women. The Greek word *misogyny* (*miso*, "hatred," and *gyne*, "woman") perfectly captures this horrendous phenomenon. The feminist movement has rightly stood against this mindset and the horrors that it has birthed over the centuries. But, tragically, instead of recognizing that the biblical worldview provides a solid foundation to honor women as women, radical feminists have embraced a metaphysic that undermines both the woman and the feminine.

At first, they bought into the modernism of Darwinian naturalism. As Darwin himself said in his 1896 book, *The Descent of Man, and Selection in Relation to Sex*:

> The chief distinction in the intellectual powers of the two sexes is shewn by man's attaining to a higher eminence, in whatever he takes up, than can woman—whether requiring deep thought, reason, or imagination, or merely the use of the senses and hands. If two lists were made of the most eminent men and women in poetry, painting, sculpture, music (inclusive both of composition and performance), history, science, and philosophy, with half-a-dozen names under each subject, the two lists would not bear comparison. We may also infer, from the law of the deviation

from averages . . . that if men are capable of a decided pre-emi-
nence over women in many subjects, the average of mental power
in man must be above that of woman.[1]

At its most basic level, sexism compares men to women and finds women
lacking. Radical feminists, perhaps unconsciously, accept the error of male
superiority and seek to turn women into men. This hatred of women leads
to the death of the feminine metaphysic—*femininicide*—and the death of
female—*femalicide*.

In this remorseless attack on the feminine, it is a man's world, and male
values dominate. A single, unfettered male is the ideal. Writing in *Taking Sex
Differences Seriously*, researcher Steven E. Rhoads states: "Cultural anthro-
pologist Robbie David-Floyd finds that pregnant professionals in positions of
real power tend 'to see the body as an imperfect tool that the more perfect self
should control. They tend to experience pregnancy and birth as unpleasant
because they are so out of control.' Their 'conscious choice [is] to dissociate
themselves from their biology.'"[2]

The death of women was preceded by the death of the feminine. In his
1965 book, *The Flight from Woman*, psychologist Karl Stern discussed "the
woman who finds it difficult to accept her womanly role. This is quite inde-
pendent of the injustices imposed on women in many societies: it is rather an
over-evaluation of masculine achievement and a debasement of values which
one commonly associates with the womanly; a rejection, often unconscious,
even of motherhood; an aping of man, associated with an unceasing under-
tone of envy and resentment. In either case, whether of the man or of the
woman . . . there is a flight from the feminine."[3]

Lilian Calles Barger states that these flights "allow us to become, in a
sense, invisible as women and able to navigate the male-defined public world
with less notice."[4] Raymond C. Ortlund writes: "Ironically, feminism shares
the very premise upon which male domination is founded, namely, that my
personal significance is measured according to my rung on the ladder, and
my opportunity for personal fulfillment enlarges or contracts according to my
role. By this line of reasoning, the goal of life degenerates into competition
for power."[5]

The Three Waves of Feminism

Feminism is not new. In fact, Jesus was the first pure feminist. He held a high view of humanity and thus had, unlike his culture, a high view of women. He spoke of them and to them with dignity, and he treated them with respect. Ashamedly, too seldom has the church that bears his name heeded his example.

Feminism has had three waves in history. We will examine each in turn.

First-wave Feminists

Active in the nineteenth and early twentieth centuries and largely operating consciously or unconsciously from a biblical worldview, first-wave feminists saw women as *women* and as *human*. For them a woman was not to be judged by a masculine standard but by the equally valued feminine standard.

Also called "maternal feminists," they were interested in motherhood, children, family, and the good of the larger community. Many were committed Christians or were at least working from the memory of a more biblical worldview. They reacted to the sexist cultural stories that often brutalized women. Affirming the dignity of women and their unique functions of homemaking, succoring, and mothering, they had a high view of women, children, and the family and had a social and familial conscience.

In the United States they led the fight to get women and children out of sweatshops and into the home. They fought for a family wage that would permit a husband to earn enough money to support a family so that his wife and children would not have to work outside the home. They wanted to allow women to be homemakers and mothers and to engage in the philanthropic and social needs of the larger community. They wanted children to get an education. Their instinct for motherhood made the first-wave feminists strong pro-life advocates, leading the movement against abortion.

Some of the leaders of this movement were:

- Susan B. Anthony (1820–1906): Raised in a godly Quaker family, she stood against slavery, against abortion, and for women's suffrage.

- Elizabeth Cady Stanton (1815–1902): Mentored by a Presbyterian pastor, she challenged sexism both in society and in the church.
- Sarah Grimke (1792–1873) and Angelina Grimke (1805–1879): Daughters of a slave-owning judge and denounced by certain elements in the church, they helped to lead the fight against slavery and for woman's suffrage.
- Sojourner Truth (ca. 1797–1883): Born a slave, this evangelist became a leader of the abolitionist and feminist movements. While at the Women's Convention in Akron, Ohio, in 1851, she responded to a heckling clergyman with what would become her most famous speech, known as "Ain't I a Woman?"

That man over there says that women need to be helped into carriages, and lifted over ditches, and to have the best place everywhere. Nobody ever helps me into carriages, or over mud-puddles, or gives me any best place! And ain't I a woman? Look at me! Look at my arm! I have ploughed and planted, and gathered into barns, and no man could head me! And ain't I a woman? I could work as much and eat as much as a man—when I could get it—and bear the lash as well! And ain't I a woman? I have borne thirteen children, and seen most all sold off to slavery, and when I cried out with my mother's grief, none but Jesus heard me! And ain't I a woman? . . .

Then that little man in black there, he says women can't have as much rights as men, 'cause Christ wasn't a woman! Where did your Christ come from? Where did your Christ come from? From God and a woman! Man had nothing to do with Him.

If the first woman God ever made was strong enough to turn the world upside down all alone, these women together ought to be able to turn it back, and get it right side up again! And now they is asking to do it. The men better let them.[6]

Missionaries William Carey, Amy Carmichael, and Hudson Taylor were also first-wave feminists, fighting against child prostitution and widow burning in India and foot binding in China.

Second-wave Feminists

As the predominant Western worldview shifted from biblical theism to secularism, feminism shifted along with it. Feminism became less interested in others and more interested in the self. Family and community were jettisoned for the individual. Motherhood was jettisoned for the marketplace. Self-sacrifice was exchanged for self-serving.

Second-wave feminists, becoming active in the mid-twentieth century, agreed with their predecessors that women are fully human, but they downplayed the feminine aspects of their natures. They foolishly accepted a masculine standard and demanded that women be graded by it. By surrendering to this value system, women inadvertently acknowledged male superiority and surrendered the glory and honor that are uniquely theirs as women.

A number of strands fed this movement.

- Margaret Sanger (1879–1966) was a leader of the modern eugenics movement in the United States. In *The Pivot of Civilization*, she linked poverty and sex and zeroed in on the breeding habits of the poor, advocating widespread abortion. After the world's outcry against the eugenics espoused by fascists like Hitler, Sanger changed the name of her organization, the American Birth Control League, to Planned Parenthood. It was a stroke of marketing genius.
- Sigmund Freud (1856–1939) linked sex with psychological health. Freud argued that Christianity was antisex, whereas people need to satisfy their natural sexual inclinations. (As an aside, Freud must never have read the Book of Genesis or the Song of Solomon; God created sex for human beings to enjoy.)
- With the rise of national socialism, human beings were transformed into mere "instruments of production." A woman's ideal place was no longer in the home, but on the assembly line.
- Alfred Kinsey (1894–1956) laid the foundation for the normality of sexual deviancy through his now-discredited research.[7] Kinsey loosed the bonds between morality and sex

and laid the foundation for cultural, behavioral, and policy change in the West.

- Hugh Hefner (1926–), the founder of *Playboy*, was a disciple of Kinsey and became the popularizer and conveyor of Kinsey's vision and values.

The late Peter Drucker, one of the world's leading business gurus, stated the goal of the second-wave feminists: "We are busily unmaking one of the proudest social achievements in the nineteenth century, which was to take married women out of the work force so that they could devote themselves to family and children."[8]

Third-wave Feminists

Advocates from this group, becoming active in the late twentieth century, don't want women to become like men. Instead, they reject masculine and feminine standards, building their lives on asexual, postmodern standards.

Postmodern feminists reject any notion of absolute truth and deny any essential distinctions between men and women. Working from the metaphysical foundation of monism, they assume there are no transcendent differences. In this movement, both male and female disappear. This leads to a fusion of masculine and feminine sexuality, in which gender roles are interchangeable.

Language Manipulation

Whoever controls the language controls the culture. Thus the "sacredness of life" has devolved to the "quality of life." "Abortion" becomes "pro-abortion." "Baby" becomes "tissue" or "product of conception." "Sex," which implies distinctions between male and female, has been replaced by "gender," an elastic sociological term that may be used for heterosexuals, homosexuals, bisexuals, transvestites, and "transgendered" or "transsexual" people who have undergone surgery to "change" their sex.

Language not only changes, but the very definitions of words change. Witness the twenty-first-century debate over the word *marriage*. For generations, Scripture has shaped people's understanding of marriage as a sacred institution between one man and one woman—"until death do us part." But as the cultural story shifted from biblical theism to secularism, marriage came to be known as a social contract, with the idea of mutual faithfulness shriveling to faithfulness to yourself. Now marriage is between "consenting adults" and can include two women, two men, or even one man and many women or one woman and many men.

Such language adroitness even slips into so-called gender-neutral versions of the Bible or hymnals. Now words translated for centuries in male or female terms are translated in ways deemed less offensive to postmodern sensibilities. "Son" becomes "child," and "God the Father" becomes "Creator God."

Philosophical Roots

In our postmodern world, secular materialism is being combined with a pagan spirituality to shape a new language and ultimately a whole new world order. Neo-Paganism is rooted in the monistic or pantheistic assumption that all is one. All distinctions blur and finally disappear. This is the case in the metaphysics of sexuality as well. In the end, there is no distinction between male and female, masculine and feminine. The sexual ideal of this Neo-Paganism is androgyny.

The word *androgyny* is a combination of the Greek words *andros* ("male") and *gyne* ("female"). The Greek word *andrognos* literally means "male and female in one."

Androgyny is the state of indeterminate gender. Given this definition, human sexuality is "constructed" by the sociological impulses of a culture or the personal whim of each individual.

Two pop icons exemplify the coming androgynous order: Madonna, the epitome of the postmodern constructed personality, and Michael Jackson, who has gone beyond Madonna's "sculpting" of her persona to the sculpting of his body. Jackson, while born a male, is playing out a postmodern role of appearing androgynous. These celebrities assert that sexual identity is not fixed; it is a personal preference.

In postmodern society, the transcendence of sexuality is gone. There is no ultimate meaning to our sexuality or to our bodies. There are no role distinctions between men and women. This interchangeability takes place in the workplace, in the military, in the home, and in the church. It is even being argued that this is the case in the act of procreation, as we will see below. Equality, in modern feminism, means sameness. Equality, in postmodern feminism, means a blank slate. We can shape ourselves and even our bodies however we may want.

In post-modern culture our bodies reveal nothing. They are a blank canvas upon which to paint, a blank piece of paper upon which to write, a whiteboard on which to draw. Today people write on their bodies with tattoos, pierce their bodies with jewelry, do "plastic surgery" to cut away skin or change the shape of a face, and use instruments to remove fat—all in order to re-create who they are.

Author and journalist Danielle Crittenden has stated that women want lives "unhampered by our biology."[9] For women to reach their potential, they must be child free. Knives and chemicals will make this happen. Abortion is one way. The birth-control pill—which allowed sex to be separated from the archaic language and culture of marriage, family, and motherhood—is the other.

Sex is now "casual" and "recreational." Barger writes, "For the average woman, the pill has provided a way to divorce sex from procreation, so she can make herself available to any sexual partner she chooses at the moment. Woman is now considered to be available 24/7/365."[10]

In abortion, the medical community uses chemicals and "reproductive technologies" to rid a woman of unwanted "tissue." Like a sculptor, the doctor uses tools to transform the place of compassion (a woman's womb) into a chamber of death. Barger perceptively notes, "The widely practiced violence of abortion is not a sign of progress but a sign that women's reproductive ability needs to be exterminated in order for society to go 'forward.' In an environment hostile to women's bodies and through abortion, women participate in a war against their own bodies, objectifying them."[11]

Researchers are now working to blur the line of biology even further. Hans Schoeler and Karin Huebner have turned mouse embryonic stem cells into eggs that can be fertilized. As this technology develops, a lesbian or homosexual couple could have children with one partner providing the genetic makeup for an egg and the other for a sperm.[12]

Androgyny, however, is not evolution; it is *devolution*. In the creation order, androgyny is represented in the lower forms of life, such as paramecia and amoebas. The higher forms of life, in contrast, exhibit greater design, complexity, and differentiation.

Against Motherhood

This drift of culture has produced a selfishness that leads men to sire children but not to father them. It has led women to kill their babies before they are born (through abortion) and after they are born (by abandoning them in toilets or trash bins or drowning them in a convenient water source). Until the recent U.S. Supreme Court ruling, some women in America were killing their children *as* they were born—via partial-birth abortion.

The radical feminist movement, of the modern and postmodern varieties, is part of a culture of self that seeks to stamp out motherhood. Growing numbers of websites reflect this phenomenon. Some are related to feminism, others to the radical ecology movement. What they have in common is animus to anything maternal. A few of the sites in this antimaternal network are Child-Free Zone, Voluntary Human Extinction Movement, No Kidding! and Planned Parenthood.

No wonder, then, that postmodern industrial societies have experienced a decline in birthrates. John and Barbara Wilkke describe the "death of the West" when they write that "Europe and Japan are dying. Japan has a total fertility rate of 1.4 [children per woman, with a rate of 2.1 needed to maintain population parity]. If this continues in the next century, its population will drop from 125 to 55 million. Europe is in a similar fix. Eighty-three countries are now below replacement fertility levels. These encompass 2.7 billion people, 44 percent of the world's total."[13]

Worth Found in the Marketplace

As worldview has shifted from biblical theism to secular materialism, so our identity has shifted from our having intrinsic worth because we are made in the image of God to our worth being defined by the marketplace.

An atheistic, materialistic paradigm assumes that the only thing that is real is matter. Therefore, the only things that have value are material things. One's worth is defined by the marketplace. Retired Brandeis University professor Linda Hirshman captures this well when she writes that "money is the marker of success in a market economy; it usually accompanies power, and it enables the bearer to wield power, including within the family."[14]

People who are not making money in a job have little or no value. Thus women who work long hours at homemaking, succoring, and motherhood have no value, because, in a material-oriented culture, they are not seen as "productive members of society."

Betty Friedan contributed profoundly to the idea that worth is found in the marketplace when she wrote *The Feminine Mystique* in 1963. Friedan states that "man . . . was set apart from other animals by his mind's power to have an idea, a vision, and shape the future to it. . . . When he discovers and creates and shapes a future different from his past, he is a man, a human being."[15]

Friedan is correct in noting that humans are distinct from the animals in their ability to dream, discover, and shape the future. This is, in fact, a biblical assumption. Her error is to assume that this ability only applies to people working in the marketplace. Friedan assumes that women who choose to work in their home are functioning at a less-than-human level. She likens women who make homes and succor children to mere animals. Again, she writes: "Vacuuming the living room floor—with or without makeup—is not work that takes enough thought or energy to challenge any woman's full capacity."[16] She finds the nurturing of children, building the next generation of a nation's leaders, creating a home that can be a refuge for a family, succoring friends and strangers, and "entertaining angels unawares" to be mindless.

Likewise, Professor Hirshman states that women who devote their time to changing their babies' diapers have "voluntarily become untouchables."[17] Neither Hirshman nor Friedan understands the powerful role of the nation-building, culture-creating woman and mother of Proverbs 31.

The radical feminist metaphysic, either consciously or unconsciously, is redefining marriage and attempting to reorder society. But the family is the building block of society; therefore, as the family devolves, the society will slide into anarchy and poverty.

Where are the honor and dignity of women to be found? Not in second-wave and third-wave feminism.

Evangelical Feminism

So where do evangelical feminists, who stand strongly against the unbiblical crushing of women, fit in?

First, we must note that evangelical feminists and so-called Christian feminists are not the same. The latter, despite their self-appointed title, are conscious secularists who routinely challenge the authority of Scripture. They are usually found in the liberal wing of the church. By contrast, evangelical feminists (also known as "biblical feminists") tend to have a high view of scriptural authority. What they challenge is the traditional interpretation of Scripture that calls for a hierarchy of roles in the church and in the family. Instead of recognizing the dignity of women and their roles, they have followed the siren call of third-wave feminists into egalitarianism, a belief in the ultimate sameness of all people.

Of course, all human beings, young and old, slave and free, Jew and Gentile, big and small, healthy and broken, female and male, are made in the image of God. But philosophical egalitarianism is rooted in the monistic tenet "god is one," in contrast to sexism's absolute differentiation. Thus, the egalitarian asserts that to be equal means to be *the same*—undifferentiated, interchangeable, identical, and indistinguishable. Egalitarians see distinctions as (almost) immoral. There is no place for hierarchy or subordination in the vocabulary or practice of egalitarians. They ultimately are promoting role interchangeability for men and women.

Evangelical feminists unconsciously tend to allow monism, not Trinitarianism, to create the framework for their hermeneutics. This framework alters their understanding of the Bible. Scholar Susan T. Foh states: "The most crucial question the biblical feminists have raised is how to interpret the Bible. Deculturization is a part of the biblical feminists' hermeneutic; they think that since the Bible was written in a patriarchal culture, the biblical writers are prejudiced by that culture against women's rights. . . . According to this approach, the Bible is fallible and it can contradict itself. In effect, this view exalts human reason, by which man then determines what is and what is not God's authoritative word."[18]

Mary Kassian writes of the new metaphysic in *The Feminist Gospel,* saying, "Religious and secular feminism were of the same essence. They were based on the same presuppositions, and were therefore destined to intersect and merge. . . . The alteration of God-language and the increasing hermeneutic liberty employed by feminist theologians had catapulted the religious movement forward onto the same path as that of secular feminism."[19]

Some evangelical feminists go so far as to say, "There is no hierarchy in the Trinity, only absolute equality."[20] They refuse to allow God to define himself as unity and diversity. Instead, they seek to define God as absolute unity. Their hermeneutic leads to a paradigm of role interchangeability, which is a secular ideal. They project this paradigm onto texts that relate to men and to women and onto God himself. Kassian continues:

> With this definition in hand, Biblical feminists turned to the Bible. They found that while the Bible did teach the essential equality of women and men, it also taught role differentiation. In order to harmonize the Bible's teachings with their view of equality, these feminists found it necessary to determine which Scriptural texts were dynamic and which were static, which were inspired and which were the author's bias, which were true and which were in error. In doing so, Biblical feminists adopted a feminist mind-set. . . . Christian feminists adopted this mentality when they used their own definition of equality to judge the validity and applicability of the Bible. . . . Even for conservative evangelical feminists, women's experience became the new norm for Biblical study and theological interpretation.[21]

Changing Language

In their laudable attempt to stamp out sexism, evangelical feminists brought feminist language into the church. Worse, they infused biblical terminology with feminist meanings. So while they continue to use language common to Christians with a high view of biblical authority, the definitions of the words have changed. Some have even sought to change the language itself. One way is to make the Scriptures "gender-neutral." For example, "Father, Son, and Holy Spirit" become "Creator, Redeemer, and Sustainer." Some Christian feminists go so far as to speak of God as "Mother/Father" (androgyny) or to affirm God as "Mother" (paganism). They move from describing the feminine nature of God to calling God "Mother" or using female personal pronouns when referring to God.

Let me reiterate that there is a distinction between the language of metaphor (God *is* a mother) and the language of simile (God is *like* a mother). In God's self-disclosure he uses simile to reflect his maternal heart. But God uses masculine personal pronouns—*he* and *his*, not *she* and *hers*.

Mary Kassian notes how language is employed to change the church:

> The phenomena of inclusive language recognized and further served to reinforce the paradigm offered by feminist theology. It, more than theological rhetoric, brought the feminist debate to the level of the ordinary believer as women's studies had done. Feminist theology was thereby translated from an academic philosophy to the level of practical daily worship of the Christian community. Feminists had named themselves and their world, and now, through inclusive language, they and their Christian communities began to name God.[22]

Critiquing the Church

Mary Pride is a current-day maternal feminist. She warns that third-wave feminists, including evangelical feminists, may bring about the destruction of Christianity in the West. She says these feminists rob men and women of the glory of their uniqueness, as they have misplaced their priorities: "The evangelical feminists are really *much* more anxious to convert us to feminism than they are to convert feminists to Christ."[23]

This problem is not confined to evangelical feminists, of course. Too many Christians of all kinds, in violation of Romans 12:2, are conformed to our culture. Christian men are too often sexists, contributing to the crushing of women and the disparaging of the God of the Bible. In reaction, some

Christians are courageously challenging sexism and chauvinism, recognizing the injustice they inflict on women, girls, mothers, daughters, and sisters. However, instead of leading a truly biblical, countercultural movement that honors women as women, they align themselves with feminism. In so doing, they contribute to the disappearance of women, exchanging the glory of the "one and many God" for the "all is one god" of Neo-Paganism.

Nevertheless, the unbiblical extremes that either crush women or lead to their disappearance are not the end of the story. There is a third way that we will meet in the pages ahead. This way recognizes that women and men are made in the *imago Dei*, equal in their being but diverse in their roles and functions.

Notes

1. Charles Darwin, *The Descent of Man, and Selection in Relation to Sex* (New York: D. Appelton and Company, 1896), chap. 19; available at http://www.biologie.uni-hamburg.de/b-online/e36_descent/descent_chap19.htm.

2. Steven E. Rhoads, *Taking Sex Differences Seriously* (San Francisco: Encounter Books, 2004), 36.

3. Karl Stern, *The Flight from Woman* (New York: The Noonday Press, 1965), 6.

4. Lilian Calles Barger, *Eve's Revenge* (Grand Rapids: Brazos Press, 2003), 25.

5. Raymond C. Ortlund Jr., "Gender, Worth, and Equality: Manhood and Womanhood according to Genesis 1–3," in *Recovering Biblical Manhood and Womanhood: A Response to Evangelical Feminism,* John Piper and Wayne Grudem, eds. (Wheaton: Crossway, 1991), 112.

6. Rendered in a modern dialect; originally recorded by Frances Gage in *History of Woman Suffrage*, produced by Elizabeth Cady Stanton, Susan B. Anthony, Matilda Joslyn Gage, and Ida Husted Harper in six volumes from 1887 to 1922; available at http://en.wikipedia.org/wiki/Ain%27t_I_a_Woman%3F.

7. For example, Judith Reisman questions the validity of "scientific" data gained from pedophiles' interactions with young children; Judith Reisman, "Kinsey and the Homosexual Revolution," in *The Journal of Human Sexuality*, George A. Rekers, ed. (Addison, TX: Lewis and Stanley Publishers, 1996); available at http://www.leaderu.com/jhs/reisman.html.

8. Peter Drucker, in Cullen Murphy, "A Survey of the Research," *The Wilson Quarterly* (Winter 1982): 75.

9. Danielle Crittenden, *What Our Mothers Didn't Tell Us: Why Happiness Eludes the Modern Woman* (New York: Simon & Schuster, 1999), 108.

10. Barger, *Eve's Revenge*, 71.

11. Ibid., 73.

12. Chuck Colson, "Science without Limits: Reinventing Parenthood," *BreakPoint Commentary* , May 21, 2003, http://www.breakpoint.org/listingarticle.asp?ID=4683.

13. John C. Willke and Barbara H. Willke, *Abortion Questions and Answers: Love Them Both* (Cincinnati: Hayes Publishing, 2003), 291.

14. Linda Hirshman, "Homeward Bound," *The American Prospect Online Edition*, December 2005, http://www.prospect.org/web/printfriendly-view.ww?id=10659.

15. Betty Friedan, *The Feminine Mystique*, in Hirshman, "Homeward Bound."

16. Ibid.

17. Hirshman, "Homeward Bound."

18. Susan T. Foh, *Women and the Word of God: A Response to Biblical Feminism* (Phillipsburg, NJ: Presbyterian and Reformed Publishing, 1979), 2.

19. Mary A. Kassian, *The Feminist Gospel: The Movement to Unite Feminism with the Church* (Wheaton: Crossway, 1992), 184.

20. Loren Cunningham, "How We Know What We Believe," in Loren Cunningham and David J. Hamilton, *Why Not Women: A Biblical Study of Women in Missions, Ministry, and Leadership* (Seattle: YWAM Publishing, 2000), 43.

21. Kassian, *The Feminist Gospel*, 212.

22. Ibid., 147.

23. Mary Pride, *The Way Home: Beyond Feminism, Back to Reality* (Wheaton: Good News Publishers, 1985), 11 (italics in the original).

PART 3

THE BIBLICAL FOUNDATIONS

CHAPTER 6

Worldview and God's Word

In the West, we are privileged to enjoy many marvelous things: automobiles, DVD players, dishwashers, and so on. They bring us pleasure, expand our capabilities, and generally make our lives easier. Yet when we drive a new car off the sales lot or pull new electronic devices out of their boxes, most of us wouldn't dream of operating them without first looking at the instructions. What tire pressure is recommended for safe driving? The owner's manual will say. Where do you plug in the red wire? The instructions tell you. Skipping the instructions not only invites frustration in operating complex machinery, but it could well be dangerous.

Yet without giving it a second thought, many people ignore the most important instructions we have ever received: the Bible, God's written Word. And the consequences, both on this earth and for eternity, can be disastrous. As we have seen, the devaluation and abuse of women are some of those disastrous consequences. Now that we have seen the power of a faulty metastory to destroy lives, we need to move on to a true metastory that will preserve them. Before we can do that, however, we need to lay the foundations. We need to make clear the basis for our beliefs.

In this short chapter we will look at an absolutely essential element of a proper worldview: God's written Word. Of course, many people claim to follow the teachings (or at least the spirit) of the Bible, but their applications can vary radically. Some claim the Bible encourages them to crush women through sexism. Others claim the Bible allows us to redefine womanhood out of existence through feminism. I am proposing a radical middle way: biblical complementarianism.

Before we can get there, however, we need to agree on the ground rules of scriptural interpretation, also known as hermeneutical principles. That's what this chapter is all about.

Revelation

Biblical scholars agree that God not only *can* communicate but that he *has* communicated to human beings in four ways. These four means of revelation may be grouped into two categories:

- God's *works*, which reveal something of himself to all mankind. These works are: (1) the creation, from the farthest galaxies to the smallest subatomic particles, encompassing the physical and spiritual realms, the seen and the unseen; and (2) the creation of mankind, specifically, as the *imago Dei*. Theologians call this "general revelation."
- God's *Word*, by which God reveals himself to those who would be saved. This Word has two aspects: (1) the written Word (the Bible, both Old Testament and New Testament); and (2) the living Word, Jesus Christ (John 1:1, 14). Theologians call this "special revelation."

While all four means of revelation provide important ways we can learn about our Creator, this chapter will focus on properly understanding and applying God's written Word, the Bible.

What is the final authority upon which we base our life and thinking? Some people say it is the government. Others say it is the experts, or cultural norms, or the self. Still others claim the church as their final authority. While each of these things has its sphere of validity, for the Christian who believes that the Bible is God's inspired revelation, there can be only one ultimate authority. Scripture alone (or, as the Reformers said, *sola scriptura*) gets the last word.

Of course, this commitment to follow the dictates of the Bible is meaningless if we don't properly understand and apply it. That's what the science of hermeneutics is all about.

Hermeneutics

According to the 1828 Webster's Dictionary, hermeneutics is "the art of finding the meaning of an author's words and phrases, and of explaining it to others." There are two aspects of hermeneutics:

- *Exegesis* brings out of any text "the meaning the writers intended to convey and which their readers were expected to gather from it."[1] Exegesis answers the questions *What does the text say?* and *What does it mean?*
- *Exposition* shows how the text is relevant to people today in their cultural settings. Exposition answers the question *How does this apply?*

These two hermeneutical principles are the fundamental building blocks of scriptural interpretation. The framework for scriptural interpretation, however, is something called the *grammatical-historical approach*. As the name implies, this method is interested in both the grammar of the text and the history behind it. Knowing these helps us understand what the text means.

Throughout the history of the church, a number of assumptions have accompanied the grammatical-historical approach:

- God is infinite (transcendent) *and* personal (immanent).
- God has revealed himself through his works *and* his Word.
- God has revealed himself in the Scriptures truly, but not exhaustively.
- The Holy Spirit used human beings to record God's written Word.

With this approach, the focus is on the text itself to answer the questions *What does it say?* and *What does it mean?* The grammatical-historical method assumes that Scripture is, as the apostle Paul said, "God-breathed" and that the task of Christians is to sit under its authority.

But with the rise of secularism, we saw a shift in fundamental assumptions and thus in the understanding of hermeneutics. Operating either consciously or unconsciously from a man-centered, naturalistic set of assumptions based on Enlightenment thinking (there is no God and there are no miracles), a skeptical view of the Scriptures was inevitable. Biblical scholars call this the *historical-critical method*. This approach sees the authors of Scripture as godly men who nonetheless wrote from their own personal experience and perceptions of God. Proper historical-critical interpretation seeks to understand the mind of the author at the moment he wrote the text. This method views the Bible as nothing more than any other classic or good literature.

There is a third approach we need to mention, called the *imaging* method. Built on a postmodern mindset, the focus is neither on the text itself nor on the writer's perception of God, but on the reader's perception of God. In postmodernism, there is no metanarrative. On this barren landscape, there is skepticism both of the claimed absolute truth of an older age and of the rationalism of the modern world. In the imaging method, the individual creates all "truth." The imagination the reader brings to the text establishes the meaning of the text.

Basic Principles

If we compare God's Word to a forest, we quickly see that there are two ways to look at it. The first is to stand *in* the forest and study the individual trees (individual verses).

The second is to stand *outside* the forest and examine it from a distance, perhaps from the top of a mountain. This is the worldview or metanarrative perspective. Both have their place, and later in this book, when we come to the transforming story, we will view Scripture from both the mountaintop and inside the forest.

For now, I want to alert you to the basic hermeneutical principles that will guide our interpretation of Scripture. There are, of course, many excellent volumes on this important subject that treat it in more depth.[2] But the principles below will suffice for now.

- Christ is the central focus of the Bible. Jesus, the living Word, makes clear the written Word.
- The Bible interprets the Bible. The Bible provides checks and balances within itself.
- An individual text should be interpreted within
    1. the immediate context,
    2. the biblical book itself,
    3. the body of work of the particular author (e.g., Moses or Paul),
    4. the given testament (Old or New), and
    5. the entire Scriptures.
- The metanarrative—the big story—must interpret the smaller details. Elements of the biblical metanarrative or worldview include: (1) the existence of the one true God, (2) man—both female and male—being made in the image of God, (3) the reality of the Fall, (4) the fact that history is going somewhere, and (5) the fact that human beings are free moral agents and can affect history.
- We are to understand the less clear passages in Scripture in light of the clear passages.
- The explicit teachings (prescriptions) interpret the examples (descriptions). We are to build principles for living based on the commands rather than on the examples.
- Where the Bible speaks, we speak; where the Bible is silent, we are silent.
- We are not to be dogmatic on nonessential doctrines. At the same time, we must not flee the essentials of the faith simply because they are difficult or unpopular.
- There is a range of clarity in Scripture. Not all doctrines are equally clear.
    1. Some things are unquestionably true (or, as Francis Schaeffer called them, "true truth"). The deity of Christ, the virgin birth, and Christ's death and resurrection are examples. We need to defend them confidently and be ready to die for them.

2. Other doctrines, however, are merely probable or even just possible. We must come to conclusions about them, but hold our conclusions lightly, with a certain amount of humility. In areas such as the mode of baptism or the structure of church governance, we need to exhibit charity toward those who believe differently. As the old saying attributed to Augustine goes, "In essentials, unity; in nonessentials, diversity; in all things, charity."

- The Bible critiques culture; culture does not critique the Bible.

With these principles in mind for interpreting God's instruction book, we are ready to move on to the true metastory. This worldview will reinforce the God-given dignity of women.

Notes

1. Walter A. Elwell, ed., *Evangelical Dictionary of Theology* (Grand Rapids: Baker Academic, 2001), 611, s.v. "exegesis."

2. An excellent and readable book on hermeneutics from a solidly evangelical perspective is Robertson McQuilkin's *Understanding and Applying the Bible* (Chicago: Moody, 1992).

CHAPTER 7
The Trinity as a Model

One of the many reasons I believe Christianity is true is because it is so counterintuitive. The Christian faith is not something that a philosopher thought up after spending a week meditating in the mountains. For example, the heroes of the Bible are often some of the worst sinners you will ever come across.

Unlike the gods of the other world religions, the God portrayed in the Bible cannot be bribed and is not impressed with outward signs of religiosity. He is concerned not just with the rich and powerful, but with the poor and weak. He wants not our money nor our religious performances, but our hearts. This God is holy, and he hates sin. Scripture says, in fact, that all people are spiritually dead and under God's judgment. Yet Christianity teaches that this same God has provided a way of escape by coming to earth in the form of a man, dying on the cross for our sins, and offering forgiveness and eternal life to all who believe.

One of the most astoundingly counterintuitive claims of Christianity is that this God is a Trinity, three in one. Before the beginning of the universe, there was individuality *within* community. This one God exists as three eternally divine persons: Father, Son, and Holy Spirit. In his own perfect being, this God encompasses both diversity and unity. Each person is fully God; yet there are not three Gods, but one.

Figure 9: Trinity

No one could (or would) make this up. The paradox is too great. Again, that's one reason I believe Christianity is true. Another reason is because doctrines such as this are not esoteric religious knowledge with no application in the real world. As we will see in this chapter, the Trinity not only helps us make sense of our salvation in Christ; it also provides the intellectual and moral foundation for the equal dignity of men and women. The Trinity leads us to the glorious revelation of the individual within community. With a good grasp of this great doctrine, we are ready to see women as equal actors in the great drama of the kingdom.

An Ancient Question

For thousands of years, philosophers have struggled to make sense of the unity and diversity that are present in the universe. When we look at creation, we see both incredible diversity (plants, animals, peoples, cultures, languages, etc.) and incredible unity or similarity. There are many different breeds of dogs, for example, yet all share a common "doggyness." The same is true of other types of animals, and it is also true of people. All peoples share a core of similarity, both in physical characteristics and in psychological makeup. These simple observations create the two poles of unity and diversity. Most metanarratives emphasize one and de-emphasize the other. Only the biblical worldview holds both in balance, and the balance is rooted within the Trinity.

Is reality defined by unity or diversity? How do we resolve the age-old question of the one or the many? The fall of humankind left philosophers polarized and, to borrow a metaphor from Paul, "[seeing] through a glass, darkly" (1 Corinthians 13:12 KJV). Beginning with human wisdom, they developed two different understandings.

The ancient Greeks helped to frame the debate on the issue. Parmenides of Elea (ca. 510–450 BC) emphasized unity over diversity. According to Parmenides, all is one, and all is unchanging. Following in the footsteps of Parmenides, the Greek philosopher Plato (ca. 428–348 BC) opted for unity over diversity, metaphysical meaning over scientific fact, and the ideal over common sense. Plato said that things move from this world (the physical) to the eternal (spiritual), from lower to higher, from appearances to reality, from becoming to being.

Some scholars believe that these ideas were imported from Greece to India by means of Alexander the Great and his eastern conquests of present-day Iran and India. Today we see a similar idea at the core of Hinduism—ultimate reality is *one*. This approach holds that only the spiritual is really real.

Plato and Parmenides did not have the philosophical playing field to themselves, however. Heraclitus of Ephesus (ca. 540–480 BC) went the other way, postulating diversity over unity. According to Heraclitus, all is many, and all the particulars are in flux. In this system, the tangible is what is really real. Plato's pupil Aristotle (ca. 384–322 BC) broke with his master and sided with Heraclitus, emphasizing diversity over unity, the temporal over the eternal, scientific fact over metaphysical meaning, and common sense over the ideal. Like modern secularists, Aristotle held that only the tangible was real.

Despite the this-worldly appeal of Aristotle's approach, Aristotle and his followers lost the debate to Plato and the Platonists; and history would never be the same. Notwithstanding the Bible's appreciation of God's creation, Platonic philosophy came into the church via Gnosticism, elevating the spiritual over the physical. Thus people concluded that the physical world, including the human body, is bad and that sex, by its very nature, is profane. Plato's approach dominated the Western world until the Reformation.

One versus Many in Religious Thought

The matter of unity and diversity has also profoundly shaped religious thought down through the ages. The great monotheistic religions of Judaism, following the Jewish rabbi Moses Maimonides (1135–1204), and Islam emphasize the unity of God, viewing him as absolutely *one* in both essence and person. Both emphasize

- God as transcendent over immanent,
- God as infinite over personal,
- God as Creator over Lord and Savior, and
- God as powerful over compassionate and loving.

At the other end of the spectrum is a host of ancient polytheistic religions that worship distinct, separate, and often local deities. In the ancient world, the Egyptians, Assyrians, Babylonians, Greeks, Romans, and Norse were polytheists. Today polytheism continues to define animistic or folk religions throughout the world, particularly in Africa and Asia.

Over and against both monotheism and polytheism, Christianity holds to the radical middle: Trinitarianism. Rather than going to either pole, classic Christian theology affirms both unity and diversity in the Godhead—God the Father, Son, and Holy Spirit—and in his creation.

Resolving the Question

In the middle, of course, the Scriptures advocate two things at the same time, both the unity[1] and the diversity[2] of the Godhead. Before we get too deep into the theology, we can easily see this combination manifest in creation. In human creation, we see individuals within communities. Family units are generally made up of mothers, fathers, and children. In nonhuman creation, we see a marvelous amount of diversity in plants, animals, and minerals. Within the species, we see definite specialization. For example, while all dogs are related, their differences are stark (and often amusing).

In contrast to unitarianism on the one side and tritheism on the other, the early church fathers struggled to articulate a biblically balanced Trinitarianism.

Studying the Scriptures that hint at or imply the Trinity,[3] they articulated the mysterious doctrine that all orthodox Christians believe.

- Athanasius (ca. AD 296–373) spoke of the "coequality of three persons." He was the first to articulate that the members of the Trinity were *identical* in essence (*homoousion*) rather than *similar* in essence (*homoiousion*).

- At the pivotal Council of Nicaea (ad 325) church leaders agreed upon the Nicene Creed, which handled this topic with great care:

> We believe in one God,
> the Father, the Almighty,
> maker of heaven and earth,
> of all that is, seen and unseen.
>
> We believe in one Lord, Jesus Christ,
> the only Son of God,
> eternally begotten of the Father,
> God from God, Light from Light,
> true God from true God,
> begotten, not made,
> of one Being with the Father.
> Through him all things were made.
> For us and for our salvation
> he came down from heaven:
> by the power of the Holy Spirit
> he became incarnate from the Virgin Mary,
> and was made man.
> For our sake he was crucified under Pontius Pilate;
> he suffered death and was buried.
> On the third day he rose again
> in accordance with the Scriptures;
> he ascended into heaven
> and is seated at the right hand of the Father.
> He will come again in glory to judge the living and the dead,
> and his kingdom will have no end.

We believe in the Holy Spirit, the Lord, the giver of life,
who proceeds from the Father.
With the Father and the Son he is worshiped and glorified.
He has spoken through the Prophets.
We believe in one holy catholic and apostolic Church.
We acknowledge one baptism for the forgiveness of sins.
We look for the resurrection of the dead,
and the life of the world to come. Amen.

- Gregory of Nazianzen (ca. AD 329–389) stated, "I cannot think of the One, but I am immediately surrounded by the glory of the three; nor can I discover the three, but I am suddenly carried back to the One."[4]
- Augustine (AD 354–430) gave us the classic formulation of God being "three persons [who] are coequal and coeternal."

The Athanasian Creed, written sometime between the fourth and sixth centuries, affirms: "And the Catholic Faith is this, that we worship one God in Trinity and Trinity in Unity. Neither confounding the Persons nor dividing the Substance."[5]

Different Roles

Trinitarian faith affirms two things: both the oneness and the many-ness of God, both his unity and his diversity. Each person of the Trinity possesses the fullness of the divine essence (is coequally God). Yet each person of the Trinity may be distinguished by his individuality. Each member of the Trinity also has a different role, function, or mission in carrying out the divine plan.

In salvation, the Father is the author of the plan;[6] the Son executes the plan through his life, death, and resurrection;[7] and the Holy Spirit actuates the plan in the life of the believer through his works of regenerating, sanctifying, sealing, and indwelling.[8]

Yet here is an important point in our examination of the dignity of women. Though the members of the Trinity are equal in divine being, there is a *subordination of function*. According to the teaching of Scripture, the Father has authority over the Son,[9] while both Father and Son have authority over the Holy Spirit.[10] The Father is Father in his paternity and in sending his Son; the Son is Son in his being begotten of the Father and in his loving obedience to his Father's will; and the Holy Spirit is the Spirit of God in that he glorifies the Father and the Son. The Son deflects glory from himself and glorifies the Father;[11] the Holy Spirit deflects glory from himself and glorifies the Son.[12]

Theologian Stephen D. Kovach summarized the biblical framework well when he said, "Take away equality of being and you no longer have the Son and Spirit as fully divine. Take away differences in role and you no longer have three distinct persons; there is nothing that makes the Son to be the Son rather than the Father, or the Spirit to be the Spirit rather than the Father or the Son. If we abandon eternal differences in role, then we also abandon the Trinity."[13]

God's Self-Revelation

The Creator, just like a human artist, reveals something of himself through the things he has made. God has left his fingerprints on his work. The creation is a reflection of the Creator. This includes males and females created in his image. As Romans 1:19–20 affirms: ". . . because that which is known of God is manifest in them; for God manifested it unto them. For the invisible things of him since the creation of the world are clearly seen, being perceived through the things that are made, even his everlasting power and divinity; that they may be without excuse" (1901 American Standard Version).

When people or cultures deny God, they end up worshiping either man or nature. The apostle Paul describes this in Romans 1:21–23: "For although they knew God, they neither glorified him as God nor gave thanks to him, but their thinking became futile and their foolish hearts were darkened. Although they claimed to be wise, they became fools and exchanged the glory of the immortal God for images made to look like mortal man and birds and animals and reptiles."

And yet humble humanists, Muslims, Hindus, Christians, and animists, because they are made in the image of God, have the ability to see God's fingerprints throughout creation.

These fingerprints point to God's unity and diversity—and to our own.

The Mystery of Trinity

Now we must admit that the nature of the infinite, personal God transcends human reason. But we must also acknowledge the truth of the Trinity because God has revealed himself this way, as both one and many, in his Word and in his creation. In God we find unity without uniformity and diversity without superiority. God is the archetype for the unity and diversity we find in creation.

Let me be clear that God's transcendent attributes—his omnipotence and omnipresence, for example—separate him from creation. However, his personal attributes provide the pattern for all that is human: the image of God, both male and female. As such, we would expect to see this pattern repeated in creation—and we do.

We can find a surprising number of analogies, or pictures, of the Trinity, in creation:

- In *nature*, we see analogies to the Trinity in water (liquid–gas–solid), in the atom (neutron–electron–proton), in time (past–present–future), in space (length–width–height), the primary colors (red–blue–yellow), and music (pitch–harmony–rhythm).

Figure 10a:

Analogy: Trinity in Water

Figure 10b:

Analogy: Trinity in the Atom

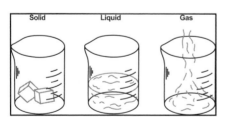

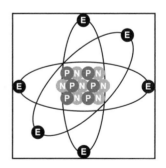

- In *man*, we see threefold pictures of the Trinity in our inner makeup (spirit–soul–body) and our familial relationships (mother–father–child).

God's threefold nature, to which these aspects of creation point, is anything but static. Clark Pinnock writes: "Early theologians spoke of the divine nature as a dance, a circling round of threefold life, as a coming and going among the Persons and graciously in relation to creation."[14]

Other Christians agree: "We call the Inner Life of the Trinity the *Perichoresis*, or The Great Dance, circling about. It is an image of profound peace in dynamic flow, of eternal give and take. The Persons of the Trinity are equal but different, each deferring to the other in the Love of the Great Dance."[15]

Educator and theologian Greg Uttinger captures the essence of The Great Dance when he writes: "The metaphor [of The Great Dance] is apt. In a ballroom dance or a folk dance, each participant is responsible for his own role. He cannot see the whole, let alone shape the whole. But as he dances his part well, as he submits himself to the rules of the dance, he helps to create a thing of wondrous complexity and great beauty. Such is the universe, and such is the church. But the root of this all lies in the inner life of the Triune God."[16]

When we come to Christ for salvation, we are invited to "come, join the dance!"

Effects on Society

So what difference does belief in the Trinity make for our discussion about women? In brief, it solves the age-old question about the relation of unity and diversity. And this is not just an academic question. How we answer it will determine the order of a society. If we value diversity over unity, we will face evils such as tribalism, racism, Nazism, or radical multiculturalism. If we choose unity over diversity, we will slip into egalitarianism or communism.

In the realm of relations between the sexes, diversity accentuates the differences between males and females. One of the most obvious differences is the general greater physical strength and muscle mass of males when compared to females. This leads many people to believe that males are superior to females. This is sexism, pure and simple; and it leads, as we have seen, to the crushing of females.

However, valuing unity over diversity leads to another evil: radical feminism. This philosophy holds that male and female are equal. But it often goes beyond that to say that they are *the same*. This approach promotes not equality so much as androgyny, which leads to the supposed interchangeability of the sexes. In this well-meaning but misguided scenario, *female* disappears.

Community in the Godhead

Plato and Aristotle each affirmed half of the truth and thus lost the whole. Only Trinitarianism resolves the age-old question of the one and the many. On a practical level, Trinitarianism affirms both the unity and the diversity of the human social order.

The idea that God is community is fundamental to human society. An overemphasis on individualism leads to loneliness, tribalism, and sexism. An overemphasis on diversity, on the other hand, leads to full integration with one's community. On a familial level, it leads to the misguided concept of interchangeability.

To fail to acknowledge the reality of the Trinity not only undermines the Christian faith, but it denies God's design for relationships in society. The Father, Son, and Holy Spirit are three distinct persons in community. They exist in relationship. They cannot and do not exist independently of one another. There are no role confusions of egalitarianism or sexist power plays in the Trinity, only perfect harmony. Following this pattern, we are hard-wired for community.

What we need is not a male world but a human world, a world where the *imago Dei* is appreciated. No other religion gets us there. Neither Aristotle's atomism (which exalts diversity) nor Platonic monism (which accentuates unity) has the intellectual capital to bring us this truly human world, a place that properly honors both men and women. The following chart delineates the differences.

Only Trinitarianism encourages us to honor and value one another while

Figure 11: Conflicting Views of Valuing Men and Women

Monism (Unity)	Trinitarianism (Unity - Diversity)	Atomism (Diversity)
Feminism	*imago Dei*	Machismo
Egalitarianism	Complementarianism	Male Domination
Equal = Identical	Equal & Different	Different = Unequal
Maleness Valued	Femaleness & Maleness Valued	Maleness Valued

celebrating our distinctiveness. Thus reflecting God's divine nature, we are free to revel in our equality in being and our diversity in role and function.

The unity and diversity of the Trinity, so counterintuitive to our finite minds, provide the pattern for the unity and diversity between men and women. They also provide the pattern for healthy, God-honoring relationships.

Notes

1. Many Scriptures teach that God is one, including Deuteronomy 6:4 and Isaiah 44:6–8.

2. Many Scriptures teach or imply that God is more than a simple unity, including Genesis 1:26–27; 3:22; Matthew 3:16–17; Mark 1:9–11; Luke 3:21–22; John 14:15–17; Ephesians 3:14–19.

3. Genesis 1:26–27; 3:22; 11:7; Matthew 3:16–17; 28:19; Mark 1:9–11; Luke 3:21–22; 2 Corinthians 13:14; Ephesians 4:4–6.

4. Gregory Nazianzen, *Orations of Saint Gregory Nazianzen*, Oration XL, para. 41, "Oration on Holy Baptism," *A Select Library of the Nicene and Post-Nicene Fathers of the Christian Church*, second series, vol. 7 (Grand Rapids: Eerdmans, 1983), 375; quoted in James A. Fowler, "Three Divine Onenesses," 2002, http://www.christinyou.net/pages/3divineonenesses.html.

5. The Athanasian Creed, Catholic Encyclopedia, http://www.newadvent.org/cathen/02033b.htm.

6. Luke 22:42; John 3:16; 4:34; 17:4.

7. John 3:14–15; Romans 4:25; 1 Corinthians 15:3–8; Ephesians 2:13–18.

8. John 14:16,26; 15:26; 16:7–15; Ephesians 1:13–14; Titus 3:3–7.

9. Luke 22:42; John 4:34; 17:4; 1 Corinthians 11:3.

10. John 14:26; 16:7,13–14.

11. John 17:4.

12. John 16:13–14.

13. Stephen D. Kovach, "Egalitarians Revamp Doctrine of the Trinity," *CBMW News*, vol. 2, no. 1 (December 1996): 4.

14. Clark H. Pinnock, *Flame of Love* (Downers Grove, IL: InterVarsity, 1996), 22.

15. "Byzantine Wisdom: Trinity," http://members.aol.com/theloego/byzantine/page3.html.

16. Greg Uttinger, "The Theology of the Ancient Creeds Part 4: The Athanasian Creed," August 27, 2002, http://www.chalcedon.edu/articles/0208/020827uttinger.php.

CHAPTER 8
The Two "S" Words

These days *authority* is a dirty word. How many times have we heard people say (or said ourselves), "Don't tell me what to do," or, "Who died and made you king?" To modern men and women, the concept of authority is rankling. We want to be the master of our fate, the captain of our ship—and woe to anyone so foolish as to make a claim on us! Power, pride, and self-service are virtues for modern man. Service and humility are vices.

To have authority over another is good. To be under authority is bad.

While people have always fought for power and control, this pervasive antiauthoritarian mindset emerged during the Enlightenment, when modern man began to revolt against ecclesiastical power structures and, ultimately, against God himself. The philosophy of the Enlightenment—"Man is the center of all things"—seemingly put men and women at the center of the universe.

Following in this train, we want absolute freedom and autonomy. We revolt against any form of authority, beginning with God and his Word. Our rebellion, no matter how freeing it appears in the beginning, ends in a revolt against nature itself. Those who break God's laws eventually end up broken. This chapter describes this breaking process, as well as how we can begin putting the pieces back together.

Freedom without Form

As the British Roman Catholic statesman Lord Acton has so famously said, "Power tends to corrupt, and absolute power tends to corrupt absolutely." This is certainly true in marriage and in relations between the sexes. In this social realm, authority too often morphs into an ugly male tyranny of women, in which angry men dominate cringing and servile women. Hierarchy or patriarchy defined outside scriptural parameters spells tyranny.

Right in rejecting such abusive patterns, secularism, and the radical feminism that springs from it, rejects all authority in favor of absolute personal autonomy. Denying God and his sovereignty, individual human beings become sovereign and the center of the universe. By definition, to be absolutely free is to be unbound by any authority. The goal is freedom without restriction. By definition, to be under authority is to be inferior. Also by definition, to be equal means to be autonomous, to be under no other authority.

Those who pursue absolute personal autonomy say that to obey God or any human authority is to have one's freedom restricted. We have seen the fruits of this radical freedom in the last four decades throughout the United States: surging rates of sexually transmitted diseases, the explosion of divorce, and the collapse of family structures in. Freedom without form eventually leads to anarchy. And anarchy in a society will soon lead to tyranny.

Effects in the Church

A culture that rebels against God will create a framework that will lead to a church in rebellion against God. Just before his death, Francis Schaeffer stated, "Tell me what the world is saying today, and I'll tell you what the church will be saying seven years from now."[1] It is well past seven years since our culture started proclaiming the sameness of men and women. Too many who call themselves evangelical feminists have bought into this philosophy of radical freedom. I hope this chapter will convince them—and the rest of us—that *authority* is not a dirty word.

In the last chapter we looked at how the Trinity lays the intellectual foundation for unity and diversity in human relations. Here we shall examine how the threefold Godhead provides the pattern for authority in human relations.

Biblical Authority

There is a pattern of authority throughout the visible and invisible creation. There is an authority structure between kinds: God over all creation, angels over people, people over the rest of creation, husbands over wives, parents over children, and so on. Other than God's authority, this authority structure places equality and subordination in two different and complementary categories. Just because one is in authority over another does not mean that the one is more important than the other.

Pastor Raymond Ortlund writes, "Authority does not authenticate my person. Authority is not a privilege to be exploited to build up my ego. Authority is a responsibility to be borne for the benefit of others without regard for oneself. This alone is the Christian view."[2]

Biblical authority structures between people recognize two key requirements:

- Equality of being
- Diversity of function

There is no relationship between a person's function and his or her worth. People's dignity is established not by what they do, but by who they are (the image of God).

Husbands, wives, and parents in the family; employers in the workplace; and elders in the church all have roles that carry authority. But this does not mean that parents are superior in being to their children, that employers are superior in being to their employees, or that elders are superior in their being to members of the larger congregation. Subordination denotes a difference in function. It is a far cry from subjugation, which leads to evils such as apartheid, slavery, caste, racism, tribalism, and sexism.

Related to subordination is submission, which refers not to an inferior mission, but to being under authority in a complementary aspect of a mission.

The key issue for our discussion concerning the dignity of women is how authority is wielded. Is it tyrannical, dictatorial authority, or self-giving leadership? We find the answer in the Godhead, which models not only human complementarity and diversity, but also the proper way to serve and submit. Just as the Father honors the Son and the Son honors the Father *as equals*, so the man honors the woman and the woman honors the man *as equals*. Though *equal* in *kind*, they are *diverse* in *role*.

Archetype for Servant-Leadership

God's triune nature stands as a challenge to modern man's arrogance. Down through the ages, fallen man has viewed service and humility as vices and power and pride as virtues. However, God honors humility, self-sacrifice, and subordination in man. As Scripture says, "God opposes the proud but gives grace to the humble" (1 Peter 5:5). These virtues reflect God's *love*.

There are four types of love highlighted in the Bible, so I want to be specific. I am not talking about love for a detail of life, such as, "I love my dog." Nor am I thinking of *phileo*, which is affectionate love for a friend or brother. Finally, I am not referring to *eros*, or romantic love. No, the love we are examining in the very nature of God is humble and self-sacrificing and offered to undeserving sinners like you and me. This is *agape*, self-sacrificing love.

In John 17:24, Jesus reveals that love existed before the creation, saying to the Father: "You loved me before the creation of the world." Agape is the love of Christ, and it is to be the love Christians exhibit toward their fellow human beings. This is expressed in Philippians 2:1–8 (emphasis mine):

> If you have any encouragement from being united with Christ, if any comfort from his *love*, if any fellowship with the Spirit, if any tenderness and compassion, then make my joy complete by being like-minded, having the same *love*, being one in spirit and purpose. Do nothing out of selfish ambition or vain conceit, but in humility consider others better than yourselves. Each of you should look not only to your own interests, but also to the interests of others.

Your attitude should be the same as that of Christ Jesus:

> Who, being in very nature God,
> did not consider equality with God something to be grasped,
> but *made himself nothing,*
> *taking the very nature of a servant,*
> being made in human likeness.
> And being found in appearance as a man,
> he humbled himself
> and became obedient to death—
> even death on a cross!

This is agape. It is humble and selfless, thinks of others first, is self-sacrificing, and serves others. In a beautiful passage that captures the essence of agape—while pointing to Christ—the prophet Isaiah states:

> See, my servant will act wisely;
> he will be raised and lifted up and highly exalted.
> Just as there were many who were appalled at him—
> his appearance was so disfigured beyond that of any man
> and his form marred beyond human likeness—
> so will he sprinkle many nations,
> and kings will shut their mouths because of him.
> For what they were not told, they will see,
> and what they have not heard, they will understand.
>
> Who has believed our message
> and to whom has the arm of the LORD been revealed?
> He grew up before him like a tender shoot,
> and like a root out of dry ground.
> He had no beauty or majesty to attract us to him,
> nothing in his appearance that we should desire him.
> He was despised and rejected by men,
> a man of sorrows, and familiar with suffering.
> Like one from whom men hide their faces
> he was despised, and we esteemed him not.
>
> Surely he took up our infirmities
> and carried our sorrows,

yet we considered him stricken by God,
smitten by him, and afflicted.
But he was pierced for our transgressions,
he was crushed for our iniquities;
the punishment that brought us peace was upon him,
and by his wounds we are healed.
We all, like sheep, have gone astray,
each of us has turned to his own way;
and the Lord has laid on him
the iniquity of us all.

He was oppressed and afflicted,
yet he did not open his mouth;
he was led like a lamb to the slaughter,
and as a sheep before her shearers is silent,
so he did not open his mouth.
By oppression and judgment he was taken away.
And who can speak of his descendants?
For he was cut off from the land of the living;
for the transgression of my people he was stricken.
He was assigned a grave with the wicked,
and with the rich in his death,
though he had done no violence,
nor was any deceit in his mouth.

Yet it was the Lord's will to crush him and cause him to suffer,
and though the Lord makes his life a guilt offering,
he will see his offspring and prolong his days,
and the will of the Lord will prosper in his hand.
After the suffering of his soul,
he will see the light of life and be satisfied;
by his knowledge my righteous servant will justify many,
and he will bear their iniquities.
Therefore I will give him a portion among the great,
and he will divide the spoils with the strong,
because he poured out his life unto death,

and was numbered with the transgressors.
For he bore the sin of many,
and made intercession for the transgressors.
—Isaiah 52:13–53:12

We see the beautiful spirit of agape throughout the New Testament, especially in the willing sacrifice of the Son of God as payment for our sins. The Father sacrifices his one and only Son (John 3:16), and the Son willingly sacrifices himself for us (Matthew 26:39). Edward Nason West was right to describe *agape* as "a profound concern for the welfare of another without any desire to control others, to be thanked by that other, or to enjoy the process."[3]

The love of God, according to his very nature, is characterized by service, self-denial, self-sacrifice, and subordination. Professor Henry Krabbendam of Covenant College has said: "love in its fullness. . . meets two criteria. First, it will never make withdrawals, but only deposits. Second, it seeks to fill vacuums not in oneself, but in the other."[4]

God honors those who willingly subordinate themselves to the interests of others. We see this described in the concluding verses of the wonderful passage in Philippians 2:

Therefore God exalted him to the highest place
and gave him the name that is above every name,
that at the name of Jesus every knee should bow,
in heaven and on earth and under the earth,
and every tongue confess that Jesus Christ is Lord,
to the glory of God the Father.
—Philippians 2:9–11

My good friend and colaborer Bob Moffitt has captured this in his book *If Jesus Were Mayor:* "Because Jesus voluntarily and sacrificially became a servant, God exalted Him. He gave Jesus the highest position that could be given, a name that supercedes every name. Every tongue will confess that this Servant is Lord. He is exalted more than any other being. God honored Jesus in this manner *because* Jesus fully reflected what God intended when He created man. Jesus fully expressed the highest example of God's image—voluntary and sacrificial servanthood. God is a servant, and Jesus modeled that servanthood!"[5]

Simply put, God's Word exalts what the world despises. The values of the kingdom of God are right side up; the world's values are upside down.

The Servant God

Figure 12a: Differing Value Systems

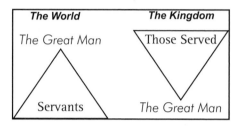

Figure 12b: The Word Exalts What the World Despises

The World	The Kingdom of God
pride	humility
self-serving love	self-sacrifice
power	service

We have a God who serves. But as we speak of God being a servant, we are speaking archetypically, not anthropomorphically. In other words, God is a serving God; his character provides the pattern for our own activity. The love of God is manifested in his service and self-sacrifice. It is seen in his character and in the incarnation.

The Old and New Testaments describe God as a serving God. The Hebrew word *hesed* ("lovingkindness") occurs some 250 times in the Old Testament. It refers to God's loyal and steadfast love. It describes his kindness and mercy toward us in practical, everyday terms. In the harsh environs of the Middle East, the Hebrew people, like many modern Arabs today, made serving the stranger a virtue of life.

Psalm 23 reveals the very *hesed* nature of God in two images:

- Shepherd (verses 1–4)

  > The LORD is my shepherd, I shall not be in want.
  > He makes me lie down in green pastures,
  > he leads me beside quiet waters,
  > he restores my soul.
  > He guides me in paths of righteousness
  > for his name's sake.
  > Even though I walk
  > through the valley of the shadow of death,
  > I will fear no evil,
  > for you are with me;
  > your rod and your staff,
  > they comfort me.

- Servant-Host (verses 5–6; emphasis mine)

  > *You prepare a table before me*
  > in the presence of my enemies.
  > You anoint my head with oil;
  > my cup overflows.
  > Surely goodness and love will follow me
  > all the days of my life,
  > and I will dwell in the house of the LORD
  > forever.

In the New Testament, we learn about God's servant heart through the incarnation, when the second person of the Trinity took on human flesh to serve us. As Mark 10:45 says: "The Son of Man did not come to be served, but to serve, and to give his life as a ransom for many." Jesus came to serve, not to be served. This service is not a contradiction to his being God, but a confirmation of his status as a serving God. Jesus is the Servant-King. Similarly, Jesus is both the "good shepherd" (John 10:11,14) and "the Lamb that was slain from the creation of the world" (Revelation 13:8).

Serving defines the nature of his authority. In his sermon "The Excellency of Christ," Jonathan Edwards showed the *complementariness* in Christ of the infinite and finite, the temporal and eternal:

> . . . infinite highness and infinite condescension . . . infinite justice

and infinite grace . . . infinite glory and lowest humility . . . infinite majesty and transcendent meekness . . . deepest reverence towards God and equality with God . . . infinite worthiness of good, and the greatest patience under sufferings of evil . . . an exceeding spirit of obedience, with supreme dominion over heaven and earth . . . absolute sovereignty and perfect resignation . . . self-sufficiency, and an entire trust and reliance on God.[6]

The nature of the triune God is self-denial and self-sacrifice. There is an authority structure in the Trinity. And that structure is manifest through self-sacrifice among the members of the Trinity. John 14:31 illustrates this: "The world must learn that I love the Father and that I do exactly what my Father has commanded me."

Henry Krabbendam writes:

Behavior in reality by the believer is ethically determined by the inner Trinitarian conduct of God. This is characterized by self-denial in the divine One and Many sphere, and by self-sacrifice and submission in the divine authority structure. That is to say, in the Trinity the "Parties" are there not for themselves but for the others in a radical and total manner. For example, in the Trinity, as an authority structure, the Father, who is in authority, exemplifies self-sacrifice in a rather astounding fashion, when he transfers life, authority and judgment to the Son, who is under authority (John 5:20–22,26–27). At the same time, the Son exemplifies submission to an equally astounding fashion, when he refuses to proceed on his own initiative or to implement his own will, but rather determines only to please his Father and to do his will (John 5:30; 6:38–40; 8:28–29,42).[7]

Krabbendam continues: "The cross would have been an impossibility without self-denial, self-sacrifice and submission. In the divine One and Many sphere, the cross was a model of self-denial on the part of both the Father and the Son. In the divine authority structure, the cross was equally a model of the Father's self-sacrifice and the Son's submission. It hardly needs to be argued that the cross, or anything even remotely resembling it, could never have been initiated or achieved by man. Self-interest, self-service, and self-preservation would have precluded that."[8]

The cross is an affront to the modern virtues of power, pride, and self-fulfillment.

Submission within the Godhead

The Bible is full of examples of deference, or submission, by the various members of the Trinity:

- The Holy Spirit defers to Christ.[9]
- The Son defers to the Father in his suffering for our salvation.[10]
- The Father reveals his humility by allowing man to serve as vice-regent[11] and in giving his Son.[12]

But let me be clear: While there is a hierarchy in function or mission by the members of the Trinity, there is no hierarchy in being. To carry out God's purposes, the Son and the Holy Spirit are under the Father's authority. This is true not just in time,[13] but also in eternity.[14] Some Christians, however, argue that if Jesus were eternally subordinate, then he would not be the Father's equal. They are confusing being and function. Contending that to be subordinate in function is to be inferior in being, they argue that Jesus must have been subordinate only while he was on earth. Again, the assumption is that subordination of function implies inferiority of being. This is not a biblical assumption.

As Wayne Grudem observes in *Biblical Foundations for Manhood and Womanhood:* "When did the idea of headship and submission begin then? *The idea of headship and submission never began!* It has *always existed* in the eternal nature of God Himself."[15]

Stuart Scott writes: "The Trinity is a relationship in which three eternal persons . . . reveal, know, and love each other tenderly and perfectly for the other's good within the context of eternal commitment. When they decide to set and accomplish a goal, for the purpose of order and economy, God the Son and God the Spirit voluntarily subordinate themselves to God the Father in order to function according to their perfect plan. As they work together, they are totally unified in desire, thought and action until the goal's completion."[16]

There is no rivalry, resentment, or animosity among the members of the Trinity.

There is a complementary nature between the equality of being and the subordination of function within the Trinity. Self-sacrificial love and servant-hood are godly virtues because they arose from the Godhead. This is at the heart of the glory of God.

Elisabeth Elliot speaks of *glorious hierarchy*.[17] Hierarchy is glorious because authority and subordination are rooted in the nature of God. Unfortunately, the Fall brought a terrible distortion of hierarchy. From an order defined by service and self-sacrifice, we live in an order defined by tyranny and oppression. But the distortion is no reason to redefine the nature of the Trinity and to deny the glorious order that God has manifested from his own nature into creation.

The Imperative of Service

If service is so important within God's very being, it is also vitally important for us, who are made in his image. If God is love[18]—as manifested in self-sacrificing service—and man is made in the image of God, then it goes without saying that we were made to serve.

What was the last thing that Jesus modeled to the disciples before he went to the cross? Service, by washing the disciples' feet.

We are meant to serve

- God in worship,
- our fellow human beings with self-sacrificing love, and
- creation via our stewardship.

Thus, our service touches God, people made in God's image, and God's creation. We were made to serve, not as slaves, but as reflections of the divine Servant himself. Bob Moffitt writes:

> God does not command compassionate and sacrificial service for its own sake. He commands it because it results in the demonstration

of His greatest attribute, love. Jesus told us to love God and to love our neighbors as ourselves. We demonstrate our love for God by loving our neighbor as we would want to be loved. Similarly, God's love was demonstrated to the world through Christ's compassionate service. Sacrificial service is the way that the full character of God is still expressed in the world today. When God's love is expressed through human agents, it expresses itself not only in words, but in sacrificial service.[19]

To despise service is to despise the heart of God. But when we serve with a servant's heart, we honor God.

The Necessity of Submission

Convincing modern people that a related concept, *submission*, is a good thing is not easy. When we hear the term we think of people who are doormats, who are easily bullied, who have no minds or wills of their own. This is not biblical submission!

The word has two parts:

- *sub*, a Latin preposition, which denotes "under" or "below," used in English as a prefix to express a subordinate degree; and
- *mission*, which usually denotes being sent to transact business.

Taking both parts together, *submission* means to be on a mission under the authority of someone else. We can easily see this in the roles of spokespersons, diplomats, and stewards. Submission, despite the ugly modern connotations the word has picked up, is a high calling. There is nothing menial about it.

Submission is a key component of our growth as Christians. Justified by faith, we are sanctified by obedience to God's call and his commands and by submission to one another. John Frame writes: "It is often by submitting to others that we best display the ethical components of the divine image. How better to demonstrate God's love, His patience, His gentleness, His self-control, then by submitting to others?"[20]

Does submission mean inferiority? Not at all! As I have been saying, there is a huge distinction between *being* and *function*. In *being*, there is no inferiority. In *function*, we are recognizing a distinction in rank or degree.

Submission recognizes *authority*, the legitimacy of governance, administration, and leadership.

Hierarchy in Creation

Unfortunately, that old-fashioned word *authority* gives many of us moderns the willies. It shouldn't. All of creation reveals the existence of legitimate spheres of authority, which in turn depend on a related concept: *hierarchy*.

Elisabeth Elliot describes this as the *glorious hierarchical order*. Elliot writes, in an essay titled "The Essence of Femininity," that her statements about femininity are validated by both God's world and his Word. She writes about "what I see as the arrangement of the universe and the full harmony and tone of Scripture. This arrangement is a glorious hierarchical order of graduated splendor, beginning with the Trinity, descending through seraphim, cherubim, archangels, angels, men, and all lesser creatures, a mighty universal dance, choreographed for the perfection and fulfillment of each participant."[21]

But to egalitarians who deny any hierarchy in the created order, a subordinate position implies inherent inferiority. They say there is no inferiority because there is no subordination. Compared to the biblical witness, this is an arid view indeed. The angels are created beings and are thus a lesser being than God. Man was made "a little lower than the heavenly beings" (Psalm

Figure 13: Hierarchy in Creation

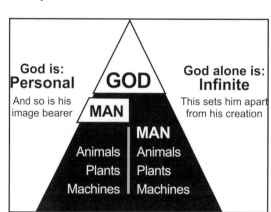

8:5), and God "set eternity in the hearts of men" (Ecclesiastes 3:11). But because we are made in the image of God, we are higher than the rest of creation.

Sadly, sin corrupts hierarchy. Satan rebelled against God and the angelic order. Humankind's caring dominion over nature too often turns into environmental rape. The husband's loving headship becomes domination over his wife.

Hierarchy in Society

Properly appalled by abuses of authority, some Christians have decided to oppose authority structures in the created order, including in the social order. To do so, they have denied the authority structure in the Trinity. Some even go so far as to say, "There is no hierarchy within the Trinity."[22] But denying hierarchy in the Trinity leads eventually and logically to denying other aspects of diversity in the Trinity, including the individuality and personality of each member and their differing roles. Krabbendam writes:

> Let it be underscored that at times deep seated antagonism against both the fact and the nature of this authority structure has dire consequences. Since it is embedded in created reality as a reflection of the being of God, its radical opponents, bent upon eradicating it in an all-embracive egalitarianism, recognize that they will never succeed in reaching their goal unless they can wipe out God's self-disclosure of himself as the archetype of all created authority structure. Attempts to this effect are on the increase. In an all-embracive egalitarianism it is bluntly denied that the headship of the Father over the Son implies any sort of authority. . . . Thus the rage against the created order becomes a rage against God who brought that created order into being as a reflection of Himself.[23]

Headship, within the Godhead and human relations, must always be defined in the context of servanthood. Within the Godhead, God solved his demand for justice by giving his only Son to die on the cross. Likewise, Jesus is the head of the universal church. But how does he lead the church? Not tyrannically, but as a servant. This is the glory of the Trinitarian hierarchy.

Just as serving was essential to Christ's identity as God, it is essential to our identity as human beings. As with him, our service is a virtue, a voluntary act. We subordinate ourselves not under threat but according to the design and plan of a loving God. We submit for the sake of Christ and his kingdom. As Martin Luther said: "A Christian man is the most free lord of all and subject to none; a Christian man is the most dutiful servant of all and subject to everyone."[24]

Men and women are both servants of the living God and vice-regents of creation. They are to mutually submit to one another as sons of Adam and daughters of Eve. But just as Jesus was both King *and* Servant, a man may provide headship for his wife *and* serve her. At the same time, he is subject to church leaders and civil authorities.

A woman also plays multiple roles. She may provide leadership for her children, her household, and her employees and yet be under the authority of her husband, the church leaders, and civil government. Women, like men, are to be involved in leadership, ministry, and service. The issue is not leadership at the exclusion of service or service at the exclusion of leadership. Men and women are called to do both.

According to biology, all service roles are open to men, except birthing and nursing a baby. Because there is freedom, except where Scripture sets limits, all leadership roles are open to women, except headship in the home and eldership in the church.[25] We should focus not on a particular "leadership role," however, but on service.

St. Francis of Assisi understood this:

> O Divine Master,
> grant that I may not so much seek to be consoled as to console;
> to be understood as to understand;
> to be loved as to love;
> for it is in giving that we receive;
> it is in pardoning that we are pardoned;
> and it is in dying that we are born to eternal life.[26]

The world sees greatness as "having the most servants." The kingdom sees greatness as "serving the most people." Servanthood is not the prerequisite for greatness; it is the standard of greatness.

As we continue our study, let us remember the importance of understanding the distinction between *being* and *function.* The archetype for human relations is the glorious Trinity: one God, three persons. The persons of the Trinity are *equal in their being* and *diverse in their function.* This same pattern applies to the *imago Dei*: female and male. This is manifest, for instance, in the husband-wife relationship in the family. Both husband and wife are the *imago Dei*—equal in their being. Yet they are diverse in their function. The God-ordained order of the family, as we shall see later, is for the husband to be the loving servant-leader and the wife to be the loving, respectful helper.

Many Christians who are rightly concerned about the exploitation of women fall into the error of equating function and worth. They feel that unless husband and wife share the same roles, then somehow the wife has less worth or value than her husband. While the intention is laudable, the result is tragic. Those who would argue for egalitarianism in the family or the church are unwittingly diminishing the glory of both servanthood and submission that is rooted in the Godhead. This moves to the denial of God's self-sacrificing love found in the most fundamental of biblical revelation: "For God so loved the world that he gave his one and only Son" (John 3:16).

Notes

1. Quoted in Elisabeth Elliot, "The Essence of Femininity: A Personal Perspective," in *Recovering Biblical Manhood and Womanhood: A Response to Evangelical Feminism,* John Piper and Wayne Grudem, eds. (Wheaton: Crossway, 1991), 395.

2. Raymond Ortlund Jr., "Male-Female Equality and Male Headship: Genesis 1–3," in *Recovering Biblical Manhood and Womanhood*, 112.

3. Quoted in Elisabeth Elliot, *The Mark of a Man* (Old Tappan, NJ: Fleming H. Revell Company, 1981), 78.

4. Henry Krabbendam, *A Biblical Pattern of Preparation for Marriage* (Lookout Mountain, GA: Covenant College, 2000), 44.

5. Robert Moffitt, *If Jesus Were Mayor* (Phoenix: Harvest Publishing, 2004), 80 (italics in the original).

6. Jonathan Edwards, "The Excellency of Christ," in *The Works of Jonathan Edwards,* vol. 1 (Edinburgh: Banner of Truth, 1974), 681–82; quoted by John Piper, "A Divine and Supernatural Light Immediately Imparted to the Soul by the Spirit of God," 2003 Desiring God National Conference, October 12, 2003, http://www.desiringgod.org/ResourceLibrary/ConferenceMessages/ByDate/146_A_Divine_and_Supernatural_Light_Immediately_Imparted_to_the_Soul_by_the_Spirit_of_God/.

7. Henry Krabbendam, *Sovereignty and Responsibility* (unpublished, 1998), 52.

8. Ibid.

9. John 14:26; 15:26; 16:13–15.

10. Matthew 26:39,42,44; 27:46; Philippians 2:5–8.

11. Genesis 1:26–28; 2:19–20.

12. John 3:16.

13. Matthew 11:27; 20:23; 26:39,42; Mark 14:36; Luke 4:18–19; John 4:34; 5:19, 26–27.

14. Romans 8:34; 1 Corinthians 11:3; 15:24–28; Hebrews 1:3,13.

15. Wayne Grudem, "Key Issues in Manhood-Womanhood Controversy and the Way Forward," in *Biblical Foundations for Manhood and Womanhood,* Wayne Grudem, ed. (Wheaton: Crossway, 2002), 51 (italics in the original).

16. Stuart Scott, class notes on "Relationship," Grace Community Church, Sun Valley, CA, 1994; quoted in Martha Peace, *The Excellent Wife* (Bemidji, MN: Focus Publishing, 1999), 30.

17. Elliot, "The Essence of Femininity," 394.

18. 1 John 4:8,16.

19. Moffitt, *If Jesus Were Mayor,* 81.

20. John M. Frame, "Men and Woman in the Image of God," in *Recovering Biblical Manhood and Womanhood,* 228.

21. Elliot, "The Essence of Femininity," 394.

22. Loren Cunningham and David Joel Hamilton, *Why Not Women?* (Seattle: YWAM Publishing, 2000), 170.

23. Krabbendam, *A Biblical Pattern of Preparation for Marriage,* 34.

24. Martin Luther, "The Freedom of a Christian," http://wsu.edu/~dee/REFORM/FREEDOM.HTM.

25. Dealing with the issue of the roles of women in the church is not the purpose of this book. Many others have focused on this very important subject. After years of discussions and study, I have concluded that there is freedom for women in leadership and ministry in every arena with the exception of these two that are proscribed in Scripture. These issues will be dealt with in more detail later in the book. To restrict women in areas that the Bible does not is to do a disservice to Scripture, women, the church, and the larger world.

26. St. Francis of Assisi, "Instrument of Peace," http://www.franciscanstor.org/prayers.htm.

CHAPTER 9
The Transcendence of Sexuality

At an economics conference in 2005, Harvard president Larry Summers suggested three explanations for why there are such small numbers of women holding tenured math and science positions at elite universities. Summers postulated that women with young children might not be willing or able to put in the grueling hours these positions require. He also noted that girls generally have lower scores on math and science tests than do boys and that these differences might be innate. Third, Summers acknowledged discrimination might be a factor.

Incensed MIT biologist Nancy Hopkins walked out halfway through the speech and later told reporters she felt "physically ill" when Summers mentioned basic sexual differences in the sciences. Hopkins said that if she hadn't left, "I would have blacked out or thrown up." Later, one hundred Harvard professors took their president to task in an open letter that said such comments "serve to reinforce an institutional culture at Harvard that erects numerous barriers to improving the representation of women on the faculty."

Actually, more and more women are choosing to stay home, regardless of their innate abilities. The United States Census Bureau reports that in 2003 about 5.4 million mothers with children age fourteen and under stayed home, an increase of a million since 1995. According to the U.S. Bureau of

Labor Statistics, in 2001 a majority of women with kids under age six worked only part-time or not at all. Just 42 percent worked full-time.

In addition, thirty years of scientific studies show that men and women indeed have different aptitudes. Men do better, generally, in mathematical reasoning, mechanical understanding, and spatial relationships. Women tend to do better in language, reading, and other verbal tasks. Even when women do as well as men in the hard sciences, they often choose to work in fields with a higher social component.

Yet despite these facts, Summer's comments ultimately cost him his job. Any suggestion that women and men are not basically the same is met with shock and outrage. While any child knows that boys and girls are different, almost any adult who says so is the object of scorn and derision. But men and women, although equal in dignity and worth, are different in aptitudes and roles. In fact, the masculine and feminine attributes of human beings are rooted in the very heart of God.

The Role of Worldview

As we have seen, your worldview will determine how you understand the world, including how you understand sexuality. Men and women generally live their lives against the backdrop of presumed male superiority, which, as we have seen, is the lie that leads to *sexism* or *machismo*. This view sees only the differences in men and women and fails to recognize their inherent equality. While rightly reflecting the diversity of the Godhead, sexism denies its unity. Sexism stresses the differences between men and women while downplaying or ignoring the ways they are the same. And men, because they are physically stronger, are seen as more valuable than women.

In response, *radical feminism* asserts the radical equality of men and women. Rightly reflecting the unity of the Godhead, this approach, as seen in the agitated responses to Larry Summers, overlooks God's inherent diversity, leading to the denial of reality. This is not surprising. If you begin from a secular, materialist starting point, you will end up believing there is no transcendent reality. This view reduces sexuality to "plumbing," and those who hold it tend to believe that sexual differences are learned through socialization.

These two positions seem radically different, but in fact they both depreciate femaleness in favor of maleness. There are several fearsome consequences:

- The first consequence is to depreciate *God's transcendent qualities* of nurture, compassion, self-sacrifice, love, and a servant's heart that he chooses to manifest most fully in females.
- A second consequence is to depreciate women by failing to honor their *equality* to men in their *being*. Like man, woman is made in the *imago Dei*. She, too, is to be treasured because she, too, is fully human, made in the image of God.
- A third consequence is to depreciate the unique *function* of women, robbing society of the qualities of the *maternal heart*.
- A fourth consequence is to rob both men and women of their *counterpart*. The ideal becomes a metaphysical homosexuality.

Forcing women to live against the backdrop of male values may reduce them to hating men or drive them to hate being women (because by definition this is inferior) and to try to transform themselves into males. If the latter, they will seek to think, feel, and act as male and (on a practical level) to cease being females. Either way, the unique glory of being female disappears.

By Design

In Genesis 1:26–28 we see what has rightly come to be known as the "creation mandate":

> Then God said, "Let us make man in our image, in our likeness, and let them rule over the fish of the sea and the birds of the air, over the livestock, over all the earth, and over all the creatures that move along the ground."

> So God created man in his own image,
> in the image of God he created him;
> male and female he created them.

God blessed them and said to them, "Be fruitful and increase in number; fill the earth and subdue it. Rule over the fish of the sea and the birds of the air and over every living creature that moves on the ground."

God created the world and delegated to us the shaping of that world through the creation of culture. At the end of God's work, creation was *perfect*, filled with potential. *But it was not finished.* God made humankind—male and female—in his image to function as his vice-regents or stewards of creation. As such, we are to make the earth's potential flourish by expanding the garden, so to speak. This is why we are driven by some subconscious urge to plant orchards and vineyards and to create music, dance, literature, poetry, and fabrics. We have been called in a multitude of ways to fill the earth with the knowledge of the glory of God as the waters cover the sea (Habakkuk 2:14). By doing these stewardly tasks we move creation from the garden of Eden (Genesis 2:8,15) to the Garden-City, the New Jerusalem (Revelation 21:1–2).

Human beings, created male and female, find their joint purpose in shaping the world God has made, creating unique cultures that glorify God. To glorify God, these cultures must in some sense reflect the One who gave us this awesome task. Human culture cannot bring glory to God if it explicitly denies the truths about him that we learn directly from his Word and indirectly from his works.

One simple principle we will follow here is that design predicts function. Another is that function reveals design. The great naturalist biochemist Jacques Monod, who was a co-recipient of the 1965 Nobel Prize in medicine for his work in genetics, recognized that all living things reveal the purpose for which they have been made in their design. He writes about "one of the fundamental characteristics common to all living beings without exception: that of being *objects endowed with a purpose or project*, which at the same time they exhibit in their structure and carry out through their performances."[1]

Monod calls this purposefulness *teleonomy*. He says that scientific objectivity "obliges us to recognize the telenomic character of living organisms, to admit that in their structure and performance they act projectively—realize and pursue a purpose."[2] *The American Heritage Dictionary* does not recognize the word *teleonomy*, but instead uses a more traditional word, *teleology*, to capture the same concept: "the study of design or purpose in natural phenomena."

Applying the concept to the human body, we see God's purposes expressed in our mortal frames. Capturing its essence is Elliot, who profoundly states, "In order to learn what it means to be a woman, we must start with the One who made her."[3]

While men and women are more alike than they are dissimilar, it is equally obvious that men and women differ in dramatic ways. Gloriously, the male and female bodies differ in complementary fashion. Likewise there are basic emotional, psychological, and biochemical differences. These differences not only reveal purpose; they also reveal something of the nature and character of the living God. Writing in *If the Foundations Are Destroyed*, historian K. Alan Snyder states: "The Biblical concept of individuality can be stated succinctly: God has created all things distinct and unique and for a specific purpose. He has given an identity to all parts of His creation, whether material objects, animals, or human beings."[4]

Unity and diversity go together in this. While all flowers share certain characteristics, think of the incredible diversity expressed in different kinds of flowers. The same unity and diversity go for dogs and snowflakes, just to name two more examples. It's safe to conclude that the Creator likes diversity.

What is the purpose behind the uniqueness of women? I suggest that a woman reveals in her body something of the motherly heart of God—of his nurturing, compassionate, and self-sacrificing love. Her body also reveals the metaphysical purposes for which she has been born. Among other things, a woman was uniquely designed to carry and nurture babies.

Sadly, much of the sexual confusion in our world has followed from the fact that we have forgotten that the form and function of living things reveal something of their purpose. Separate the physical from the transcendent and the physical loses its meaning. The sexual confusion of postmodern society has occurred because we have separated creation from the Creator, design from the Designer.

While men and women share the same *being*, made in the image of God, they have different *functions*. We can see their functions in how God designed them.

Essentialism versus Nurture

Parents often remember when their young children discovered that boys and girls have different "private parts." But do these differences have anything to do with transcendence? Or are they simply accidental differences in "physical plumbing"?

Elliot writes: "It's dangerous and destructive to treat sexuality as if it were meaningless. Much of the church, which is being strongly influenced by the world's ideologies, is ignoring the fact that sexuality means something."[5]

Our world is witnessing a debate between those who say that that sexuality is inborn and fixed and those who argue that it is learned through a process of socialization. The first believe in what is called essentialism; the second believe in the primacy of nurture. I am a member of the first camp. There is an essential nature to our sexuality. That essence is rooted in the transcendent nature of God.

To see why this is so, let us return for a moment to the beginning. In creation, God created two basic classes of living things: first spiritual beings (exemplified by angels) and then physical beings (animals). Actually, there is a third kind of life: spiritual-physical beings (humans). We are the only part of creation that bridges the physical and spiritual realms.

As embodied spirits, or spirit-infused organic bodies, we alone are made in the image of God. While the Bible does not spell out precisely the factors that constitute this image, it is safe to assume that they help us reflect our transcendent origin in physical form. Further, our sexual identity is *essential* in manifesting some of the transcendent nature of God, in whose image we are made.

While God is not a physical being with visible sexual characteristics, our human sexual differences—taken together—help us see more clearly the divine pattern or archetype for the created order. Our human sexuality, male and female, reflects the masculine and feminine characteristics of God's very character. As C. S. Lewis writes, "The male and female of organic creatures are rather faint and blurred reflections of masculine and feminine."[6]

Our sexual identity is a physical manifestation of the heart of God, who is the origin of all that we call male and female. The Father heart of God leads, initiates, protects, and provides. God's heart also is the origin of the motherly characteristics of following, responding, nurturing, and receiving. Note in Genesis 1:27 (emphasis added) the sexual manifestation of the transcendent maternal/paternal nature:

> So God created man in his own *image*,
> in the image of God he created him;
> *male* and *female* he created them.

One man cannot fully reflect the fullness of the image of God, nor can one woman. There needs to be community, the smallest unit being the family. Further, two males or two females cannot fully reflect the fullness of the image of God. It takes male and female to create a family. It takes male and female to reflect the unity of *being* and diversity of *function* found in the Trinity. There is a complementary convergence of male and female that mimics the unity and diversity of the Trinity.

Elliot captures this when she writes in *Let Me Be a Woman*: "Recent scientific research is illuminating, and as has happened before, corroborates ancient truth which mankind has always recognized. God created male and female, the male to call forth, to lead, initiate and rule, and the female to respond, follow, adapt, and submit. Even if we held to a different theory of origin the physical structure of the female would tell us that woman was made to receive, bear, to be acted upon, to complement, to nourish."[7]

There is a nonmaterial or transcendent component to sexual distinction. Sexuality is built into the soul. Payne writes:

> Masculinity and femininity are attributes of God, and we, in His image, are most surely—in our spiritual, psychological, and physical beings—bipolar creatures. Our Creator, holding all that is true and real within Himself, reflects both the masculine and the feminine, and so do we. The more nearly we function in His image, the more nearly we reflect both the masculine and the feminine in their proper balance—that is, in the differing degrees and aptitudes appropriate to our sexual identities as male and female.[8]

As figure 14 shows, God is both Protector and Nurturer. Indeed, he is the archetype of these characteristics, which have equal value. Since God manifests his character in creation, especially here in the *imago Dei*, both characteristics are discernible in male and female *imago Dei*. The attribute of protector was

Figure 14: God's Character Given to *imago Dei*

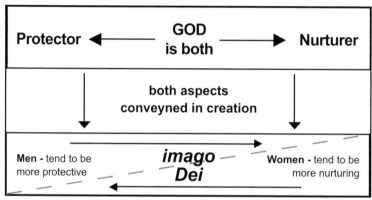

given primarily, but not exclusively, to men, and God imprinted women with more of the nurturing aspect. Men do have some nurturing elements, of course, but this is not their strong suit. Likewise, women do have a protective trait, yet this is not manifest to the same extent or degree as it is in men. This is not say that some men are not more nurturing than some women or that some women are not more protective than some men. This does not tend to be the norm, however.

The masculine and feminine polarities are complementary in marriage and reflect something of the mystery of the eternal unity and diversity in the Trinity. In Scripture, we see this in God's husbanding of Israel during the Old Testament period and, in the New Testament, in the mysterious and beautiful union, at the end of time, of Christ and the church.

The Creation Mandate

Genesis 1:26–28 establishes God's divine purpose for humankind on earth:

Then God said, "Let us make man in our image, in our likeness, and let them rule over the fish of the sea and the birds of the air, over the livestock, over all the earth, and over all the creatures that move along the ground."

So God created man in his own image,
in the image of God he created him;
male and female he created them.

God blessed them and said to them, "Be fruitful and increase in number; fill the earth and subdue it. Rule over the fish of the sea and the birds of the air and over every living creature that moves on the ground."

Some have called this the creation mandate or cultural mandate. Either way, the mandate has two tasks:

- The societal: multiply and fill the earth.
- The developmental: have dominion over creation.

To fulfill this purpose, females and males are essential. As we have seen, God has made men and women equal in *being* and diverse in *function* in order to fulfill the creation mandate. And we have also seen that when societies order around the *one,* a philosophical egalitarianism results. Uniqueness and individuality disappear, and people blur equality of being with equality of function. This leads to confusion of identity, including sexual identity, and purpose.

But when societies order around the *many,* inequality results. Unity of being disappears, and people tend to see those differences in function as signs of inherent inequality. This leads to slavery and indenturing of other human beings.

The Bible, however, brings a healthy balance, lifting up individuality *within* community. Modeled after the Trinitarian order, equality of *being* and diversity of *function* are affirmed at the same time. Therefore, the apostle Paul made two seemingly paradoxical statements:

- Referring to *being,* Paul states in Galatians 3:28: "There is neither Jew nor Greek, slave nor free, male nor female, for you are all one in Christ Jesus."

- Referring to *function*, Paul writes in Ephesians 5:22–24: "Wives, submit to your husbands as to the Lord. For the husband is the head of the wife as Christ is the head of the church, his body, of which he is the Savior. Now as the church submits to Christ, so also wives should submit to their husbands in everything."[9]

Because all humans are equal in being, they are free

- to fulfill the purpose for which they have been created without fear and
- to celebrate the incredible diversity of the human family.

Similarities and Distinctions

Paul's analogy of the body of Christ in 1 Corinthians 12:12–20[10] profoundly demonstrates the interconnectedness of unity and diversity in God's world. God has built unity and diversity into all of creation and into the human family as well.

Another way to approach this topic with men and women is to examine similarities and distinctions. Similarities describe what male and female share in common, but they do not imply interchangeability. Distinctions describe where female and male are dissimilar, but they do not imply inequalities.

To get a full-orbed picture, we will examine the similarities and differences of men and women using the motifs of creation, fall, and redemption.

Similarities

- *Creation*

Dorothy Sayers, a writer and Christian apologist, observes: "The fundamental thing is that women are more like men than anything else in the world."[11] Our shared position as God's image bearers means we are more like God than any other created thing. We are equally valuable; we both have the responsibility for the creation mandate.

Biologically, we have been made from the same DNA. Eve was made from Adam's rib (Genesis 2:21–23). We share the same blood[12] and body. Unlike the angels or the physical creation, women and men bridge the spiritual and physical realms. Fused into our physical being is a soul and spirit. We were made to walk side by side in intimacy with our Creator (Genesis 3:8).

- *Fall*

The moral fall of human beings, which occurred at a particular place in the very distant past, continues to have global effects in the present. Men and women are both affected. We are equally sinners (Genesis 3:6–7; Romans 3:23), both culpable in this disaster. While some would argue from 1 Timothy 2:14 ("Adam was not the one deceived; it was the woman who was deceived and became a sinner") that Eve caused the Fall, Paul states in Romans 5:12–17 that Adam, as the first (representative) man, bears ultimate responsibility. But both feel the horrible results of the curse (Genesis 3:16–19). Men and women also have an equal need for grace.

- *Redemption*

Thankfully, in Christ women and men are equal recipients of grace (Galatians 3:28): We are called to the same gospel (John 3:16), have the same Holy Spirit dwelling in us (Acts 2:17–18), are baptized into the body of Christ (Acts 2:4), have received spiritual gifts to edify the church (1 Corinthians 12:7,11), and are called to manifest the same fruit (Galatians 5:22–23).

Distinctions

While men and women are alike in kind, they are also very different. As MIT professor David C. Page of the Whitehead Institute for Biochemical Research told the *New York Times*: "We all recite the mantra that we are 99 percent identical and take political comfort in it, but the reality is that the genetic difference between males and females *absolutely dwarfs all other differences in the human genome*."[13]

So despite the political and social pressure to call men and women the same, the truth is that the differences between the sexes are far greater than the differences between races and ethnic groups. These distinctions reflect the distinct responsibilities or *functions* given to us in the creation mandate. Call it a "division of labor," but remember that this division is played out against the backdrop of Adam and Eve being made in the image of God, not against the backdrop of maleness.

These distinctions gloriously establish the absolute uniqueness of each individual in the unfolding of God's eternal purposes. But we must not confuse *individuality* with *individualism*. We are made for community. Rather, one's distinctions are to be complementarily bound to the family, the extended family, and the larger community for the fulfillment of the creation mandate.

- *Creation*

While each human shares certain physical characteristics, each of us is an absolutely unique individual. We see this in any of the myriad biological differences including height and weight, skin complexion and color, hair texture and color, sexual organs, male and female hormones, and so on.

Even our cerebral cortexes display our distinctions. Psychologist Mary Stewart Van Leeuwen writes, "The most salient *biological* fact about human beings is the size and plasticity of the cerebral cortex, which enable us to be adaptive, culture-creating persons who are called to be under the cultural mandate."[14] Biology professor Gregg Johnson adds, "Indeed, as we survey the biology of mammals and humans in particular, we find sex-related differences in all of the organ systems, including the brain and nervous system."[15]

But the differences go far beyond the physical. Our differing internal characteristics display a *one of a kind* human being to the world. These soul differences include how we think (abstractly or practically), how we process languages, and how we feel and express emotions.

In the main, men and women exhibit two equally valid ways of knowing. The masculine tendency is toward the rational. The feminine tendency is toward intuition. To be fully human requires both the rational and the intuitive. Thus, men and women need one another in community to fully express the image of God. Reason and intuition, science and art, have their fount in the Creator himself. Yes, women are capable of rational thinking, but generally their gifting is intuitive. And men are capable of intuitive perception, though for the most part their strength is in the rational.

As we examine distinctions between all human beings evident in the created order, we must study the distinctions given by God at the creation of man and woman. Rather than pure egalitarianism, the Bible teaches that there is an order of creation. The male comes first (Genesis 2:7), then the woman (Genesis 2:18,22; 1 Timothy 2:13). There is also a distinction in the means of creation. The man is made from the dust of the ground (Genesis 2:7), while the woman is created from the rib of the man (Genesis 2:22).

Woman is called a "suitable helper" for man (Genesis 2:20). Again, this in no way implies inferiority. It only implies complementarity. The further implication is correspondence. The woman and man fit together physically—and spiritually. The woman is suitable to be man's helper in the cultural mandate. Man is, likewise, the woman's suitable helper in their combined task.

We also can easily note many basic differences between the sexes via anthropology.

> Anthropologists find similar kinds of universal sex-specific behaviors among human cultures. Of two hundred fifty cultures studied, males dominate in almost all. Males are almost always the rule makers, hunters, builders, fashioners of weapons, workers in metal, wood, or stone. Women are primary care givers and most involved in child rearing. Their activities center on maintenance and care of home and family. They are more often involved in making pottery, baskets, clothes, blankets, etc. They gather food, preserve and prepare food, obtain and carry firewood and water. They collect and grind grain.[16]

As Wayne Grudem, research professor of Bible and theology at Phoenix Seminary, writes: "From the beginning God designed our sexuality so that it reflects unity and differences and beauty all at the same time. As husband and wife, we are most attracted to the parts of each other that are the most different. Our deepest unity—physical and emotional and spiritual unity—comes at the point where we are most different."[17]

- *Fall*

While both the man and the woman were accountable for the Fall, their roles were different. The Bible tells us that Eve was tempted first, then Adam (Genesis 3:1–6). Satan challenged Eve directly and Adam indirectly, through his wife. The *weight* of responsibility, however, falls on Adam, because Adam heard the command not to eat the fruit of the tree (Genesis 2:16–17) and *deliberately* disobeyed. Adam's choice affected all people because he was head of the race (Romans 5:12). But Eve was *deceived* by the serpent, succumbing to a half-truth (Genesis 3:1–5).

Unfortunately, some use Eve's deception to imply that women are somehow responsible and therefore inferior to men.[18] This is patently false. As stated in Romans, Adam, as the *representative man,* carries the full weight of responsibility.

The results of the Fall also produce distinctions between the sexes. While both will labor, the woman will labor in childbearing (Genesis 3:16), but the man will labor because of the thorns and thistles in the ground (3:17–18). Perhaps even worse, the Trinitarian model of unity of being and diversity of function is lost as new paradigms begin to shape the marriage relationship. Starting with Genesis 3:16, the man ceases to *husband* (lovingly serve) his wife and begins to compulsively *dominate* her. The wife ceases to *help* (respectfully follow) her husband and begins to compulsively be *servile* to him or challenge him. We see this in Genesis 3:16: "Your desire will be for your husband, and he will rule over you." We will examine this in more detail in chapter 12.

- *Redemption*

God's expectations of men and women in marriage differ. For Christian couples, marriage is to reflect the mystical union of Christ and the church (Ephesians 5:22–33). Reflecting on scriptural teaching, Elliot notes that the man is the "head" of the woman, representing the very person and glory of God.[19] The husband is the "head" of the wife in the same way that Christ is the head of the church and the Savior of the body. The husband must give his wife the same sort of sacrificial love that Christ gave the church. Men ought to give their wives the love they naturally have for their own bodies. A man will leave his father and mother and will be united to his wife. Husbands are to love their wives as they love themselves; they are to try to understand their wives, honoring them as physically weaker yet equal heirs of the gracious gift of life (1 Peter 3:7).

Wives, like their husbands, no longer have full rights over their own persons. Men and women are interdependent. The woman reflects the person and glory of the man and is called to adapt to her husband, submitting herself to the Lord. This submission is not a cringing servility, but a picture of the loving, reverent, and joyful trust that the church has for its head, Jesus Christ.

So, yes, men and women are gloriously the same . . . and gloriously different. We need to keep both similarities and distinctions in balance, recognizing they exist in large part because they reflect the transcendent nature of our Creator.

Notes

1. Jacques Monod, *Chance and Necessity* (New York: Alfred A. Knopf, 1971), 9 (italics in the original).

2. Ibid., 21–22.

3. Elisabeth Elliot, *Let Me Be a Woman* (Wheaton: Tyndale, 1976), preface.

4. K. Alan Snyder, *If the Foundations Are Destroyed: Biblical Principles and Civil Government* (Marion, IN: Principle Press, Foundation for Biblical Government, 1994), 16.

5. Elisabeth Elliot, *New Covenant*, February 1982, in Leanne Payne, *Crisis in Masculinity* (Grand Rapids: Baker, 1985), 76.

6. C. S. Lewis, *That Hideous Strength* (New York: Collier, 1962), 315, in Payne, *Crisis in Masculinity*, 70.

7. Elliot, *Let Me Be a Woman*, 59.

8. Payne, *Crisis in Masculinity*, 86.

9. The rest of this passage (Ephesians 5:25–33) makes clear that husbands are to exercise a gentle, loving, Christlike leadership in the home: "Husbands, love your wives, just as Christ loved the church and gave himself up for her to make her holy, cleansing her by the washing with water through the word, and to present her to himself as a radiant church, without stain or wrinkle or any other blemish, but holy and blameless. In this same way, husbands ought to love their wives as their own bodies. He who loves his wife loves himself. After all, no one ever hated his own body, but he feeds and cares for it, just as Christ does the church—for we are members of his body. "For this reason a man will leave his father and mother and be united to his wife, and the two will become one flesh." This is a profound mystery—but I am talking about Christ and the church. However, each one of you also must love his wife as he loves himself, and the wife must respect her husband."

10. "*The body is a unit, though it is made up of many parts; and though all its parts are many, they form one body.* So it is with Christ. For we were all baptized by one Spirit into one body—whether Jews or Greeks, slave or free—and we were all given the one Spirit to drink. [emphasis added]

"Now the body is not made up of one part but of many. If the foot should say, 'Because I am not a hand, I do not belong to the body,' it would not for that reason cease to be part of the body. And if the ear should say, 'Because I am not an eye, I do not belong to the body,' it would not for that reason cease to be part of the body. If the whole body were an eye, where would the sense of hearing be? If the whole body were an ear, where would the sense of smell be? But in fact God has arranged the parts in the body, every one of them, just as he wanted them to be. If they were all one part, where would the body be? As it is, there are many parts, but one body."

11. Dorothy L. Sayers, *Are Women Human?* (Grand Rapids: Eerdmans, 1971), 37, in Lilian Calles Barger, *Eve's Revenge* (Grand Rapids: Brazos Press, 2003), 84.

12. "And hath made of *one blood* all nations of men for to dwell on all the face of the earth, and hath determined the times before appointed, and the bounds of their habitation" (Acts 17:26 KJV; emphasis added).

13. "Boys Will Be Boys: The Science of the Y Chromosome," *The New Atlantis: A Journal of Technology and Society,* no. 2 (Summer 2003): 107; available at http://www.thenewatlantis. com/archive/2/soa/boys.htm (italics added).

14. Mary Stewart Van Leeuwen, "Summary Concept Statement" to unpublished manuscript, "My Brother's Keeper: Masculinity in a New Millennium (2001)," 2, in Mardi Keyes, "The Mystery of Gender," paper delivered at L'Abri, Southborough, MA, July 20, 2001, 25 (italics in the original).

15. Gregg Johnson, "The Biological Basis for Gender-Specific Behavior," in *Recovering Biblical Manhood and Womanhood: A Response to Evangelical Feminism,* John Piper and Wayne Grudem, eds. (Wheaton: Crossway, 1991), 282.

16. G. Murdock, "The Common Denominator of Cultures," in *The Science of Man in the World Crisis*, R. Linton, ed. (New York: Columbia University Press, 1945), 123–42; quoted in Johnson, "The Biological Basis for Gender-Specific Behavior," in *Recovering Biblical Manhood and Womanhood,* 282.

17. Wayne Grudem, "The Key Issues in the Manhood-Womanhood Controversy, and the Way Forward," in *Biblical Foundations for Manhood and Womanhood,* Wayne Grudem, ed. (Wheaton: Crossway, 2002), 54.

18. First Timothy 2:11–15 is a divisive passage for the church today. Too much of the discussion in the church in our generation has not been helpful and has failed to deal with the larger question of the dignity of every woman. Some use this passage to argue that women are inferior to men and thus all women are to be under the authority of all men in any and every situation. Others argue that the principle of women's silence in the church is not universal and permanent, but is a local response to some women in Ephesus who were aggressively challenging the leaders of the church and were engaged in false teaching. This "camp" would thus argue that there is never to be any limitation upon any woman regarding teaching authority in the church. This polarized situation is indeed unfortunate. It keeps us from dealing with the larger issue of the dignity of women. And it freezes too many women from exercising their teaching gifts and leadership ability inside and outside of the church. Those who do this neglect the larger Trinitarian principle that men and women are equal in dignity and value and diverse in person, role, and function. While the church is arguing, women are being raped, beaten, enslaved, and murdered. One hundred million women are "missing." Hundreds of thousands of baby girls are being killed, either in the womb or after birth, in India alone each year. Hundreds of thousands more are being killed or abandoned in China. Where are our priorities?

19. Elisabeth Elliot, *The Mark of a Man* (Old Tappan, NJ: Fleming H. Revell Company, 1981), 83–84.

CHAPTER 10

God's Motherly Love

In recent years, some avant-garde theologians in mainline churches have sought to extinguish sexism—the mistaken idea that men are intrinsically superior to women—by eliminating what they see as sexist theology. They say that referring to God in exclusively male terms has encouraged patriarchy and abuse. Apparently believing what is bound on earth shall be bound in heaven, these theologians are attempting to give God an extreme makeover.

Gone, therefore, are old-fashioned, "patriarchal" names for God, such as Father, Son, and Holy Spirit. In their place are the "gender-neutral" terms of Creator, Redeemer, and Sustainer. Some radical feminists, mixing paganism and the Book of Proverbs, have taken to worshiping the goddess Sophia, claiming this female deity is Wisdom personified.

While this is blasphemy, pure and simple, I can appreciate the desire to find a firm theological foundation for one's ecclesiology. These radical feminists at least grasp the truth that what we believe about the nature of God has a profound impact on how we live our lives. In fact, we build our cultures and lives to be like the gods we worship.

The fact is that you don't have to reinvent God to find ample justification for treating women with the respect and dignity they deserve. All the women-affirming facts you need to know about him in this regard are readily accessible in the Bible, and have been for millennia. The problem is that for too long we have been reading these data with patriarchal eyes, thereby ignoring the parts that don't fit with our preconceived sexist worldviews. I hope this chapter will help give us new eyes to appreciate the wonderful nurturing heart of God—and the women he has made in his image.

Several years ago a popular book postulated *Men Are from Mars, Women Are from Venus.*[1] If that thesis—that there are basic differences between the sexes—is true, then a completely natural question comes to mind: *From what planet is the God who made them?* My answer: God is from both Mars and Venus. Male *and* female come from God. That is, the attributes that make men *men* and women *women* have their origin in him. He created them to reflect his complete nature and character.

God's Nature

Another fairly recent title encouraged Christians to think about *The Father Heart of God.*[2] This was a noble effort to get God's children to appreciate the fatherly love of their Creator. This chapter, I hope, will help us appreciate the motherly qualities of God's nature and character. Maternal and paternal qualities find their resting place in the heart of God.

But let me assure you that my intent is not to introduce some strange heresy of God as Mother or Christ as Daughter. Rather, my intent is to help you see old truths in fresh ways. While the journey may be, at times, difficult or uncomfortable, it is necessary if we are to recognize the wonder of the female.

I am not saying God is feminine, any more than I would say God is masculine. God is spirit (John 4:24) and thus is neither biologically male nor biologically female. God created our biology but transcends it. Our masculine and feminine qualities reflect something basic about God's nature. Male and female together, as created in the image of God, provide a more complete picture of that God than either could alone.

As many have noted before, the Bible describes God in male and female terms. But God reveals himself in predominately masculine language. The two major Hebrew names for God, *Yahweh* and *Elohim,* are masculine. God is referred to as Father 250 times in the Bible (not once as Mother). God is called Master (not Mistress), Shepherd (not Shepherdess), King (not Queen), Lord (not Lady), and Husband (not Wife). When referring to God, Scripture uses the masculine personal pronouns he (not she), his (not hers), and him (not her).

And yet feminists, as we have seen, move from describing aspects of the nature of God that express themselves most often in humanity via females to calling God "Mother" or using female personal pronouns for God. Or they replace *who God is* as Father, Son, and Holy Spirit with *what God does* as Creator, Redeemer, and Sustainer. This approach is unscriptural and theologically illegitimate. God has the right not only to name himself but also to reveal something essential about himself by his self-designations. God truly is Father, not Mother; King, not Queen.

Metaphor and Simile

These theological innovators also make a basic grammatical error that fatally weakens their argument. The Scriptures that describe God in masculine terms invariably use metaphors, while those that describe him in feminine terms use similes. What's the difference? Everything, when it comes to understanding God's divine being.

To see why, let's review our grade-school grammar for a moment. A *metaphor* is a figure of speech that refers to something that it does not literally denote in order to suggest a similarity between the whole of one thing and the whole of another thing. For example, saying, "God is our rock," as several Scriptures do, is a metaphorical way to describe God's strength and dependability.

A *simile*, by contrast, compares part of one thing to part of another, suggesting a resemblance between things of different kinds, often using the words *like* or *as*. For example, saying *God is like a mother* is scriptural, because the Bible agrees that there are some aspects of God's personality that are motherly. But saying *God is a Mother* says something else completely.

We need to bear this important distinction between metaphor and simile in mind while studying the Scriptures. As Roland M. Frye writes in the *Scottish Journal of Theology:* "Simile differs from metaphor in that it merely states resemblance, while metaphor boldly transfers the representation, and again while the simile gently states that one thing is like or resembles another, the metaphor boldly and warmly declares that one thing is the other."[3]

The Bible uses simile to state that God is *like* a mother, but never that God *is* a mother. God *is like*:

- a woman giving birth (Isaiah 42:14; 46:3)
- a nursing mother (Isaiah 49:13–15; 66:10–13)[4]
- a mother hen (Matthew 23:37; Luke 13:34)
- a mother eagle (Exodus 19:4; Deuteronomy 32:10–12)

While God is named Father, he is never called Mother. Noteworthy passages, however, reveal God's motherly *and* fatherly attributes.

- In Deuteronomy 1:31, Moses reminds the Israelites about God's provision for them in the desert: "There you saw how the LORD your God carried you, as a father carries his son, all the way you went until you reached this place."
- Matthew 23:37 quotes Jesus: "O Jerusalem, Jerusalem, you who kill the prophets and stone those sent to you, how often I have longed to gather your children together, as a hen gathers her chicks under her wings, but you were not willing."
- And in an intriguing juxtaposition of both, Deuteronomy 32:18 says, "You deserted the Rock, who fathered you; you forgot the God who gave you birth."

On a human level, we can begin to grasp God's all-encompassing love by looking at how it is expressed—incompletely and imperfectly—in men and women.

Physical Body, Transcendent Purpose

Typically, men and women express two different sides of the same coin when it comes to God's heart. Let's look more closely at the side of the coin more frequently associated with women. These attributes are manifested through the feminine qualities of

- nurture,
- self-sacrifice,

- compassion and caring, and
- patience and long-suffering.

Yes, of course men can and do express these qualities, too, but they are most often associated with females. As a matter of fact, we find these attributes not just in the personalities of women, but also in their very physical beings. One might say that women's bodies reflect God's motherly love in a way that the male anatomy does not. The principle of *teleonomy* helps us here. The form and structure of an object reveal its purpose and function. The purpose reveals something of the glory of the maker of the object.

While one cannot make a one-to-one correspondence between the Creator and the thing created (after all, we live in a fallen world), it stands to reason that we should expect to discover clues about the Designer from the things he has designed—especially when we are talking about people, whom he has made in his very image.

Just as we learn something about God's nature from studying men, we can learn equally valuable insights about God by studying women. I contend that *God reveals his transcendent compassion, nurture, and protection in the female body.* A woman's body is not merely functional; it also points us to the motherly heart of God.

Motherly Characteristics

The most common denominator of being a human is having a mother. God, like the mothers he has made, conceives and brings life into being. A woman who does this manifests something of the nature of God that no man is capable of manifesting. Every human being was carried inside a womb.

Further, most of us received our first nurturing at a mother's breast. God has designed women, in their transcendent and physical natures, to nurture and protect weak and helpless children. As the Bible says, a mother is the source of comfort (Isaiah 66:13), a teacher (Proverbs 1:8; 6:20; 31:1), and a discipler (2 Timothy 1:5).

Scripture expresses these truths in three powerful similes: womb love, nurturing breasts, and sheltering wings. To continue with these similes, we might say that a female is a human being with a womb, breasts, and "wings."

A mother's love is compassionate and secure (womb), nurturing and comforting (breasts), and a protective covering (wings). We will look at each simile in turn to see the intimate connection between women and God's tender, motherly heart.

Womb Love[5]

God made humankind—man—as male and female. As Leanne Payne, founder of Pastoral Care Ministries, wrote in *Crisis in Masculinity*, "Woman . . . even though her sexual and gender identity is gloriously feminine, is man, man with a womb."[6]

It goes without saying that the womb is unique to women. Males do not have them and thus are unable to express, in their bodies, the motherly love of God the way a woman can. God made half of humankind—women—to have a womb (womb + man). God is compassionate, merciful, and loving. He has manifested these characteristics most profoundly in a woman's womb or uterus. He is the God of the womb. He made the womb to express his nature.

- The womb is the place of *origin*: where something is *conceived* and *nurtured*.[7]
- The womb is a place of *security*: it offers *protection* and *shelter*.[8]

Interestingly, the Hebrew word for *womb*, *racham*, is also translated *compassion*. It is derived from a Hebrew word that means "to love, love deeply, have mercy, be compassionate, have tender affection, have compassion."[9] It is translated *mercy* thirty times, *compassion* four times, and *womb* four times.

This link between *compassion* and *womb* helps us understand the very heart of God in a wonderful, woman-honoring way. Remember when God told Moses his name? "Then the LORD came down in the cloud and stood there with him and proclaimed his name, the LORD. And he passed in front of Moses, proclaiming, 'The LORD, the LORD, the *compassionate* and *gracious* God, slow to anger, abounding in love and faithfulness'" (Exodus 34:5–6; emphasis added).

We see here that God is the God of compassion and that compassion is essential to who God is. God's heart is the wellspring of compassion for the world. The cross is God's compassionate response to our sin. A woman's womb expresses this compassion physically.

The moving story in 1 Kings 3:16–28 tells of two prostitutes who lived in the same house. They had baby boys three days apart. One of the babies died. The woman whose son died switched the dead infant for the living one. Her housemate quickly discovered the deception, and both of them brought their dispute to King Solomon.

Slyly, the king offered to "solve" the dispute by cutting the living baby in two and giving each mother half. The mother whose child had died, perhaps out of deadly jealousy, told the king to go ahead. But the mother of the living child told the king to give him to the other woman. Why? "The woman whose son was alive was *filled with compassion* for her son and said to the king, 'Please, my lord, give her the living baby! Don't kill him!'" (1 Kings 3:26; emphasis added). This woman, the true mother, was filled with "womb love." Solomon's wisdom allowed him to recognize it when he saw it.

The ultimate source of such womb love is the very heart of God. Phyllis Trible, professor of sacred literature, writes:

> The Hebrew noun *rah min* [compassion] connotes simultaneously both a mode of being and the locus of that mode. . . . Accordingly, our metaphor lies in the semantic movement from a physical organ of the female body to a psychic mode of being. It journeys from the concrete to the abstract. "Womb" is the vehicle; "compassion," the tenor. To the responsive imagination, this metaphor suggests the meaning of love as selfless participation in life. The womb protects and nourishes but does not possess and control. It yields its treasure in order that wholeness and well-being may happen. Truly, it is the way of compassion.[10]

> This womb is a *sacred* space where the spiritual and physical are fused in a unique human being. The womb is the place where human beings are formed, their purpose is established, and the future of nations is found.[11] God is, to use Trible's term, the "God of the womb."[12]

Psalm 22:9–10 completes the story of womb love and moves the story to the nurturing of the mother's breasts. It is God who was the midwife for the psalmist. God delivered the baby and immediately put the baby in the safest and most nurturing place in the world, at his mother's breasts:

> You brought me out of the womb;
> you made me trust in you
> even at my mother's breast.
> From birth I was cast upon you;
> from my mother's womb you have been my God.

Webster's 1828 dictionary captures the significance of this when it equates mother with womb. The basic definition of *mother:* "womb: a woman who has borne a child."

Nurturing Breasts

Often our sexually dysfunctional society reduces a woman's breasts to sex objects. In so doing, we ignore the metaphysical nature of the physical breasts, as well as the many other critical feminine roles they represent. God, who designed the breast, is the God of nurture. He is comforting, nurturing, and providing. He has revealed his motherly heart profoundly, not just in Scripture, but also in the physical structure of a woman's breasts.

Maternal-infant bonding provides a compelling, precious picture of the bonding relationship between God and his creatures. Here are two striking Scripture passages that support that picture, using powerful similes that God is like a nursing mother:

Isaiah 49:15:

> Can a mother forget the baby at her breast
> and have no compassion on the child she has borne?
> Though she may forget,
> I will not forget you!

Isaiah 66:10–13:

> "Rejoice with Jerusalem and be glad for her,

all you who love her;
rejoice greatly with her,
all you who mourn over her.
For you will nurse and be satisfied
at her comforting breasts;
you will drink deeply
and delight in her overflowing abundance."

For this is what the LORD says:
"I will extend peace to her like a river,
and the wealth of nations like a flooding stream;
you will nurse and be carried on her arm
and dandled on her knees.
As a mother comforts her child,
so will I comfort you;
and you will be comforted over Jerusalem."

The Hebrew word for *breast* in this last passage is *shad*, the root of one of the names of God, *El Shaddai*, which means *God Almighty*. The word *Shaddai* is found forty-eight times in the Old Testament. The root word *shad* occurs twenty-one times in the Old Testament and is translated "breast" or "bosom." Eight of these verses are found in the love song Song of Songs. Yet there is no "blushing" here, no diminution of the female to a sex object, but only wonder and beauty of how God has made woman.

Nathan J. Stone states, in *Names of God in the Old Testament*, "As connected with the word *breast*, the title *Shaddai* signifies one who nourishes, supplies, and satisfies. Connected with the word for God, *El*, it then becomes the One mighty to nourish, satisfy, and supply. Naturally with God the idea would be intensified, and it comes to mean the One who 'sheds forth' and 'pours' out sustenance and blessing. In this sense, then, God is the all-sufficient, the all-bountiful."[13]

Theologian R. C. Sproul catches the wonder of God's feminine imagery in Scripture. He writes in *Family Practice*: "The Bible itself not only describes God in the masculine image of Father but also borrows from feminine imagery at times. Some scholars argue that the semitic, linguistic roots of the divine title *El Shaddai* referred to the "multibreasted one," the one who provides the nation with succor and nourishment."[14]

So we see that breasts (1) give life, (2) provide all that is needed, (3) bring total satisfaction, (4) bring comfort, (5) bring delight, (6) provide abundantly like a river, (7) respond to particular needs, (8) and give wealth.

The themes of womb love and nurturing breasts continue in the New Testament. As examples, Jesus compares the pain of a woman giving birth, and the joy that follows, to the pain of the disciples as he goes to the cross, followed by the joy of seeing him after the resurrection (John 16:20–23). Paul uses motherly language to describe the birth and nurture of young churches (Galatians 4:19–20; 1 Thessalonians 2:6–9).

A woman's glory is to reveal the motherly heart of God to a watching world. On a fundamental level, this is the glory of all women, even those who choose not to marry or those who are unable to have children. Women may nurture children who are not their own. They also bring the nurturing heart into the marketplace, teaching, nursing, ministry, and missions.

So while physically carrying a baby in the womb and nursing a baby manifest God's maternal heart, so too does the maternal metaphysic of love, self-sacrifice, and nurturing of all women. This is the essence of being female.

Nursing Mother

God reveals himself to be like a nursing mother. To nurse, in the Hebrew, means both to suckle and to give milk. Isaiah 66:10–12 provides a picture of the satisfaction and comfort associated with nursing a child:

> "Rejoice with Jerusalem and be glad for her,
> all you who love her;
> rejoice greatly with her,
> all you who mourn over her.
> For you will nurse and be satisfied
> at her comforting breasts;
> you will drink deeply
> and delight in her overflowing abundance."

For this is what the LORD says:
"I will extend peace to her like a river,
and the wealth of nations like a flooding stream;
you will nurse and be carried on her arm
and dandled on her knees."

The concept of nursing is closely associated with nourishing, which goes far beyond the physical act of dispensing milk. The Hebrew word *kuwl* means "to bear, to forbear, to guide, to hold, to nourish, to make provision, to be present, to set aright, to set forth, to be stable, and to be established." Note the need for the mother's role in guiding a child. Webster's 1828 dictionary defines *nourish* as "to feed and cause to grow." Note the significance of nurturing for the health of the child now and in the maturation process.

We get a clear picture of this process of spiritual maturation in the physical characteristics of breastfeeding. While we can't always draw a one-to-one link between God's creation and God's character, in this case the lessons are too obvious to miss.

Marie Davis, registered nurse and lactation consultant states:

> Breastfeeding provides continued close contact between mother and child. Social interaction is frequent and prolonged. The breast-fed infant is in control of the feeding. Breast-fed infants show more body activity at one to two weeks of age, are more alert and have stronger arousal reactions. Mother's breast is the source of warmth and comfort. The baby associates his mother with nourishment and interacts with her rather than with a bottle. Breast-fed infants started walking an average of two months earlier than their bottle-fed counterparts. It is believed that breast-fed infants are more secure and will later become more independent than bottle-fed infants because they are held so often throughout infancy. The longer an infant is breast-fed, the more striking developmental differences become.[15]

As Davis puts it, "Research is repeatedly proving that breastfeeding is more than the act of transferring milk. Breastfeeding is nurturing."[16]

In their book *Maternal-Infant Bonding*, physicians Marshall Klaus and

John Kennell describe the maternal-infant bond that begins in the womb and continues at the nurturing breasts. They say it "is characterized as an intense *physical, emotional, spiritual bond* that exists between the two." Klaus and Kennell describe this bond as "a sensitive dance that occurs between them, where each relies on the cues of the other and interacts in an intense intertwined fashion."[17]

Klaus also notes that if mothers and newborns are left alone directly after birth, within an hour the babies will "crawl when they are placed near the tip of the sternum to their mother's breast, open their mouths widely, and latch on all on their own."[18] Klaus continues to describe the wonder of the maternal-infant bonding in "the crawling ability of the infant, the sensitivity of the mother's nipple, the decreased crying when close to their mother, and the warming capabilities of the mother's chest."[19]

The beauty and wonder of maternal-infant bonding are not a result of evolution but are a manifestation in creation of the reality that we are made for community and bonding—by the first bonded community, the Trinity.

Vikki Franklin writes, "The nutritional benefits of breast-feeding are associated with at least a 3.2-point difference in cognitive development compared to formula feeding after adjustment for key factors. This increase is in addition to the 2.1 IQ points that appear related to maternal bonding. . . . The longer a baby was breast-fed, the greater the increase in cognitive developmental benefit."[20]

My wife, Marilyn, spent six months studying the female breast and breastfeeding to become certified as a lactation consultant. Many an evening she would tell me that the female breast leads to the conclusion that there is a God. Marilyn writes, "As with any organ of the body, the breast function is so complex, intrinsic, and specific to its purpose. But mother's breast is absolutely unique in that it is precisely and perfectly linked to *all* the needs, physiologically, mentally, socially, emotionally of another human being, the newborn. Its hundreds of provisions have no adequate substitute."[21]

The secular worldview now ascending to dominance in the West has reduced women in general, and their breasts in particular, to sex objects, and sex itself to a recreational sport. Lost is the real wonder and beauty of the female. Lost, too, is the awesome manifestation of the motherly heart of God in his creature, woman.

In an essay titled "Anatomy of the Breast: How the Breast Makes Milk," Davis states, "The breast is not merely a passive container of milk. It is an organ of active production. When the infant suckles, a series of events takes place within the mother's body. . . . Continued milk production is governed by the infant."[22] The needs of the particular suckling infant are actually recognized by the mothers' body and her breasts adjust the quantity of milk as well as a vast myriad of qualities according to the specific baby's needs.

Breastfeeding is not merely a mechanical plumbing process. It is a natural, beautiful relationship between the mother and child. The woman was made (in her metaphysic and in her physical body) to manifest the nurturing nature of God. What is taking place is a life-giving, life-sustaining symbiotic relationship. The mother-child bonding at the breast is, at its most basic, a reflection of the eternal bond of the members of the Trinity.

Milk of Life

Human milk has many factors needed to provide for the baby's nutritional health. Davis writes: "We now know that breast milk also contains many nonnutritive, bioactive substances that have direct effects on the infant's physiology."[23] She goes on to list some of these marvels of creation:

- Protein: "The proteins in human milk are specific to human mammary production and are not found elsewhere in nature."
- Lipids: "Lipids provide 50 percent of the energy content in human milk. . . . Maternal diet affects the constituents of the lipids but not the total fat content. When a mother's caloric intake is poor, *fat is mobilized from maternal fat stores* (primarily in the hips and the thighs). The cholesterol level of breast milk will remain constant despite manipulation of the mother's cholesterol intake."[24]

Note the self-sacrificing nature built into the biology of the mother. Her body will not let the baby suffer from her own lack of caloric intake. Instead, her body sacrifices her own health by converting body fat into milk. That's why poor mothers in developing countries, unless at the point of starvation, will still provide adequate breast milk to their babies. What does this seemingly simple biological fact reveal about the nature of women? About the nature of God? Clearly, we see a reflection of God's self-sacrifice (John 3:16). Transcendent femininity is self-sacrifice.

- Minerals: "The mineral content of milk is *species specific*. The type and amount of minerals present in milk reflect the growth rate and bone density of the offspring. The mineral content of cow or elephant milk therefore is higher than in human milk because of the animal's larger bone mass."[25]

Note the specificity of creation. This affirms diversity and individuality. It reveals the perfection of God's design. Human babies were meant to be nurtured by the milk from a human breast, not from a cow or elephant. As Davis notes, "Mature milk [the predominant milk type within nine days of birth] provides all needed nutrients for normal growth and development. Breast milk will meet all of the infant's nutritional needs for six months."[26]

These are just a few of the tiny miracles of the female breast. These alone should cause us to worship the One who made us male and female. It should also spark us to honor women *as women*.

All science and art find their germ in the mind and creative expression of God. Nowhere is this reflected more clearly than in the anatomy of the female breast. The mother's breast is a scientific marvel. Yet its sculpting has stirred painters and poets for millennia.

Brooding (Sheltering) Wings

As many well-known Scriptures teach, God is a refuge and a protector.[27] He manifests this aspect of his character most profoundly in the metaphor of the wings of a mother bird. As Psalm 91:1–4 says:

> He who dwells in the shelter of the Most High
> will rest in the shadow of the Almighty.
> I will say of the LORD, "He is my refuge and my fortress,
> my God, in whom I trust."
>
> Surely he will save you from the fowler's snare

and from the deadly pestilence.
He will cover you with his feathers,
and under his wings you will find refuge;
his faithfulness will be your shield and rampart.

As shade protects from the hot desert sun, a *shadow* is a Hebrew metaphor for God's shelter from oppression. *Wings* is a metaphor for God's protection.

Next we come to the idea of brooding (Hebrew *rachaph:* "to brood, to flutter, to move").

In its definition of *brood*, Webster's 1828 dictionary returns us to the idea of a bird:

- "To sit on and cover, as a fowl on her eggs for the purpose of warming them and hatching chickens, or as a hen over her chickens, to *warm* and *protect* them" (emphasis added).
- "To have the mind uninterruptedly dwell a long time on a subject."

We see an illustration of brooding in Luke 2:19, where we read that "Mary treasured up all these things and pondered them in her heart." Mary was *brooding* about all that she had heard about her son Jesus.

In the beginning, it is the Spirit of God who broods over creation. As Genesis 1:2 says: "Now the earth was formless and empty, darkness was over the surface of the deep, and the Spirit of God was *hovering over* the waters" (emphasis added). The word translated "hovering over" is literally "fluttering." The image here is of a mother bird stirring the nest or hovering over her brood.

The Holy Spirit is called the paraclete, called to come alongside to help and succor God's people. Notice there is no inferiority in this role. The Holy Spirit does not have an inferior status. Just as the Spirit is the paraclete for redeemed mankind, so a woman is also called to help and succor.

Another definition of brooding is "to sit over, cover and *cherish*; as a hen broods her chickens" (Webster's 1828 dictionary; emphasis added). In the song of Moses recorded in Deuteronomy 32, Moses sings of God's care for Israel as a mother bird:

In a desert land he found him,
in a barren and howling waste.

He shielded him and cared for him;
he guarded him as the apple of his eye,
like an eagle that stirs up its nest
and hovers over its young,
that spreads its wings to catch them
and carries them on its pinions.
The LORD alone led him;
no foreign god was with him.
—Deuteronomy 32:10–12

Pastor Kip Ingram describes the mother eagle:

> The female eagle, larger and heavier than the male, bears the ea-
> glets on her wings when it is time for them to leave the nest. The
> mother eagle stirs up her nest to get the young out on their own
> to hunt their own food. Then she takes them on her wings and
> swoops down suddenly to force them to fly alone. But she always
> stays close enough to swoop back under them when they become
> too weary and weak to continue to fly on their own. Through
> this powerful image of God as a mother eagle, we can understand
> God as nurturing and supporting us when we are weak, yet always
> encouraging us to grow and mature.[28]

Jesus used a similar image when he mourned over Jerusalem: "O Jerusalem,
Jerusalem, you who kill the prophets and stone those sent to you, how often
I have longed to gather your children together, as a hen gathers her chicks
under her wings, but you were not willing" (Matthew 23:37).

Though likely fictional, we see a beautiful illustration of this concept in
the following legend:

> After a forest fire had devastated the back country, forest rangers
> began the process of assessing the inferno's damage. One ranger
> found a bird literally petrified in ashes, huddled on the ground
> against the base of a tree.
>
> Somewhat sickened by the eerie sight, he nudged the bird with
> a stick. To his great surprise, three tiny chicks scurried from under
> the dead bird's wings.
>
> The protective mother, aware of impending disaster, had

sheltered her offspring against the base of the tree and had covered them with her wings. She could have flown to safety but had chosen, instead, to remain steadfast when the blaze arrived and the heat began to scorch her small body.

Because she had been willing to die, those under the cover of her wings continued to live.

I told this story during a conference in Guatemala. After I finished, a young Guatemalan man stood up. With tears flooding his eyes, he told how one day his father, in a drunken rage, came after him with a gun, and how his mother jumped between them just as the father pulled the trigger. She took the bullet meant for her son. The young man blurted out that now he understood the heart of God. So did we all.

"Scars of Love," a poem written by Rebekah (Holsapple) Jack for her mother, beautifully captures the motherly, self-sacrificing heart of God:

If a man came to me and said, "I am your Christ," I would ask him to show me his hands. I know my Christ by the love which defines His character—the love that gave Him the strength and desire to give His life in exchange for mine.

"There is no greater love than this—that a man lay down his life for his friend."

I have never seen Jesus, but He knew me and loved me even before I was born. He gave me life, and when my own sin threatened that life, He died on the cross to save it, and no mark was left on me. When I see Him, I will know Him by the scars that bear witness to the unfathomable magnitude of His love for me.

I know my mother by the love which defines her character—the love that gave her strength and desire to offer her life in exchange for mine.

"There is no greater love than this—that a man lay down his life for his friend."

My mother knew me and loved me even before I was born; she gave me life. When I was a baby, twelve stone steps threatened that life, but she held me so tight and close that every cut and bruise fell on her own body, and so no mark was left on me.

So, Mother, if when I get to heaven I don't recognize you, show me the scars on your arms that bear witness to the unfathomable magnitude of your love for me.[29]

Notes

1. John Gray, *Men Are from Mars, Women Are from Venus* (New York: Harper Collins, 1992).

2. Floyd McClung, *The Father Heart of God* (Eugene, OR: Harvest House, 1992).

3. Roland M. Frye, *Scottish Journal of Theology*, 463, in Faye Short, "Biblical Language: A Brief Study of Inclusive Language for God," http://www.renewnetwork.org/Reports%20Pages/biblical%20language%20a_brief_study.htm.

4. Though it might be argued that Isaiah 49:15 refers to a human mother, we see that God's care is the archetype of the care of a nursing mother. The trait of being a nursing mother is derived from the primary nature of God's character imprinted in the *imago Dei*. As we will see, a mother's love is compassionate and secure (womb), nurturing and comforting (breasts), and a protective covering (wings). These characteristics did not simply materialize out of nothing. Where did they come from? These female characteristics are a reflection of God's "maternal" heart.

Likewise, regarding Isaiah 66:10–13, it might be argued that the "woman" in verses 11–12 refers to Jerusalem rather than God. But verse 13 clearly refers to God. As the God of comfort and provision, he values these characteristics and their images. The whole of Isaiah 60 and Revelation 21:23–26 speak of the glory of the nations being brought into the City of God, the New Jerusalem, at the end of time. Isaiah 66:12 describes this. So we find, in verse 11, that Jerusalem is the mother; in verse 12, Jerusalem will be provisioned by the wealth of nations; in verse 13, the mother will provide for and comfort her child. Why all these images of comfort and provision? Because God is the God of provision and comfort. He is the source of the maternal heart.

5. For the concept of "womb love," I am indebted to Phyllis Trible, *God and the Rhetoric of Sexuality* (Minneapolis: Augsburg Fortress Publishers, 1978), 51.

6. Leanne Payne, *Crisis in Masculinity* (Grand Rapids: Baker, 1985), 13.

7. *Encarta Dictionary*, s.v. "origin."

8. Ibid., s.v. "security."

9. *Enhanced Strong's Lexicon*, s.v. "racham."

10. Trible, *God and the Rhetoric of Sexuality*, 33.

11. Job 31:15; Psalm 139:13–16; Jeremiah 1:5; Galatians 1:15.

12. Trible, *God and the Rhetoric of Sexuality*, 36.

13. Nathan J. Stone, *Names of God in the Old Testament* (Chicago: Moody, 1944), 27.

14. R. C. Sproul Jr., ed., *Family Practice: God's Prescription for a Healthy Home* (Phillipsburg, NJ: Presbyterian & Reformed Publishing, 2001), 46.

15. Marie Davis, "Breastfeeding: The Lost Art," http://www.lactationconsultant.info/lostart.html.

16. Ibid.

17. "Maternal-Infant Bonding," http://www.rivershrink.com/mib.html (italics added).

18. Marshall Klaus, "Perinatal Care in the 21st Century," American Academy of Pediatrics, *Developmental and Behavioral News*, vol. 7, no. 1 (Fall 1998), http://www.dbpeds.org/section/fall98/klaus.html.

19. Ibid.

20. Vikki Franklin, "UK Study: Breast-feeding Increases Babies' IQ," *University of Kentucky Chandler Medical Center News*, September 22, 1999, http://www.uky.edu/PR/News/MCPRNews/1999/breastfeeding.htm.

21. Marilyn Miller, "Thoughts on Breastfeeding, by an OB Nurse and Mother" (unpublished article, February 2003).

22. Marie Davis, "Anatomy of the Breast: How the Breast Makes Milk," http://www.lactationconsultant.info/how.html.

23. Ibid.

24. Ibid. (italics added).

25. Ibid. (italics added).

26. Ibid.

27. Psalm 17:8; 36:7; 57:1; 61:3–4; 63:7; 71:1; Ruth 2:12.

28. Uncited quotation in Kip Ingram's sermon "The Nurture God Gives," Twinbrook Baptist Church, Rockville, MD, September 5, 1999, http://members.aol.com/Twinbrookb/sermons/1999/nurture_god_gives.htm.

29. Given to me by Rebekah's mom, Diane Holsapple.

PART 4

THE TRANSFORMING STORY

CHAPTER 11

The Big Story

To this point, we have been building a case, brick by brick, for the uniqueness and worth of women in God's economy. Individually, these bricks encourage us to let go of old patterns of thinking when it comes to the sexes. But together, they reveal a structure that compels us by its very beauty and undeniable design to value and esteem women into the life of the community, recognizing their unique God-given role in the cultural mandate and in the nurturing of families and nations.

This chapter is about stepping back from the individual facts and seeing how they fit together into God's marvelous story of creation, fall, redemption, and consummation. Cultures and nations are enlivened by stories, at times naively dismissing the hard facts of reality. Because we live in the world that God has made, the facts of reality are the same for all human beings. They inform us of what is true. Our cultural stories explain "what we see." As we saw earlier in chapter 4, the stories that power the imaginations of nations and cultures are called metanarratives. They explain the basic questions of life: who we are, why we are here, and where we are going. The Bible has a metanarrative, too, and it is more transforming than any other—because it matches reality like no other.

We will explore the Bible's transforming story in overview fashion in this chapter, then focus on some of the details and their implications in later chapters as we close out the book. Hold on tight, because it promises to be an exhilarating ride.

Figure 15: God's Transforming Story

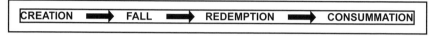

The Transforming Story

The Bible is God's story, the sacred narrative that reveals the interaction between the Creator and his creation. It begins and ends in wonder. It begins in a garden—the garden of Eden, a perfect place—with a couple, Adam and Eve. It ends in a garden-city—the New Jerusalem—with another couple, Jesus Christ and his glorious bride.

From beginning to end, we witness humankind's rebellion against God and the utter depravity that affects all human relationships, including those between women and men. Along the way, we observe God taking Israel for his bride (Ezekiel 16:1–14; Hosea 1–3) and Jesus preparing to take the church as his bride (2 Corinthians 11:2; Ephesians 5:22–33). In both testaments we see the harbingers of the glory that will be fully manifest at the second coming of Christ (Revelation 19:6–9; 21:2).

God's transforming story, like any great novel, has both breadth and depth (see figure 16). Its breadth, from Genesis to Revelation, may be called the flow of HIStory; for in fact, history is ultimately *his* story, the story of Christ Jesus. The breadth of the biblical narrative reveals the creation, fall, redemption, and consummation. The depth of the story reveals the worldview of the narrative; it describes reality the way God made it. The Bible answers questions of meaning: *What is true? What is good?* And *What is beautiful?*

In the following graphic, we see in iconic form the Bible's answers to the questions (from left to right): *What is the nature of creation? What is the nature of man?* And *Where is history going?* Like all metanarratives, the Bible answers questions on the nature of being a woman and a man. *Are men and women equal? Are men and women the same?*

Figure 16: The Flow of Biblical History

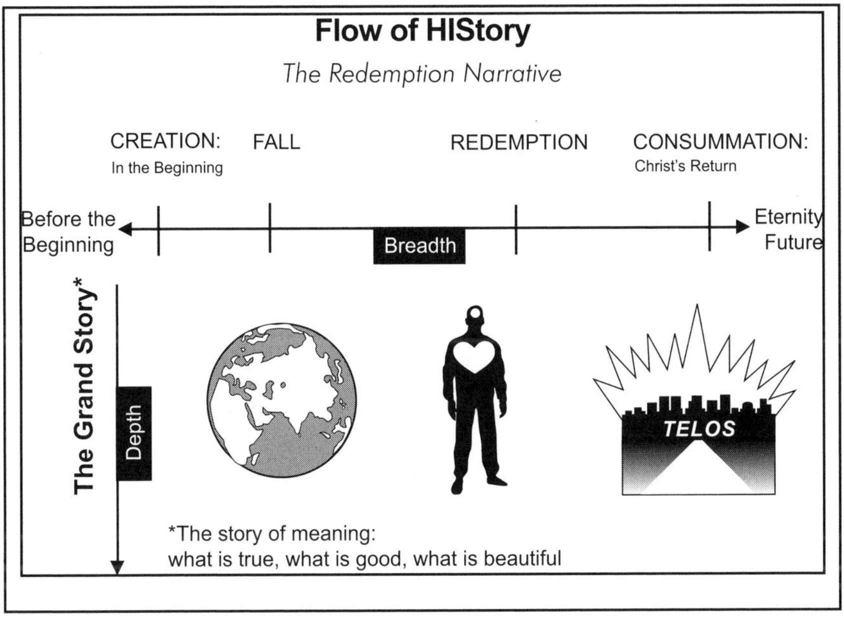

Flow of HIStory
The Redemption Narrative

CREATION: FALL   REDEMPTION   CONSUMMATION:
In the Beginning   Christ's Return

Before the Beginning — Breadth — Eternity Future

The Grand Story*

Depth

TELOS

*The story of meaning:
what is true, what is good, what is beautiful

The Greek word *telos* signifies "the end" toward which all of history is moving. It is God's ultimate purpose for creation. It is the biblical answer to ultimate questions like *Why are we here? What is the purpose of creation? Why did God create?* The *telos* is the fullness of the kingdom of God.

The biblical narrative can transform

- individuals, in their calls to salvation and to their life work;[1]
- communities, lifting them out of poverty; and
- nations, enabling citizens to build free, just, and compassionate societies.[2]

It forms a metanarrative that helps us understand the grandeur and wonder of women. German psychiatrist Karl Stern captures the glory of women in *The Flight from Woman*. He writes, "The earliest prophetic message of eschatological significance refers to Woman (Gen. 3:15). Hence it is no surprise that she appears at the end of history, bigger than life, clothed in the Sun, the moon at her feet. Everything, the entire tortuous plot of Salvation, has to fit between these two tableaux, and it does."[3]

The Opening Scenes

Christian author Gene Edwards has also captured this beautifully in his book *The Divine Romance: The Most Beautiful Love Story Ever Told*. In the first scene, the angels watch God's creation of Eve:

> Slowly the revelation subsided, giving angels a moment to wonder what *ultimate* thought had coursed through God's being. What masterpiece might now fall from his hand? At last they could pierce the light and see again the face of God. Upon that face was etched exaltation and joy.
>
> Whispered one angel as he staggered to his appointed place, "He has contemplated man's counterpart. He has *seen* her in the eye of his mind. But somewhere beyond that sight, methinks, he has glimpsed a higher, far greater, revelation. But what?"
>
> "'Tis mystery, hidden in unapproachable light," rejoined another.
>
> Now it was with trembling hands that the Builder did build, and mold, and fashion, and mold again. And while the being he fashioned took on its final form, awed and dumbfounded angels fell once more to their knees at the sight of the wonder before them.
>
> One angel, most irreverently cried aloud the thoughts of all: "He is not making another Ish. This one is alike, yet different. As the lioness is to the lion, so is this *out-of man*. But never, never," cried the wayward angel, "was lion or lioness so beautiful as this."
>
> Another angelic being broke the confines of restraint.
>
> "Nor was even Man so beautiful as this!" he exclaimed.
>
> With that, the vaults of heaven broke open, and in one full-throated shout, all heavenly beings proclaimed:
>> *Never was*
>> *nor e'er shall be*
>> *as beautiful*
>> *a thing as she.*
>> *All hosts in*
>> *heaven's court,*
>> *all creatures on*
>> *earthen sod,*

it matters not
the tribe nor race,
one sight alone can
be
more beautiful than
she.
It is the face
of God.[4]

Adam's first embrace of Eve perhaps provoked similar wonder. Let us return to Edwards to experience a taste of it:

Now holding her beside himself, he glanced quickly around, then raised his hand toward the heavens.

Creator, Lord.
Hear me!
Angels, hear me!
Seraphim and cherubim.
Creatures of the deep,
upon the land
and in the sky.
I am one once more.
Behold, my counterpart!
More beautiful, more glorious
than all realms combined.
At last!
Bone of my bone,
flesh of my flesh.
And I ... man!
Your earthen Lord ... I ...
I ... am ... no ... longer ... alone!
Hear me,
realms seen.
Hear me,
realms unseen,
The aloneness is broken
forever!

And now, my Lord,
my God,
my Creator—
It was not good for
man
to be alone.
*And I am **not** alone.*
Henceforth,
Forever,
All things are good.

"There remains but one thing, the ultimate completion of all oneness—first . . . *you* in me, now . . . *I* . . . in you!"

So it came about, there in the serene beauty of the Garden of Eden, a place more beautiful than heaven and earth, he embraced her again. And while angels rejoiced in that primordial age of innocence, the ruler of earth and his counterpart became, once more . . . one flesh."[5]

The Flow of Biblical History

The divine romance awaits its consummation in the coming final scene, when Jesus receives his bride. But we are getting ahead of ourselves. Let's take a look at the flow of biblical history, which reveals this transforming story.

We can divide it thusly:

Creation
- God creates male and female, complementarian by design, to depict his Trinitarian nature.
- Genesis 1 describes the man and woman as *equal in being* because they are both made in the image of God.
- Genesis 2 describes the man and woman as gloriously *different in function.*

Figure 17: The Restoration of Women

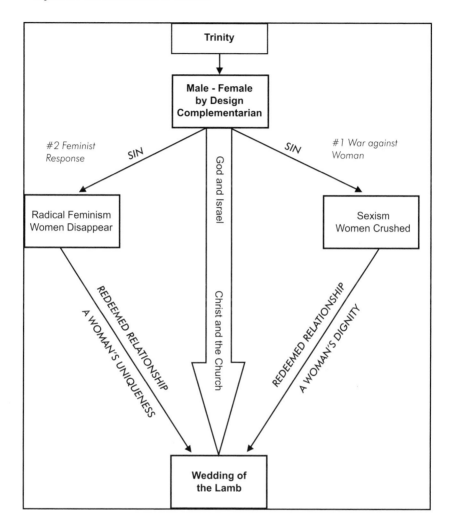

Fall

- Humankind denies the Trinitarian God.
- Genesis 3 describes the distortion of female and male, with people falsely concluding that masculine is superior to feminine.
- Two major "deviant" story lines put women in boxes and lead to the war against women.

Box 1: Sexism

This box overemphasizes the differences between men and women and holds, falsely, that woman's *being* has little intrinsic worth. As a consequence, men have responded by crushing women down through history through murder and emotional, physical, and sexual abuse.

Box 2: Feminism

This box is a response to sexism but contains evils of its own. Woman's *function* has little intrinsic worth. Women *as women* disappear. This intellectual disappearance leads to sexual confusion, including lesbianism, homosexuality, and the transgender masculinization of women and feminization of men.

Redemption

Jesus is a revolutionary when it comes to women. He is the first true feminist. In Christ, women have the opportunity and capacity to leave these confining boxes. Leaving sexism behind, we restore women's intrinsic worth of being. Jettisoning radical feminism, we restore the worth of women's design and function. Though different in many ways, men and women stand before God as equals. As Galatians 3:28 says, "There is neither. . . male nor female, for you are all one in Christ Jesus." The dignity of women is restored, as well as their unique place in the cultural mandate and their role in the nurturing of family and nations.

Consummation

Yet something even better awaits male and female followers of Christ. While we work hard to uphold one another's dignity and worth, the kingdom has not yet come in power. That glorious moment awaits its final consummation at the wedding of the Lamb.

In the meantime, however, we are to make the transforming story manifest in our lives by identifying with Christ. As Lilian Calles Barger writes: "The Word must be made flesh also in me, but in order for that to happen I need to surrender . . . resurrected with Jesus, to identify with him as, crucified, he identified with me. The divine Word can make my body a meaningful conduit of God's self-revelation instead of my being merely pliable, dumb matter waiting for the world's inscription."[6]

Notes

1. For more on the call of God, see my upcoming book, *Occupy Till I Come!* Another excellent book on the subject is Os Guinness's modern classic *The Call: Finding and Fulfilling the Central Purpose of Your Life* (Nashville: W Publishing Group, 2003).

2. For more on the nations, see my book *Discipling Nations: The Power of Truth to Transform Cultures* (Seattle: YWAM Publishing, 1998; second edition, 2001).

3. Karl Stern, *The Flight from Woman* (New York: The Noonday Press, 1965), 274.

4. Gene Edwards, *The Divine Romance: The Most Beautiful Love Story Ever Told* (Carol Stream, IL: Tyndale, 1992), 22–23 (italics in original).

5. Ibid., 43–45 (italics and bold in the original).

6. Lilian Calles Barger, *Eve's Revenge* (Grand Rapids: Brazos Press, 2003), 182.

CHAPTER 12

The Creation and the Fall

The Bible provides the primal story to explain all of human existence. This story is not simply about propositional theological truth. Relationships are at its heart. Truth in the Bible is always given in the context of relationships between

- the members of the Trinity,
- God and creation,
- God and his people,
- Christ and his bride,
- man and woman,
- members of the human family, and
- humankind and creation.

For men and women, the bookends of Scripture are nuptial. In the beginning we marvel at the glorious creation and union of Adam and Eve (Genesis 1–2); at the end we rejoice in the wedding of the Lamb and the eternal union of Christ and his bride (Revelation 19–21). But between the bookends, the Bible describes the sin-induced distortion of marriage and the male-female relationship through the worship not of the true God but of false gods, with Baal being a prime example. (We will unpack this in a later chapter.)

We need to remember that God has created *order* in the universe. This order is not burdensome. It reflects God's character and nature and leads to the fulfillment of his purposes. To have a truly fulfilling life, we must walk in that order. As John Calvin, the Swiss Reformer, stated: "We know how much every man is wedded to himself, and how difficult it is to eradicate from our minds the vain confidence of our own wisdom. It is therefore of great importance to be well convinced of this truth, that a man's life cannot be ordered aright unless it is framed according to the law of God, and that without this he can only wander in labyrinths and crooked bypaths."[1]

In contrast, to deny God and his order is to live in *disorder*. We have witnessed the power of disorder to destroy women's lives, either through sexism, which crushes women, or through radical feminism, which pushes women to disappear.

A proper understanding of the Bible's transforming story will allow us to reclaim God's order in our lives. We can discern the flow of that story by looking at it through four stages of biblical history: creation, fall, redemption, and consummation. We will cover the first two stages in this chapter, using Genesis 1–3 as our guide, and the last two stages in the following chapters.

Genesis 1: Equal in Being

Again, we need to keep in mind the all-important distinction between being and function. As we have seen, *being* refers to our existence, substance, or fundamental nature. It refers to the fact that we are created in God's image. In this all human beings are equal. *Function*, however, refers to purpose, responsibility, or role. In this men and women are diverse in person and function in a way that is complementary. While the functions of men and women may differ, they are of equal necessity and value.

Getting this basic distinction wrong leads to all kinds of problems in male-female relations. Sexism flows from seeing men and women unequal in both their being and their function. Feminism, for its part, begins with equality of being (which is right) and interchangeability of function (which is wrong). By contrast, the Trinitarian model inherent in Christianity affirms equality of being and diversity of function.

Let's look again at Genesis 1:26–28:

Then God said, "Let us make man in our image, in our likeness, and let them rule over the fish of the sea and the birds of the air, over the livestock, over all the earth, and over all the creatures that move along the ground."

So God created man in his own image,
in the image of God he created him;
male and female he created them.

God blessed them and said to them, "Be fruitful and increase in number; fill the earth and subdue it. Rule over the fish of the sea and the birds of the air and over every living creature that moves on the ground."

In Genesis 1:24 we find that God made the animals "according to their kinds." Then we learn that God makes man after *his* kind, in his image or likeness. Interestingly, the Hebrew word translated "man" (Genesis 1:26; 5:2) is *adam*. It is a generic term for the human race—both female and male. It stands in contrast to ish, which is variously translated as "man" (as opposed to "woman") or "husband," and to ishshah, which is translated as "woman" (as opposed to "man") or "wife."

Note the Trinitarian model inherent in this passage: "Then God said, 'Let *us* make *man* [humankind] in *our* image, in *our* likeness, and let *them* [male and female] rule . . . '" (emphasis added). God reveals himself as *community*. The *one* God uses *plural* references for himself and creates *one* humankind—*adam* as *ish* and *ishshah*—as the *crown of creation*.

This passage shows that our mandate is to create culture and develop the earth. Man is the one creature whose eyes are toward heaven and whose feet and hands are in the soil. Man serves as a bridge between heaven and earth by carrying out the heavenly mandate on earth.

Throughout history, theologians have made various attempts to describe what the *imago Dei* means. As we have seen, God is a serving God (see chapter 8). Man, made in the image of God, has been designed to serve and so reflect the glory of his Creator. We are to serve *God* in worship, our *fellow man* in service, and *creation* in stewardship.

Summarizing these approaches, theologian Anthony A. Hoekema states:

The image of God . . . describes not just something that man *has*, but something that man *is*. It means that human beings both mirror and represent God. Thus, there is a sense in which the image includes the physical body. The image of God, . . . includes the structural and functional aspects . . . though we must remember that in the biblical view structure is secondary, while function is primary. The image must be seen in man's threefold relationship: toward God, toward others, and toward nature."[2]

Another way to describe the image is to classify these three aspects as *structural* (man has an image that is "like God"), *relational* (man is "community"), and *functional* (what man does as the steward of creation).

Before we move on, it is worth reiterating that the Genesis 1:26–28 creation mandate to procreate and exercise dominion (see chapter 9) is given to the *imago Dei:* male and female. Note that a single human being, or a group of males, or a group of females cannot fulfill either part. It takes a team effort of male and female. The woman is not an object. She is not the property of man. She is equally the *imago Dei*. In God's design, the responsibilities of pro-*creation* and dominion are shared. The mandate is for all.

The bottom line is that human life is both *sacred* and *significant*. It is significant because we have been made for a purpose. It is sacred because of *who* we are (*imago Dei)* and because of *whose* we are (offspring of the Creator God).

Unlike other philosophies and religions, which admit little or no intrinsic worth in human beings, the Bible reveals that all of us are made in the image of God. Human life is not valued by how much we have (materialism), what we do (utilitarianism), or our social status (casteism or racism). All human life has value.

We have seen that all women and men are equal in their being. Now we will turn our attention to their difference in function.

Genesis 2: Corresponding in Function

Genesis 2 acknowledges that differences exist between men and women. They have differing roles that are nonetheless *equally valuable*. If we see Genesis

1:26–28 as the headline for the creation of the *imago Dei*, then Genesis 2 can be seen as the story. Here are the highlights:

- God finishes his creation work and rests (2:1–3).
- These startling words come: "And there was no man to work the ground" (2:5).
- God creates the man "from the dust of the ground" (2:7).
- God places the man in the garden he had planted to steward—work and care for—God's creation (2:8,15).
- Just as there had been no man to work the ground (2:5), now there is no one to help the man carry out the cultural mandate (2:18).
- Twice God states that the individual man is alone, not in the sense of having no relationships (since he had a relationship with God and creation), but in the sense of having no companion to fulfill his task; and thus he is incomplete (2:18,20).
- God creates the man's helping counterpart (2:21–22).

A Suitable Helper

The phrase "suitable helper" (Genesis 2:20) is composed of two Hebrew words: *kenegdo* and *ezer*. The Hebrew word for "helper," *ezer*, is found twenty-one times in the Old Testament. Of these, sixteen times it refers to God as "helper" of his people (for example, Deuteronomy 33:26,29; Psalm 115:9–11; 121:1–2).

There is no sense of inferiority in the word "helper." People should never assume that a helper is inferior to the one helped. Rather, isn't it often the other way around in our daily experience that the strong—by necessity and out of compassion—help the weak? We also need to remember that God, the ultimate Helper, is in no way inferior. Almighty God subordinates himself to human beings, but he does not cease to be God. Thus, this role of helper may imply humility, but it never implies inferiority.

But note: The helper is a *suitable* helper." This is the Hebrew word *kenegdo*. It means "like him," "corresponding to him," "matching him," or "counterpart."[3] Just as the individual members of the Trinity are the counterparts of one another, so the woman is the counterpart of the man and the man is the counterpart of the woman.

They are like the two parts of a latch, the two ends of a belt buckle, the two parts of a seat belt. They correspond to one another. They are not identical, like the two ends of a shoelace or a pair of earrings; they are different, by design. Yet they form a whole.

If both unique parts were not present, the mechanism would not function. By definition, a counterpart must be functionally different for it to complete what is lacking.

The man and the woman are counterparts. Note the symmetry of a counterpart. The woman is not just suitable for the man, *but the man is suitable for the woman.* Writer Dwight Hervey Small says that God created "a 'woman-sized void' in man, a void which none of the animals nor even another man could fill."[4]

As Elisabeth Elliot notes, men and women are "two creatures amazingly alike and wondrously different."[5] Men and women are, in the structural view, each the image of God. But in the relational and functional view, it takes both female and male to be the *imago Dei*. This is the secret to their unity. They are functionally different. Man, as the "head," initiates; the woman, as the "heart," responds. Together they form a whole *imago Dei* to transform the raw stuff of creation into godly culture.

The Creation of Eve

Genesis 2:21–22 brings us to the formation of Eve, the completion of God's creative activity and the high-water mark of creation:

> So the LORD God caused the man to fall into a deep sleep; and while he was sleeping, he took one of the man's ribs and closed up the place with flesh. Then the LORD God made a woman from the rib he had taken out of the man, and he brought her to the man.

Note first that while the first *adam* (the male) came from the ground, the second *adam* (the female) was formed from the first *adam*. The man's source was the ground. The woman's source was the man. The hand of God formed both.

Second, it is important to note that the woman came from the man's side. She is his counterpart, his suitable helper. She is not his property or slave. She is designed to serve alongside him. As nineteenth-century pastor and author John Angell James noted: "She was not taken from the head, to show she was not to rule over him; nor from his foot, to teach that she was not to be his slave; nor from his hand, to show that she was not to be his tool; but from his side, to show that she was to be his companion."[6]

Not only are Adam and Eve companions; they are filled with joy and wonder. When he first sees Eve, Adam exclaims:

> This is now bone of my bones
> and flesh of my flesh;
> she shall be called "woman,"
> for she was taken out of man.
> —Genesis 2:23

Raymond Ortlund comments on this passage: "These are the first recorded human words, and it is appropriate that they are poetry. 'This creature alone, Father, out of all the others—this one at last meets my need for a companion. She alone is my equal, my flesh. I identify with her. I love her. I will call her Woman, for she came out of Man.' The man perceives the woman not as his rival but as his partner, not as a threat . . . but as the only one capable of fulfilling his longing within."[7]

John Angell James catches the moment:

> I need not recite the details of the scenes of paradise, but only refer to them. It is at once a beautiful and melancholy record. We there see woman as she came from the hand of the Creator, with a body combining every charm which could captivate the being for whose companionship she was designed, and a soul possessing every virtue that could adorn her character and make her an object of reverent affection. Her creation was peculiar, but not unworthy of the Great Being who made her, of herself, or of him from whose own body she was derived. Her origin seemed to dignify both her husband and herself. She was formed of organized and vitalized

matter, and not of mere dust; here was her distinction. Who can describe or conceive the thought or emotions of this only pair at their first interview![8]

Here is no slave to be ill-treated. Here is no property to be bought and sold. Here is no sex object for male pleasure. Here is one not to be despised and crushed by sexism or denied by radical feminism. Here is the crown of creation. Here, in human form, from the hand of the Creator himself, is the manifestation of the motherly heart of God. Here is the mother of all living, the wife of the first man. Here is the prequel to none other than the bride of the Son of God.

Each stage of the creation process ascended from lower forms to higher forms, from a lower glory to a higher glory. While the crown of God's creation is *adam*, the crown of *adam*-male is *adam*-female. As the apostle Paul said, "The woman is *the glory of man*" (1 Corinthians 11:7b; emphasis added).

Naming and Serving

Let's now turn to Adam's naming of Eve. First, note the dual use of words in Genesis, both of which convey an exercise of authority: the first is to call things into existence; the second is to establish sovereignty or authority. We see this in Genesis 1:3–5: "And God said [called into existence], 'Let there be light,' and there was light. God saw that the light was good, and he separated the light from the darkness. God called [named] the light 'day,' and the darkness he called 'night.'"

Just as God established his authority over creation by naming it, so his vice-regent exercises dominion over creation by naming the animals (Genesis 2:19–20). Just as God is the Word Maker, so too are we word makers. God used words to create the universe, and man uses words to create culture and shape the universe. We see this clearly in our own lives. My wife and I discovered this awesome responsibility after we named our first child, Nathan. We realized that for all eternity God would call our son "Nathan." Why? Because that is the name we gave him.

In Genesis 2:23, Adam states, "She shall be called 'woman,' for she was taken out of man." This is a play on words in the Hebrew: "She shall be called ishshah, for she was taken out of ish." The ish is a man; the ishshah is a "wo-man." Counselor and author Leanne Payne states that "this word play points to the fact that woman too is man—*she man, womb-man,* or *female man.*"[9]

Because of the creation mandate, both the man and the woman have caretaking authority over the creation. But Adam, by naming the woman, signifies that he has loving authority over her. He is to *husband* his wife in the same way humankind is to *husband* creation in God's stead. This reflects the cultivating of the soil and the soul, leading to creating godly culture. It is modeled on God's very nature as a Servant to husband his people to salvation.

The transforming story reveals God's love for his people in the Old Testament and Jesus' love for the church in the New. Thus, God created Adam and Eve to be his first model of the transcendent. From the start, God's intention has been for the human ish to lovingly self-sacrifice himself for his ishshah.

The Record

Throughout the Bible, we see that God is the "husband" of Israel. God's love for his people (Ezekiel 16; Hosea 1–3; 11:1–11; Ephesians 5:25–33) is the pattern for ish. God defines himself in relationship to his people as a husband.[10] This covenant marriage between God and Israel was instituted at Mount Sinai. Jeff Meyers notes:

> The wedding service is recorded in Exodus 19–24. Moses is the minister officiating at the wedding. He goes up on the mountain to hear the Lord's word and brings it back down to the people. The husband's part of the wedding service begins with the Lord reminding His bride of what He has done for her (Ex. 20:1–2). Then Yahweh tells the Israelites how they are to live as His holy people (Ex. 20–23). When Moses brings these words to the people, they say basically, "I do": "All the words which the LORD has said we will do!" (Ex. 24:3). The wedding ceremony ends with a reception, a feast in the Lord's presence (Ex. 24:9–11). Then, once Yahweh and Israel are married, Yahweh moves in with His bride.[11]

Much of the Old Testament, as we shall see, describes Israel leaving her loving, self-sacrificing husband and prostituting herself before the altar of Baal, a false god worshiped by the neighboring people of the ancient Near East. The Book of Hosea, however, is a metaphor of the faithful husband who humbly woos his unfaithful wife back home.

Moving to the New Testament, we see the profound nature of Christ's self-sacrificing husbanding of the church. Romans 5:8 picks up the thread of the Book of Hosea: "God demonstrates his own love for us in this: While we were still sinners, Christ died for us." Human marriage, in fact, finds its premise in the heavenly marriage of Christ and his bride. Here are some examples:

- 2 Timothy 2:13: "If we are faithless, he will remain faithful, for he cannot disown himself."
- Hebrews 13:5: "Never will I leave you; never will I forsake you."

Before we move on, let's look at one of the functional differences established by Genesis 2:4–25. While men and women are equal in their being, they are different in both their pro-*creative* (social/relational) and developmental (functional) responsibilities related to the cultural mandate. I contend that *adam*-male will most fully manifest the Father heart of God, while *adam*-female will most fully manifest the motherly heart of God. Only together, as the *imago Dei,* will they fulfill the purpose of their creation, to create godly culture and be vice-regents of creation.

One of the differences between the man and the woman, however, comes in the very specific realm of marriage. Here the man has the authority and the responsibility to be a loving servant-leader.[12] Although Scripture also clearly makes distinctions between men and women in church leadership roles,[13] nowhere does the Bible establish a general rule of authority for all men over all women. Women's freedom for servant-leadership is found throughout the marketplace and the public square.

Theologian J. I. Packer has stated: "It is important that the cause of not imposing on women restrictions that Scripture does not impose should not be confused with the quite different goals of minimizing the distinctness of the sexes as created and of diminishing the male's inalienable responsibilities in man-woman relationships as such."[14]

Adam, the husband, is to be the loving *servant-leader* of his wife. Eve is to be the loving, respectful *helper* of Adam. Five points, or articles, establish this role distinction in Genesis 2.[15] These may be expressed as both the order and the ordinances of creation.

Order and Ordinances

The *order* of creation means simply that the man was *created first* (Genesis 2:7,22; see also 1 Corinthians 11:8 and 1 Timothy 2:13). The fact that Adam was created before Eve is the first of the five establishing articles of a man's leadership of a woman in marriage.

The *ordinances* of creation reveal reality the way God intended. He could have chosen to do things differently, but he did not. He chose to do things as he did. These creation ordinances reveal the four additional articles regarding the husband's loving servant-leadership of his wife:

- The woman was created *for* the man (Genesis 2:18); Paul reinforces this in 1 Corinthians 11:9 and Ephesians 5:22–33. Man glorifies God in his loving servant-leadership of his wife. In her loving, respectful helping of her husband, the woman glorifies him and, in so doing, glorifies God.
- The woman was created *from* the man (Genesis 2:21–23; see also 1 Corinthians 11:8).[16]
- The woman was brought *to* the man (Genesis 2:22).
- The woman was named *by* the man (Genesis 2:23).

It must be noted that the order of creation (male first) and the ordinances of creation are normative for life and practice unless and until they are explicitly modified by subsequent biblical revelation. But just as a hierarchical authority structure does not imply that some members of the Trinity are inferior, neither does the authority relationship between the man and woman in the family imply that women are inferior to men in their being or function. When men or women assume that the order and ordinances of Scripture establish male superiority, they are violating the fundamental Trinitarian principle!

The Sacred Mystery: One Flesh

Genesis 2:24 provides the glorious finale of the creation story, the "wedding" of the first couple. In this, Adam and Eve serve as a model for our lives and a picture of the events that will consummate history when Christ returns for his bride. Here we read: "Therefore shall a man *leave* his father and his mother, and shall *cleave* unto his wife: and they shall be *one flesh*" (KJV; emphasis added).

This verse is the source of the sacred mystery that we call marriage. The New Testament mentions this mystery in Matthew 19:4–6 and Ephesians 5:31–32. The mystery follows a threefold pattern to leave, cleave, and become one flesh.

Leaving

The Hebrew word means "to depart from, to be free from." Some cultures have the wife leaving her family and joining the husband's family. This often makes the woman little more than a servant or a slave in her in-laws' household. The biblical pattern is radically different. Not only must the woman leave her family, but the husband, too, must leave his family to begin a new one. God has designed marriage to create new family units. This is the beginning of something *new*.

Cleaving

The Hebrew word means "to stay close to, to join to, to be joined together." Picture gluing together two planks of wood so that the point of the bond is stronger than either plank. Here is the bonding of a covenant relationship between three parties: the woman, the man, and their Creator. Because it is a covenant relationship that includes the One who authored marriage, it is to be exclusive and for life. It is to be with no other and is enduring. This bonding of the soul leads to the bonding of the flesh. Because we are seamless physical-spiritual personalities, these two bondings must not be separated or reduced to rape, adultery, or a "recreational sport." A man and a woman are most completed in the physical and emotional embrace of sexual relations. Marriage provides for the health of individuals and society. Marriage is the first institution God created and the only one created before the Fall. As Genesis 2:25 reports: "The man and his wife were both naked, and they felt no shame."

One Flesh

Our sexuality professes a profound spiritual truth. This Scripture reveals that $1 + 1 = 1$. Unfortunately, like the radio preacher I mentioned in the beginning of this book, many Christians simply act as if the equation $1 + 0 = 1$ extends to the human sphere. But in relations between men and women, guess who gets to be the 1 and which one is assigned the 0? Many Christians think and act as if the woman is a zero.

Such thinking is not only sexist, but fails to do justice to the text. There are two major Hebrew words for the word "one": *yachid,* which means "single," "absolute," or "indivisible"; and the word found here in Genesis 2:24, *echad,* which carries the meaning "united," "compound, " or "bound together." The sense of *echad* is seen in the Shema in Deuteronomy 6:4–5: "Hear, O Israel: The LORD our God, the LORD is one [*echad*]. Love the LORD your God with all your heart and with all your soul and with all your strength."

This use of *one* reveals God's unity in diversity. Genesis 2:24 promotes a similar understanding of human beings. The united Lord is the pattern of the united Adam and Eve. The man is not to crush the woman to make her a slave so the two can become one.

The woman does not need to disappear as a woman so that the two may become one. No, they maintain their unique personalities, sexuality, and soul qualities. They are more together than the sum of their parts. They become *echad.*

Distortion in Being and Function

The Fall, described in Genesis 3, marred this wonderful unity in diversity and distorted the human understanding of being and function. With their rebellion against God, the woman and the man were separated from God. They began to lose sight of the nature and character of God and began to create gods after their own image and after created things (Isaiah 44:9–20; Habakkuk 2:18–20; Romans 1:21–23). Because the primary relationship was broken, all of the secondary relationships began to suffer.

They no longer knew who they were in relationship to one another, as male and female. Marriage began to suffer. Infidelity began and spread. Eventually sexual relations were distorted to men conquering women; eventually sex became a form of entertainment and power. Sexual confusion abounded. The concept of stewardship, of creating godly culture, was lost. Human beings began to worship creation as if it were God, or they moved to the other extreme and began to abuse and rape creation for their own selfish ends.

This deadly rebellion against God cursed humanity in two ways. First, it devastated relations between men, women, and families. Second, it brought about God's legal judgment for sin.

Let's look at what happened in Genesis 3:1–7:

> Now the serpent was more crafty than any of the wild animals the LORD God had made. He said to the woman, "Did God really say, 'You must not eat from any tree in the garden'?"
>
> The woman said to the serpent, "We may eat fruit from the trees in the garden, but God did say, 'You must not eat fruit from the tree that is in the middle of the garden, and you must not touch it, or you will die.'"
>
> "You will not surely die," the serpent said to the woman. "For God knows that when you eat of it your eyes will be opened, and you will be like God, knowing good and evil."
>
> When the woman saw that the fruit of the tree was good for food and pleasing to the eye, and also desirable for gaining wisdom, she took some and ate it. She also gave some to her husband, who was with her, and he ate it. Then the eyes of both of them were opened, and they realized they were naked; so they sewed fig leaves together and made coverings for themselves.

This is perhaps the saddest and certainly the most consequential episode in human history. All of the sin and brokenness experienced by people throughout history stem from this moment.

The rebellion against God is also a rebellion against his order, as the man and the woman abandon worship of the living God for what would become gods of their own making. This brought into being a hideous counterfeit order based on lies and injustice. One of the results was enmity between men and women.

Who Was to Blame?

For some unknown reason, Satan approached Eve. After she stepped outside the created order by rebelling against the Creator, Adam quickly chose to do the same. The *imago Dei* is male and female, and it is the *imago Dei* that rebelled. The text says that *their* eyes were "opened" (3:7), after Adam ratified Eve's choice with his own. They were both ashamed (3:7b), they both hid from God (3:8b), and they were both expelled from the garden of Eden (3:23–4:1). The rebellion was both individual and communal.

So while Eve was tempted first through deception, Adam sinned fully aware of what he was doing. Note that the responsibility for the decision ultimately falls on Adam. God called Adam to account first. In Genesis 3:9 we read: "But the LORD God called to the man, 'Where *are* you?'" (emphasis added).

Also, Adam represented all humankind, as Paul notes in Romans 5:12,14: "Therefore, just as sin entered the world through *one man*, and death through sin, and in this way death came to all men, because all sinned. . . . Nevertheless, death reigned from the time of *Adam* to the time of Moses, even over those who did not sin by breaking a command, as did *Adam*, who was a pattern of the one to come" (emphasis added).[17]

However, many Christians and theologians have placed the primary blame for the Fall at the feet of Eve. This has then become the rationale, in many Christian circles, for seeing women as inferior and for justifying male tyranny. But clearly the Bible lays the primary responsibility at the feet of the man.

Shame and Fear

Note that immediately after their rebellion, Adam and Eve were ashamed (3:7). Their internal sin changed the way they saw themselves. The results of the Fall were both individual and systemic. Adam and Eve died spiritually and as a consequence would die physically. Moral and natural evil (hurricanes, floods, earthquakes, etc.) began to reign.

In Genesis 3:8–12, we see God's response to this catastrophe.

> Then the man and his wife heard the sound of the LORD God as he was walking in the garden in the cool of the day, and they hid from the LORD God among the trees of the garden. But the LORD God called to the man, "Where are you?"
>
> He answered, "I heard you in the garden, and I was afraid because I was naked; so I hid."
>
> And he said, "Who told you that you were naked? Have you eaten from the tree that I commanded you not to eat from?"
>
> The man said, "The woman you put here with me—she gave me some fruit from the tree, and I ate it."

Here we find not only shame, but also (for the first time in world history) fear. Then we witness the first case of "passing the buck" in history. This has been the continuing pattern of all the sons and daughters of Adam and Eve.

> Then the LORD God said to the woman, "What is this you have done?"
>
> The woman said, "The serpent deceived me, and I ate."
>
> —Genesis 3:13

Eve passed the buck, too. Too often today Christians blame Satan for things for which they are responsible.

Two Curses

Two curses are pronounced. The first is on Satan (3:14–15); the second is on the ground (3:17b–18). Note that neither Adam nor Eve was cursed. Too often we think (or act) otherwise. But note that in the midst of the curse God announces hope for redemption. God is going to use that which comes from a woman's womb to seal Satan's fate. As Genesis 3:15 reports:

> And I will put enmity
> between you and the woman,

and between your offspring and hers;
he will crush your head,
and you will strike his heel.

We find this prophecy fulfilled in Christ's conquering Satan at the cross. Now we come to the heart of the relational fracture between men and women. Genesis 3:16b says:

Your desire will be for your husband,
and he will rule over you.

The word *desire* indicates "longing" or "craving." It is an ungodly lust for power and control. Adam and Eve have become self-seeking God-deniers. This new inward orientation leads to great disorder. From now on, men will largely choose one extreme or the other in their relations toward women: either irresponsibility or tyranny. Women, for their part, usually respond either by being servile or by being controlling.

Susan T. Foh summarizes the state of affairs after the Fall: "Sin has corrupted both the willing submission of the wife and the loving headship of the husband. And so, the rule of love founded in paradise is replaced by struggle, tyranny, domination, and manipulation."[18]

Domination has replaced dominion; subjugation has replaced godly subjection.

Too often Christians and non-Christians alike assume that Genesis 3:16b, "Your desire will be for your husband, and he will rule over you," is *prescriptive*—this is the way it was meant to be. But it is instead *descriptive* of how things are in our fallen world. Because Genesis 3 says there will be weeds in the garden, does this mean we should go and plant more weeds? The Fall did not destroy the created order. The Fall distorted it.[19]

Too often Christian men justify treating their wives, mothers, sisters, and daughters as second-class citizens by citing this text. What a travesty! This selfish exegesis is one of the greatest causes of poverty in the world.

Next we will turn to the outworking of the Fall in the often painful history recorded in the Old Testament. While it is painful, we also see the beginning of God's plan for redemption and consummation.

Notes

1. John Calvin, *Commentary on Psalms*, vol. 1, commentary on Psalm 19:8; available at http://www.ccel.org/ccel/calvin/calcom08.xxv.ii.html.

2. Anthony A. Hoekema, *Created in God's Image* (Milton Keyes, UK: Paternoster Press, 1986), 95 (italics in the original).

3. Alexander Strauch, *Men and Women, Equal yet Different: A Brief Study of the Biblical Passages on Gender* (Colorado Springs: Lewis & Roth Publishers, 1999), 23.

4. Dwight Hervey Small, "Christian: Celebrate Your Sexuality," in *The New International Dictionary of New Testament Theology,* Colin Brown, ed. (Grand Rapids: Zondervan, 1979), 1056.

5. Elisabeth Elliot, *The Mark of a Man* (Old Tappan, NJ: Fleming H. Revell Company, 1981), 24.

6. John Angell James, *Female Piety: A Young Woman's Friend and Guide*, Don Kistler, ed. (Morgan, PA: Soli Deo Gloria Publications, 1999), 54.

7. Raymond C. Ortlund Jr., "Male-Female Equality and Male Headship: Genesis 1–3," in *Recovering Biblical Manhood and Womanhood: A Response to Evangelical Feminism*, John Piper and Wayne Grudem, eds. (Wheaton: Crossway, 1991), 101.

8. James, *Female Piety*, 27–28.

9. Leanne Payne, *Crisis in Masculinity* (Grand Rapids: Baker, 1985), 86.

10. The Hebrew word for "husband" used in passages such as Isaiah 54, Jeremiah 3 and 31, and Malachi 2 is not the word ish found in Genesis 2. Rather, it is the common word, adopted by the Israelites, *baal*. As we will see, this is a troubling word that reflects a change in attitude toward marriage for the Hebrew people. However, as we see in these passages, when the Scriptures use this word for God's husbanding, we see God's loving, redeeming, faithful nature poured into the word.

11. Jeff Meyers, "A Little Bit of Molech in My Life," *Tabletalk*, January 2001, 15.

12. 1 Corinthians 11:3; Ephesians 5:25–33.

13. 1 Timothy 3:2; Titus 1:6.

14. J. I. Packer, "Understanding the Differences," in *Women, Authority and the Bible*, Alvera Mickelsen, ed. (Downers Grove, IL: InterVarsity, 1986), 299.

15. Much of my argument here has come from Elisabeth Elliot, *Let Me Be a Woman* (Wheaton: Tyndale, 1976).

16. Paul also argues for symmetry between the man and the woman in 1 Corinthians 11:12. He states that the first woman came from the first man, but all other men and women have come from the woman, the mother. He then adds, "But everything comes from God."

17. Romans 5:15–19 continues this theme. See also 1 Corinthians 15:22: "For as in Adam all die, so in Christ all will be made alive."

18. Susan T. Foh, *Women and the Word of God: A Response to Biblical Feminism* (Phillipsburg, NJ: Presbyterian and Reformed Publishing Co., 1979), 69.

19. Some contend that male headship originated in the Fall. It is my belief that they do this because they see headship as a bad thing and thus assume it is part of the fallen state. I have attempted to establish a biblical framework in Genesis 1 (equality) and Genesis 2 (diversity) as the pre-Fall Trinitarian pattern and that loving, serving headship is the creation pattern.

CHAPTER 13

The Dark Years and the Coming Dawn

The Bible, as we have seen, reveals the beauty, stature, and glory of the first woman. Eve is the glorious counterpart of Adam, fully his equal. The Scriptures explain why most women in the world are abused or undervalued. It also provides a framework (creation-fall-redemption-consummation) that offers women the only sure path out of this morass.

In the last chapter, we saw in Genesis 1–3 how the Fall distorted God's beautiful creation blueprint for male-female relationships. In this chapter, we will step further into the Old Testament to see the practical effects of the Fall on women. Old Testament history is largely a dark period for women, but as we work our way through the material, we will see more and more glimmers of hope as we move toward redemption and consummation.

Mardi Keyes, a L'Abri staff member, distinguishes three strands marking the treatment of women reported in the Hebrew Scriptures:

- The Dark Strand: fallen humanity's treatment of women, characterized by abuse and a lack of respect;
- The Brighter Strand: the law of God introduced to protect women, and the unusually elevated place of women in ancient Israel; and

- The Brightest Strand: the promise of the coming Messiah and his godly treatment of women.[1]

The Dark Strand

Anyone who believes that humanity is naturally good has not wrestled honestly with the testimony of either history or Scripture. Our depravity is clearly exhibited in Genesis 6:5–6: "The Lord saw how great man's wickedness on the earth had become, and that *every* inclination of the thoughts of his heart was *only evil all the time*. The Lord was grieved that he had made man on the earth, and his heart was filled with pain" (emphasis added).

It did not take long after the Fall for people to make the *great exchange* (Romans 1:21–25). In it, the apostle Paul says, our forebears exchanged the worship of God to worship and serve images of "mortal man" (pagan humanism) and "created things" (pagan animism).

This exchange was not limited to animists and polytheists but went right to God's people, the nation of Israel, "married" to Yahweh by covenant relationship. Psalm 106:19–39 records the history of Israel's breaking her marriage vows when the people worshiped the golden calf of their own making at Horeb and later the Canaanite Baal of Peor.

> At Horeb they made a calf
> and worshiped an idol cast from metal.
> They exchanged their Glory
> for an image of a bull, which eats grass.
> They forgot the God who saved them,
> who had done great things in Egypt,
> miracles in the land of Ham
> and awesome deeds by the Red Sea.
> So he said he would destroy them—
> had not Moses, his chosen one,
> stood in the breach before him
> to keep his wrath from destroying them.

Then they despised the pleasant land;
they did not believe his promise.
They grumbled in their tents
and did not obey the LORD.
So he swore to them with uplifted hand
that he would make them fall in the desert,
make their descendants fall among the nations
and scatter them throughout the lands.

They yoked themselves to the Baal of Peor
and ate sacrifices offered to lifeless gods;
they provoked the LORD to anger by their wicked deeds,
and a plague broke out among them.
But Phinehas stood up and intervened,
and the plague was checked.
This was credited to him as righteousness
for endless generations to come.

By the waters of Meribah they angered the LORD,
and trouble came to Moses because of them;
for they rebelled against the Spirit of God,
and rash words came from Moses' lips.

They did not destroy the peoples
as the LORD had commanded them,
but they mingled with the nations
and adopted their customs.
They worshiped their idols,
which became a snare to them.
They sacrificed their sons
and their daughters to demons.
They shed innocent blood,
the blood of their sons and daughters,
whom they sacrificed to the idols of Canaan,
and the land was desecrated by their blood.
They defiled themselves by what they did;

by their deeds they prostituted themselves.

The Coming of the Baals

As the above passage indicates, Israel prostituted herself to the Moabite god Baal of Peor, later even sacrificing her children to this pagan deity. Baal was the name of the local god of the various ancient Semitic peoples. The name first appeared around 1700 BC and means "master," "owner," or "husband."

Baal gained ownership of a place by providing the water needed to make the soil fertile. Often Baal had a consort, the female fertility goddess Ashtoreth, the "great mother of the earth" (Judges 2:13; 10:6; 1 Samuel 7:3–4; 12:10). She was known as Aphrodite to the Greeks and Venus to the Romans. Her worship, like that of the Baals, involved sexual practices (1 Kings 14:24; 2 Kings 23:7).

No sooner had the people ratified the covenant (Exodus 24:3) than they committed idolatry—spiritual adultery—with a god of their own making, the golden calf (Exodus 32). Aaron, taking his cue from the surrounding animistic cultures, in the Egyptian worship of Apis, the bull-god, and the Cannanite worship of Baal and his consort, Ashtoreth, allowed the Hebrews to build the golden calf. Signa Bodishbaugh, author and coworker of Leanne Payne at Pastoral Care Ministries, writes that the golden calf "was a well-known pagan symbol of the fertility cult, fashioned with a distended phallus. The golden calf also implied an invitation to participate in the sexual orgies that constitute the worship of Baal and Ashtoreth."[2]

Yet God, the long-suffering husband, accepts his people's repentance and renews the covenant with them (Exodus 33–34). But later God consigns them to wander in the wilderness for forty years because of their spiritual adultery (Numbers 14:28–35; 32:13); and he warns them not to prostitute themselves to Canaanite gods (Exodus 34:14–16):

> Do not worship any other god, for the LORD, whose name is Jealous, is a jealous God.
> Be careful not to make a treaty with those who live in the land; for when they prostitute themselves to their gods and sacrifice to them, they will invite you and you will eat their sacrifices. And

when you choose some of their daughters as wives for your sons and those daughters prostitute themselves to their gods, they will lead your sons to do the same.

However, before the new generation even entered the Land of Promise, they again broke their wedding vow. Numbers 25:1–3 reports: "While Israel was staying in Shittim, the men began to indulge in sexual immorality with Moabite women, who invited them to the sacrifices to their gods. The people ate and bowed down before these gods. So Israel joined in worshiping the Baal of Peor."[3]

Despite warnings from the prophets, the ten northern tribes of Israel worshiped this god in the time of Ahab (1 Kings 16:29–33; 18:18,22). He was also worshiped in Judah (2 Chronicles 22:2–4; 28:1–2). The high point in the struggle to rid Israel of Baal worship came when Elijah challenged the priests of Baal on Mount Carmel and killed 450 of them (1 Kings 18:16–40). But the end of this worship finally came for the northern tribes through the invasion of the Assyrians in 722 BC and for Judah with the Babylonian captivity in 586 BC.

A Choice of Husbands

When the people of Israel began to worship Baal, they exchanged the Hebrew word *ish*, which means a loving, serving husband, for the Canaanite word for husband—*baal*—which means a tyrannical, brutal owner-husband.

The things that God warned his bride against became her practice. Unfortunately, this practice influenced the Israelites' understanding and treatment of women. As recorded in Scripture, the Hebrew man, following the new god, would not only be the owner—*baal*—of his house (Exodus 22:7; Judges 19:22), livestock (Exodus 21:28; Isaiah 1:3), and wealth (Ecclesiastes 5:12). He would also be the owner—*baal*—of his wife (Exodus 21:3; Deuteronomy 24:1–4; see also Hosea 2:16).

The Israelites' exchange of the Creator God for the local pagan deity Baal led to the concurrent exchange of woman as the *imago Dei*, co-steward of creation, to woman as the property of man. Israel became like virtually all followers of pagan religions. Women were property to be owned, depreciated in their being and function.

Here is evidence of that fact:

- the many wives of David (2 Samuel 3:2–5) and Solomon (1 Kings 11:1–3);
- a woman faced reproach if she did not produce a male heir, as we see in the stories of Sarah (Genesis 12; 15–18; 21) and Hannah (1 Samuel 1–2);
- the bride-price became a dowry (Genesis 34:12; Exodus 22:16–17); and
- husbands were permitted to divorce their wives, but no provision was made for wives to divorce their husbands (Deuteronomy 24:1–4).

We find these and other provisions in the Old Testament not because they were God's ideal, but because of the hardness of the human heart. Jesus makes this abundantly clear in a confrontation with the Pharisees (Matthew 19:7–8):

> "Why then," they asked, "did Moses command that a man give his wife a certificate of divorce and send her away?"
>
> Jesus replied, "Moses permitted you to divorce your wives because your hearts were hard. But it was not this way from the beginning."

The Hebrews and their ancestors exchanged the glory of God, who manifests himself as Ish, for the pagan god *Baal*. As we have seen, the consequences of this shift have been profound. Herein is the root of chauvinism. *The spirit of Baal is the spirit of sexism.* As people put their faith in pagan humanism or pagan animism, the result is the depreciation of women.

The Brighter Strand

While the dark strand reflects, with transparency, the depth of the depravity of man, the brighter strand reveals how women were not treated as poorly as they were in other cultures and how the laws of God curbed some of the male abuses against women.

First, and perhaps foremost, the Bible establishes the fundamental principle that a woman is a human being. She is equal in being and an equal partner with the man in fulfilling God's purposes on the earth. We may take this for granted in the wake of the feminist revolution, but the fact is, the scriptural perspective on women was the true revolution.

Consider Sarah's servant, whom Sarah drove from her home. Hagar went into hiding (Genesis 16:4–6). In verse 8, the angel of the Lord addressed the maidservant, who in turn gave a name to the Lord (v. 13): "You are the God who sees me." This is remarkable. The God of the universe addresses Hagar, a supposedly lowly servant, calling her by name. Dr. Bruce Waltke, professor of Old Testament at Reformed Theological Seminary, states: "Of the many thousands of ancient Near Eastern texts, this is the only instance where a deity, or his messenger, calls a woman by name and thereby invests her with exalted dignity. Hagar is the Old Testament counterpart to the Samaritan woman (see John 4): both are women, both are not of Abraham's family, both are at a well and both are sinners, yet God treats both with compassion, gives them special revelations and bestows on them unconventional dignity."[4]

Or consider the fact that God hates divorce and calls husbands to be faithful to their wives (Malachi 2:13–16). This preference for marital faithfulness is not just a spiritual ideal. It also provides practical protection for otherwise vulnerable women. In contrast to most contemporary and many ancient societies, a daughter had a right to an inheritance if she had no living brother (Numbers 27:1–11).

Here are some other examples of the high value of women as seen in the pages of Scripture:

- Psalm 139:13–16 reveals that God declares human beings, including women, to be fearfully and wonderfully made. Women are made for his purposes.
- Isaiah 44:24 reveals that the Redeemer "formed you in the womb."
- Women, mothers, daughters, and wives are mentioned over one thousand times in Scripture, from women such as Esther

and the queen of Sheba to simple, unassuming women such as Abishag (1 Kings 1:3–4,15) and Dorcas (Acts 9:36–41). Others, such as Miriam, were prophetesses. One, Deborah, was a judge.

In a world in which women are seldom recognized by name, the Bible records the names of close to two hundred of them. Historian Thomas Cahill makes this point in his book *The Gifts of the Jews*: "In contrast to his impersonal treatment of Pharaoh [he is never given a proper name in the Bible], the god-king of all Egypt, the narrator records the names of these humble women: Shifara and Pau. Their very names seem to call them up from the distant past; and we can almost see them standing before Pharaoh, the young, beautiful one with the young, beautiful name, the old, plain one with the old, plain name."[5]

While women's primary role in Scripture is that of mother, we see them fully engaged in public life. God's Word portrays women as heroes and actors on the stage of history. Here are some examples:

- Abigail, the beautiful and intelligent wife of Nabal, was a peacemaker who saved the lives of all the males in her household (1 Samuel 25).
- Jael developed and carried out a plan to kill Sisera, the mighty commander of the Canaanite forces (Judges 4:11–22).
- Two women were the heroic and central figures in the books of the Bible that bear their names: Ruth and Esther.
- The widow at Zarephath trusted in the Lord and gave her last food to Elijah (1 Kings 17:7–16).
- Sarah, the wife of Abraham, laughed at God but lived to nurse her son and become "the mother of nations" (Genesis 17:15–16).

Then, of course, there are Rebekah, the wife of Isaac, and Hannah, the mother of Samuel. These and many other women made history. Beginning with Eve, their stories were told and ballads were sung of their lives, their virtues and vices, and their deeds. These accounts passed from generation to generation, shaping not only the little ones of Israel, but also children of today. Their lives are an integral part of the story God is telling the world.

And just as Moses desired that all the Lord's people would be prophets (Numbers 11:29), Joel prophesied that God's Spirit would be poured out on both men and women (Joel 2:28–29; emphasis added):

> And afterward,
> I will pour out my Spirit on all people.
> Your sons and *daughters* will prophesy,
> your old men will dream dreams,
> your young men will see visions.
> Even on my servants, both men and *women*,
> I will pour out my Spirit in those days.

When King Josiah discovered and read the lost Book of the Law, he sent the high priest, Hilkiah, to the prophetess Huldah to "inquire of the LORD for me and for the people" (2 Kings 22:13). Then Huldah spoke authoritatively for God: "This is what the LORD, the God of Israel, says . . ." (vv. 15–20).

Proverbs 31, meanwhile, describes the ideal wife. She is such a superwoman that it is hard to imagine any woman able to match her, but that is not Scripture's intent. The passage, rather, reveals the tremendous scope in a wife's skills. Yet we need to keep in mind that these gifts are not to be viewed as simply assets to be used in a modern, secular, and materialistic workplace. Scripture instead portrays them as employed by a wife who is making a home.

The Proverbs 31 woman is a wife (vv. 10–11,23,28b) and mother (vv. 15,28a). She is not autonomous but is part of an extended community. In her domestic role (governing her household) she complements her husband in his public role (governing the city) (v. 23).

- She cares for the poor and needy (v. 20).
- She manages her household (vv. 15,21,27).
- She is someone whose works are recognized in the marketplace and public square (vv. 18,24,31).

She is not a "housewife"—someone who is chained in a kitchen, "barefoot and pregnant." Her domain extends to the world, and she influences the larger society. With her husband she is a vice regent of creation.

What is she made of? Her virtues are many:

- reputation (vv. 12,31)
- discernment (vv. 13,16)
- work ethic (vv. 15–18,27)
- entrepreneurial (vv. 16,24)
- profitable (v. 18)
- compassionate (v. 20)
- prepared (vv. 21,25)
- personal strength (v. 25a)
- dignity (v. 25a)
- wise (v. 26)
- fear of the Lord (v. 30b)

Her skills are also many:
- weaving and sewing (vv. 13,19,22,24)
- investing (v. 16)
- farming (v. 16b)
- fabrics and interior design (v. 22)
- sales (v. 24)
- communication (v. 26a)
- education/instruction (v. 26b)
- management (v. 27)
- parenting (v. 28)

She has dignity because of both her being and her function. This is a woman who understands that her home is the center of the creation of culture. Her task is nothing less than helping her husband to build a strong and godly family and society. She is truly *more precious than rubies* (v. 10).

Finally, the female is so significant in God's plan that Wisdom is personified as a woman (Proverbs 1:20–21; 8:1–3; 9:1–6).

We will end our exploration of the Brighter Strand with the delightful words of John Angell James, a nineteenth-century Nonconformist English pastor:

There she is seen enlivening the sacred page with her narrative and adorning it with her beauty, sometimes darkening it with her crimes, at others brightening it with her virtues; now calling us to weep with her in her sorrows, then to rejoice with her in her joys. In short, woman is everywhere to be found wrought into the details of God's Scriptures, a beacon to warn us or a lamp to guide us. And all the notices written by the inspiration of the Holy Spirit are to be considered as His testimony to the excellence and importance of your sex, and the influence it is intended and destined to exert upon the welfare of mankind.[6]

The Brightest Strand

Now we will see the beginning of God's restoration of marriage and of male-female relationships. Just as two books in the Scriptures are focused on two women—Ruth and Esther—so there are two other books that deal with the glory of sex and the restoration of marriage. Let's look at them in turn.

Hosea: The God-Sized Love Story

As the prophet Hosea writes this book, Israel has rejected her husband's love and engaged in an adulterous relationship with Baal (4:13–14; 5:4; 8:5; 9:1; 10:5–6; 13:1–2). The nation's worship of Baal has led to marital infidelity (see chapter 4 of Hosea). The biblical concept of husbanding has been deformed from a loving, serving, faithful headship to a tyrannical, dominating, adulterous ownership.

Adding insult to injury, a "spirit of prostitution" inhabits the nation (4:12; 5:4). Hosea was reminded of the incident recorded in Numbers 25 when the Israelites consecrated themselves to Baal of Peor and "became as vile as the thing they loved" (9:10). Marriage, the family, and the nation have spiraled into destruction.

Yet God, Israel's faithful husband (2:19–20; 13:4–6) continues to love his adulterous wife. Hosea's marriage to Gomer becomes a living parable of God's faithful commitment to Israel. In this book, God seeks to restore the Edenic concept of a loving, caring, self-sacrificing husband and point to the coming of the heavenly husband—Jesus Christ—to redeem and restore his bride, the church, as the second Eve. The key verses are 2:16–17:

> "In that day," declares the LORD,
> "you will call me 'my husband';
> you will no longer call me 'my master.'
> I will remove the names of the Baals from her lips;
> no longer will their names be invoked."

But we are getting ahead of ourselves. Let us look at this wonderful story.

Hosea 1:1 identifies the time of this drama as the years immediately before and after the fall of the ten northern tribes of Israel to the Assyrians (722 BC). As we have seen, the people of Israel had prostituted themselves to the god Baal. The action begins as God calls the prophet Hosea to marry Gomer, who would become his adulterous wife (1:2).

Subsequent to their marriage, Gomer gives birth to three children, a son named Jezreel meaning "God scatters" (1:3–5); a daughter named Lo-Ruhamah meaning "Not loved" (1:6–7); and a second son, named Lo-Ammi meaning "Not my people" (1:8–9). The three children and their names represent the judgment that is coming upon Israel because of her unfaithfulness.

But God is faithful. After a period of judgment, the marriage will be restored because of God's faithful husbanding (1:10–11). God tells Israel that, as her husband, he has lavished incredible provision upon her (2:8), which she in turn used to worship Baal. Then God calls Hosea to do what only God can do: "Go, show your love to your wife again, though she is loved by another and is an adulteress. Love her as the LORD loves the Israelites, though they turn to other gods" (3:1).

Here we find a remarkable picture of God's love. Hosea is to love his wife, even though she was prostituting herself. What is the standard of this love to be? It is to be "as the LORD loves the Israelites." Hosea is to redeem her, to buy her back from her enslavement. This is no mere human drama. It is a living parable of God's redemption of Israel and of the future redemption price that Christ will pay, by his death on the cross, for his bride, the church.

How and why does God ask Hosea to demonstrate such love? The answer is found in Hosea 2:14–23, in what Pastor John Piper calls "one of the most tender and most beautiful love songs in the Bible."[7] God calls Hosea to model the kind of love to Gomer that God shows to Israel.

There are five things to observe about God's love song to Israel. First, the Lord is going to court her again; he will treat her tenderly (2:14). Second, though Israel is a prostitute, God will restore her to her state of innocence (2:15). The same hope she experienced when she was delivered from slavery in Egypt she will experience when she is released from being enslaved to Baal.

The third point, which we referred to earlier, is found in Hosea 2:16–17. These verses not only mark the turning point in the Book of Hosea, but also indicate the turning point in the larger narrative of the transforming story. These verses reflect the transition from the dark years of the Old Testament to the glory of the New Testament. They reveal that the glory of Eve will be restored in the glory of the bride of Christ. Here we find that the name of God will be restored. He will once again be called Ish:

> "In that day," declares the LORD,
> "you will call me 'my husband [ish]';
> you will no longer call me 'my master [baal].'
> I will remove the names of the Baals from her lips;
> no longer will their names be invoked."

Destruction has come upon Israel and all mankind because of the great exchange. Truth has been exchanged for a lie. The worship of God has been exchanged for the worship of a pagan deity: Baal of Peor. Instead of worshiping the husbanding God, Ish, mankind has worshiped the owner god, Baal. In doing so, women were no longer honored as women but have become dishonored. The spirit of Baal is the spirit of sexism. In this passage, the restoration begins: "You will call me Ish, not Baal!"

Fourth, God will betroth Israel to himself forever (2:19–20). Not only will God court Israel (2:14); now they will return to the time of engagement. Israel can have a new start, and with Christ so can each individual and each culture. The lie that "men are superior to women" may be abolished, and the truth that women are the image of God may be restored. This will not be a temporary fix, but rather a "forever" fix.

How can this be? Because the betrothal will be in Ish's righteousness, justice, love, and compassion (2:19). Notice in this formula of words the cross of Christ. It is the self-sacrificing love of Ish that is displayed in the one place in time and space where love and justice meet—the cross of Christ.

One thing that is hidden in verse 2:20 are the words "and thou shalt *know* the LORD" (KJV; emphasis added). We have seen this word "know" before. It is the Hebrew word *yada* and refers to the great soul intimacy between the believer and God (Genesis 18:19; Deuteronomy 34:10; Psalm 1:6; 37:18; Isaiah 48:8). "God knows Moses by name and face to face (Exodus 33:17; Deuteronomy 34:10)."[8] This is intimacy!

This same word, *yada*, is used for the intimacy between Adam and Eve: "Adam knew [*yada*] Eve his wife; and she conceived, and bare Cain" (Genesis 4:1 KJV). It is used similarly in Genesis 19:8, Numbers 31:17–18, and other passages. The intimacy between God and man, by name and face to face, is the pattern of the intimacy between a man and a woman. We will pick up this glorious theme in a moment in the Song of Songs.

In Hosea 2:23, we come to the end of God's love song to Israel. Here is the fifth and final observation. The marriage between God and Israel is restored. The wedding vows are renewed. In this passage, God returns to the names of Gomer's second two children: "Not loved" and "Not my people." He made a promise to Israel in Hosea 1:10–11. Now that promise is to be fulfilled. To the child he called "Not loved," he will show love. To the child he called "Not my people," he will say, "You are my people." And the renewed bride—Israel—will say, "You are my God."

Hosea was to create a space for Gomer to blossom into being all that God intended for her to be. She was not intended to be a prostitute. She was intended to be a beautiful ishshah.

Solomon's Song of Songs

While the Book of Hosea reinforces the truths that marriage is a sacred institution and the husband is to be a loving, serving head for his loving, respectful helper wife, the other biblical book focusing on marriage—the Song of Songs—presents the beauty of physical and soul union. It is also a grand love poem that reflects the intimacy of God and his people, Israel. The key Hebrew word that captures this intimacy, again, is *yada*.

The Song provides an echo of the pre-Fall intimacy of Genesis 2:25:

"And they were both naked, the man and his wife, and were not ashamed" (KJV). This book prefigures Christ and his church in Ephesians 5:31–32 and Revelation 19:9 and provides a picture of the restored intimacy available to Christian men and women (Ephesians 5:25–32).

Quaker author Richard Foster describes the Song of Songs as "eros as it should be! There is sensuality without licentiousness, passion without promiscuity, love without lust."[9] Indeed, God created unimaginable beauty in the spiritual and sexual union of a man and a woman. Let's ponder a few highlights.

- The bride calls to her husband (1:2–4):
    Let him kiss me with the kisses of his mouth—
    for your love is more delightful than wine.
    Pleasing is the fragrance of your perfumes;
    your name is like perfume poured out.
    No wonder the maidens love you!
    Take me away with you—let us hurry!
    Let the king bring me into his chambers.

- She watches her young and virile lover approach, anticipating him calling her to come away with him (2:8–10):
    Listen! My lover!
    Look! Here he comes,
    leaping across the mountains,
    bounding over the hills.
    My lover is like a gazelle or a young stag.
    Look! There he stands behind our wall,
    gazing through the windows,
    peering through the lattice.
    My lover spoke and said to me,
    "Arise, my darling,
    my beautiful one, and come with me."

- The lover calls his beloved unique among all women (2:2):
    Like a lily among thorns
    is my darling among the maidens.

- He longs for her breasts (4:5–7):
    Your two breasts are like two fawns,

like twin fawns of a gazelle
that browse among the lilies.
Until the day breaks
and the shadows flee,
I will go to the mountain of myrrh
and to the hill of incense.
All beautiful you are, my darling;
there is no flaw in you.

The Song of Songs reflects the kind of spiritual and physical intimacy—*yada*—that God intends for marriage. It challenges the secular view that sex is merely physical. It also challenges the dualism of so many Christians today who erroneously view the spiritual as a higher level of creation and sex as a natural and lower form, almost something that is "dirty." Thank God, sex is something to enjoy without guilt.

Now it is time to move from the dark years of the Old Testament to the full light of redemption and consummation. That light comes from none other than Jesus Christ.

Notes

1. Mardi Keyes, *The Question of Women in Leadership I: The Old Testament* (paper delivered at L'Abri, Southborough, MA, 20 February, 1998), 17.

2. Leanne Payne, *Crisis in Masculinity* (Grand Rapids: Baker Books, 1985), 238.

3. See also Numbers 31:15–16; Deuteronomy 4:3–4; Joshua 22:17; Psalm 106:28; Hosea 9:10.

4. Bruce Waltke, *An Old Testament Theology: An Exegetical, Canonical, and Thematic Approach* (Grand Rapids: Zondervan, 2007).

5. Thomas Cahill, *The Gifts of the Jews: How a Tribe of Desert Nomads Changed the Way Everyone Thinks and Feels* (New York: Anchor Books, 1998), 99–100.

6. John Angell James, *Female Piety: A Young Woman's Friend and Guide*, Don Kistler, ed. (Morgan, PA: Soli Deo Gloria Publications, 1999), 48.

7. John Piper, "Call Me Husband, Not Baal," sermon at Bethlehem Baptist Church, St. Paul, MN, December 26, 1982, http://www.desiringgod.org/ResourceLibrary/Sermons/By-Date/1982/372_Call_Me_Husband_Not_Baal/.

8. R. Laird Harris, Gleason L. Archer Jr., and Bruce K. Waltke, eds., *Theological Wordbook of the Old Testament*, vol. 2 (Chicago: Moody, 1980), 366.

9. Richard J. Foster, *The Challenge of the Disciplined Life: Christian Reflections on Money, Sex and Power* (San Francisco: Harper, 1985), 95.

CHAPTER 14

The Coming of the Bridegroom

Now we turn to God's story of redemption and its impact on women. At the center of God's redemptive plan stands Jesus Christ, the perfect God-man. All Christians should be thoroughly familiar with Christ's revolutionary, unprecedented treatment of women, which we will explore in this chapter. But it is good to recall first that the world Jesus entered was not at all hospitable to the idea that women have inherent dignity and worth.

Women in the Empire

At the time of Jesus' birth, Israel was under Roman occupation. The ancient world was much like modern sexist culture. Society was male-dominated; marriage was little esteemed. Historian Alvin J. Schmidt writes: "In the Roman and Greek temples sex was a common religious activity. The pagan gods of the Romans or Greeks set no precepts with regard to moral behavior."[1]

Moral depravity and prostitution of all kinds were considered normal. What Scripture deemed vice—prostitution, homosexuality, infidelity, infanticide—was applauded as virtue. The depravity that the Jewish people experienced when they worshiped Baal was commonplace in pagan Rome.

The war on women was alive and well in Jesus' day. Women were so despised in Greco-Roman society "that there were 131 males per 100 females in the city of Rome, and 140 males per 100 females in Italy, Asia Minor and North Africa."[2]

A woman had the social status of a slave. She could only leave the house in the company of a male escort, usually a slave. Girls were not permitted to go to school, and a woman could not speak in public.[3] According to Athenian law, a woman of any age was always considered a child "and therefore was the legal property of some man at all stages in her life."[4]

And no wonder. The Greek god Zeus beat his wife and flaunted his sexual exploits before her. Authors David Hamilton and Loren Cunningham rightly note, "Is it any wonder the ancients came to accept wife abuse and flagrant adultery as normal, when Zeus was their divine ideal?"[5]

Hesiod's epic poem, *The Theogony*, is the twisted Greek counterpart to Genesis 1–2. Before the creation of Pandora, "the races of men had lived on the earth without evil and without harsh labor and cruel diseases which give men over to the Fates. But the woman lifted in her hands the great lid from the jar and scattered these evils about—she devised miserable sorrows for men."[6] In this epic poem, women were made to be an eternal curse for men, and they were created as inferior to men both in their being and in their moral behavior.

In Plato's *Timaeus*, he wrote: "All those creatures generated as men who proved themselves cowardly and spent their lives in wrongdoing were transformed, at their second incarnation, into women. . . . In this fashion, then, women and the whole female sex have come into existence."[7] Aristotle, likewise, wrote "that the female is a 'monstrosity,' a 'deformed male,' and 'a deformity . . . which occurs in the ordinary course of nature.' . . . 'The male is by nature superior and the female inferior, the male ruler and the female subject.'"[8]

In a familiar theme, the Greek universe articulated by Plato and his followers was divided in two. Mardi Keyes writes: "The male was associated with mind, reason, spirit, soul and ruling; the female was associated with body, flesh, sex, reproduction, domesticity and subordination. The male was superior, the female inferior. Men were human and male . . . women were female only—defined by sex and reproduction (whether wives, concubines, slaves or prostitutes)."[9]

While a Roman woman had more freedom than her Greek sister, she had virtually no rights and privileges compared with men. The Roman law of *manus* established the husbands' "ownership" and absolute control of their wives.[10] A Roman man could kill his wife without consequence. Baby girls were often exposed—left outside to die—at birth.

A letter from a Roman soldier named Hilarion to his wife Alis shows the callous attitude toward daughters:

> Know that I am still in Alexandria. And do not worry if they all come back and I remain in Alexandria. I ask and beg you to take good care of our baby son, and as soon as I receive payment I shall send it to you. If you are delivered of a child [before I come home], if it is a boy keep it, if a girl discard it. You have sent me word, 'Don't forget me.' How can I forget you? I beg you not to worry."[11]

Women in the Jewish World

The Jewish subculture that Jesus grew up in, influenced by the surrounding paganism, was little better. Beginning in the third century BC, women were separated from men in the synagogues.[12] According to historian Rodney Stark, "Women were commonly bracketed with slaves and children by the rabbis."[13]

The Talmud requires Jewish men to pray daily: "Thank you, God, for not making me a Gentile, a woman, or a slave." Writing in the Book of Sirach in about 180 BC, Jesus ben Sirach, a Jewish scholar living in Egypt, wrote:

- Sirach 22:3: "It is a disgrace to be the father of an undisciplined son, and the birth of a daughter is a loss."
- Sirach 42:14: "Better is the wickedness of a man than a woman who does good; it is woman who brings shame and disgrace."

Despite the biblical narrative's high view of women, the Jewish world viewed women as inferior in being and in morals. Jewish women were not counted in quorums, were rarely taught the Torah (a notable exception being Mary, the mother of Jesus), and were not allowed to talk with men outside their immediate families.

Jesus, the Revolutionary

Into this sexist world stepped Jesus. His whole life and teaching challenged the culture and religious authorities of his day. With regard to women, his challenge went right to the heart of not only the sexist culture of the Jews but also the sexist cultures of all time. He came to overthrow the counterfeit, pagan-Baal influences on the Jews and restore the Trinitarian order.

As Romans 8 teaches, the whole creation groans and is waiting for redemption. Women also cry out. And their Creator has sent his Son, the Bridegroom, to redeem them equally with men. Jesus is the liberator of women from male bondage and false male values. He often frontally challenged the sexist institutions of his day, but at other times he demonstrated and taught a biblical worldview that recognized the intrinsic dignity of women and their roles.

In the pages to come, we will examine God's affirmation of women at Jesus' birth, Jesus' recognition of their intrinsic value, and his call of women into the kingdom task force. As Dorothy Sayers has said, "Perhaps it is no wonder that the women were first at the Cradle and last at the Cross. They had never known a man like this Man—there had never been such another."[14]

The Royal Bloodline

No Old Testament genealogy would include a woman, and certainly not a foreign woman. These lists normally go from father to son, tracing lineage through male ancestry. And yet we see women listed in one of the genealogies of Jesus. Let's explore the significance of this.

The New Testament provides two genealogies of the Lord, in the Gospels of Luke and Matthew. Luke gives the *paternal* bloodline leading to Joseph, Mary's husband. As such, no women are listed. But Matthew gives the *royal,* legal line of those who were or would have been the kings to sit on the throne of David, Israel's quintessential king.

Amazingly, by the standards of the time, four women are mentioned in the royal line of kings. Certainly they were not all royalty. Three of the four, in fact, were Gentiles, and three of the four were known for their sin. The four:

- Tamar (Matthew 1:3): Genesis 38 reports that Tamar, the daughter-in-law of Judah, committed the sin of incest.
- Rahab (Matthew 1:5): Joshua 2 tells the story of this woman, a prostitute who aided the Hebrew spies.
- Ruth (Matthew 1:5): The book that bears her name tells us that she was from Moab. Remember, the Moabites were pagan worshipers of Baal who unsuccessfully tried to get Balaam to curse the Hebrew people and then seduced the Israelites to indulge in sexual immorality and Baal worship (Numbers 22–25).
- Bathsheba (alluded to in Matthew 1:6): Second Samuel 11 tells us she became pregnant by David, who murdered her husband, Uriah; Bathsheba later became the queen mother through Solomon's reign.

What is remarkable about this list is that all four women had troubled pasts: one guilty of incest, one a prostitute, one a foreigner and an enemy of Israel, and one an adulterer. Yet these four "sinners" were part of the royal bloodline. The Book of Hosea, remember, described God's husbanding the harlot Israel. How fitting, then, that the blood of sinful women was part of the royal blood shed on the cross for sinners.

Mary

Next, God chose women to announce the birth of Jesus. Elizabeth, Mary's relative, prophesied about the birth (Luke 1:41–45). Then there is Mary's song, known as the *Magnificat* (Luke 1:46–55). It is similar to an Old Testament psalm and has been compared to the song of Hannah (1 Samuel 2:1–10).

Luke 1:26–38 records the announcement of God's choice for the mother of Jesus.

Mary was probably young and poor. She was pledged to a carpenter named Joseph, who was a descendent of King David. Just as God chose four unlikely women to be in Jesus' bloodline, so he chose this unlikely woman (more likely, a girl) from the backwaters of Nazareth in Galilee ("Can anything good come from there?" [John 1:46]) to carry, give birth to, and nurture his Son.

Mary was a virgin. As was the custom, she was probably no more than fourteen. Remarkably, the angel Gabriel did not appear to either Joseph, to whom she was already legally married, or Mary's father, of whom there is no mention. The angel addressed Mary as a free moral agent. Mary is an ordinary woman with an extraordinary set of circumstances and an astonishing choice, which she voiced in Luke 1:38 (KJV): "Behold the handmaid of the Lord; be it unto me according to thy word."

While the choice of Mary and the conception of Jesus were extraordinary, her pregnancy and the birth of Jesus were ordinary, sanctifying for all time this most precious of womanly roles. Think of it: the God of the universe took up residence in the womb of a woman.

Some church traditions have elevated Mary as the "Mother of God," seeing her as divinely perfect and forever a virgin. But Lilian Calles Barger, writing in *Eve's Revenge*, calls us back to reality: "Recovering Mary of Nazareth from perpetual virginity and perfection will allow us to see the possibility that God can and does work through the ordinariness of our flesh."[15]

Barger continues:

> Mary of Nazareth is the Everywoman of history, ordinary and obscure. She represents what is possible for us flesh-and-blood women who yield ourselves to God. Mary recognizes her own powerlessness and has no grand vision for herself as the model of virtue that she will become. . . . Yet her yes provided hope that in our bodies the works of God can be wrought. In her we find a sign of God's willingness to use the insignificant, even the vulnerability and symbolic nature of our bodies."[16]

Jesus will live for nine months in the womb he created (see John 1:3; 1 Corinthians 8:6; Colossians 1:16; Hebrews 1:2). He will pass through a human birth canal and will be nurtured at human breasts, the place of abundant provision. All the things we hesitate to talk about—blood, tissue, fluids—become sanctified by the habitation of the Almighty. The divine, visiting the ordinary, sanctifies it. Barger captures the wonder of this: "A holy God enters the bloodiness of the womb, considered unclean under Jewish law, and makes it a temple. In the womb of a woman the eternal and transcendent Word by which the worlds were created becomes flesh."[17]

Jesus and Women

In Jesus' day, it was considered improper for a man to speak in public to a woman who was not his wife (John 4:27). Yet Jesus initiated a conversation with the woman at the well (John 4:7–26). And she was not only a woman, but a despised Samaritan and an adulteress. Even so, Jesus took her seriously as a human being, just as he did as he spoke to the woman caught in adultery (John 8:10–11). On the way to his crucifixion, he paused—in the midst of his own suffering—to talk with a group of women who were mourning on his behalf (Luke 23:26–31).

But it is important to point out that Jesus did not *give* women dignity. He simply *recognized* their intrinsic dignity because they, every bit as much as men, are the *imago Dei*. In the same way, men cannot *give* women dignity today. Women already *have* dignity because of who and whose they are. Men can only recognize the dignity inherent in women and then treat them with the respect they deserve.

When Jesus addressed women, he spoke to them tenderly, in a way that would touch their souls:

- He addressed the woman with a bleeding disorder as "Daughter" (Luke 8:48).
- He addressed Jairus's daughter as "My child" (Luke 8:54).
- He addressed a disabled woman as "a daughter of Abraham" (Luke 13:16). Yes, Jewish men were often addressed as "sons of Abraham," but for Jesus to speak thus to a woman was to turn the world upside down.

Jesus also recognized women's dignity by treating them as free and responsible moral agents. He did not wink at their sin but lovingly confronted it. Consider these examples:

- the adulterous Samaritan woman (John 4:7–26)
- the woman caught in adultery (John 8:3–11)
- the woman "who had lived a sinful life" and who washed his feet (Luke 7:36–50)

Jesus taught women (Luke 10:38–42), something totally unheard of in his day. Again, Dorothy Sayers captures the heart of how Jesus honored women, describing him as

> a prophet and teacher who never nagged at them, never flattered or coaxed or patronized; who never made arch jokes about them, never treated them either as 'The women, God help us!' or 'The ladies, God bless them!'; who rebuked without querulousness and praised without condescension; who took their questions and arguments seriously; . . . who took them as he found them and was completely unself-conscious. There is no act, no sermon, no parable in the whole Gospel that borrows its pungency from female perversity; nobody could possibly guess from the words and deeds of Jesus that there was anything 'funny' about women's natures.[18]

Rather than making them the butt of jokes, the Lord placed women as heroines and virtuous object lessons in his stories:

- the woman in the parable of the yeast (Matthew 13:33; Luke 13:20–21)
- the Queen of the South (i.e. the queen of Sheba), representing the seeking of wisdom (Matthew 12:42)
- the widow in Zarephath, representing the blessing of service (Luke 4:26)
- the woman in the parable of the lost coin, representing diligence (Luke 15:8)
- the five wise virgins in the parable of the ten virgins, representing readiness (Matthew 25:1–13)
- the widow in the parable of the persistent widow, representing perseverance (Luke 18:1–8)

- a Canaanite woman who had "great faith" (Matthew 15:21–28)
- the widow's sacrificial offering of all she had to live on (Mark 12:41–44)

No Double Standards

As we have seen, the influence of baalism caused many Jewish men to judge women harshly as inferiors for sins the men had committed themselves. Jesus, however, saw women as complementary equals, made in the image of God. We will look at how Christ applied this understanding to cultural double standards on lust, adultery, and divorce.

Lust, wanting sexual relations with someone other than your spouse, is not a victimless crime, nor is it simply a precursor to fornication or adultery. Lust actually diminishes the sacred estate of marriage and the *one flesh* principle given in Genesis. Lust loosens sex from its moorings and reduces sexuality to conquest, mere entertainment, or "technique." Lust destroys men, women, and children. And yet women, from the Jewish male perspective, bore the social responsibility for male lust. Jesus, however, said that if a man looks lustfully at a woman, *he* has committed adultery in his heart (Matthew 5:28). As Mardi Keyes says: "In a culture which blamed woman's very nature for male lust, Jesus put the blame where it belonged—on the men who looked lustfully at women!"[19]

Adultery, having sexual relations with someone other than your spouse, also carried a double standard. Hebrew males were arrogant. In John 8:3–11, the teachers of the law and the Pharisees were ready to stone the woman—but not the man—caught in adultery. The man was caught as well, but he was free to go. Of course, in this particular case it would certainly seem that the whole "affair" had been staged as a trap for Jesus (see verse 6), the man's escape being part of the plot. Nevertheless, he lived by a different standard.

Further, these Jewish men referred to the Law of Moses *only* in regard to adulterous women being stoned. Actually, the Law reads that *both* men and women are to suffer the same punishment: "If a man is found sleeping with another man's wife, *both the man* who slept with her *and the woman* must die.

You must purge the evil from Israel" (Deuteronomy 22:22; emphasis added; see also Leviticus 20:10).

Jesus told the men in the crowd, "If any of you is without sin, let him be the first to throw a stone at her." Yes, the penalty for adultery was stoning. Jesus was saying, in effect, "If you are without sin, then you are free to judge and execute the judgment." But they were certainly guilty of sin, and many may have been guilty of adultery too. In their utter spiritual nakedness, each man put down his stone and melted into the crowd.

Regarding divorce, Jewish men were permitted to divorce their wives for almost any reason. Based on their interpretation of Deuteronomy 24:1, a wife could burn the meal and that would be grounds for the man to divorce her by writing a simple declaration. There was no judicial process to protect her rights. Yet it was almost impossible for a woman to institute the divorce.

Far from approving of this double standard, Jesus told some Pharisees that divorce was merely *permitted* because of the hardness of men's hearts (Mark 10:2–5). Then he brought them back to first principles regarding marriage: God made them male and female (v. 6). Thus, they are to leave, cleave, and become *one flesh* (vv. 7–8). Further, marriage is a permanent and holy estate, with no divorce (v. 9). Jesus calls men and women to live by first principles.

Jesus Ministered to Women

Jesus didn't merely talk a good game concerning women's dignity. He lived it, by ministering to their physical, social, emotional, and spiritual needs. As he addressed the needs of men where their lives were broken, he did the same for women. He did not favor men but treated the needs of both women and men with equal care.

- He initiated dialogue with the woman at the well, addressing her need for inner healing (John 4:7–26).
- He dealt compassionately with a woman who had a bleeding condition for twelve years (Luke 8:43–48).
- He raised Jairus's daughter from the dead (Luke 8:40–42,49–56).

- He healed a woman who had been crippled for eighteen years (Luke 13:10–13).
- He healed a Gentile woman's daughter who suffered from demon-possession (Matthew 15:21–28).
- He cared for a widow by raising her only son from the dead (Luke 7:11–15).
- He instructed the Samaritan woman (John 4:7–26) and Mary, the sister of Martha (Luke 10:38–42).
- From the cross, Jesus provided for his mother's care (John 19:25–27).
- Breaking all social custom, he allowed women to touch him, including a ceremonially unclean woman (Mark 5:25–34) and a woman who washed his feet (Luke 7:36–50).

Jesus Called Women Into Ministry

Shockingly, according to the standards of the time, Jesus called women into ministry.

Women were the first at the cradle (Elizabeth, Luke 1:39–45) and the last at the cross (Luke 23:27,49). Women were part of his traveling team and cared for Jesus' needs. Some financially supported the ministry (Matthew 27:55–56; Mark 15:40–41; Luke 8:1–3).

Luke 8:1–3 records women being part of Jesus' kingdom mission team: "After this, Jesus traveled about from one town and village to another, proclaiming the good news of the kingdom of God. The Twelve were with him, and also some women who had been cured of evil spirits and diseases: Mary (called Magdalene) from whom seven demons had come out; Joanna the wife of Cuza, the manager of Herod's household; Susanna; and many others. These women were helping to support them out of their own means."

These women not only ministered *to* Jesus, but also ministered *with* Jesus. In a day when women were rarely seen in public, their names were included in public records, the Gospels. Even today, the world knows who they are.

And, unlike the disciples, women did not abandon Jesus at the cross. It was the women who showed courage, love, and care for Jesus. God's motherly heart of compassion shined clearly through these gritty women. Many were at the cross, "watching from a distance" (Matthew 27:55; Mark 15:40). Some even stood near the cross (John 19:25).

All four Gospels honor the women who came to the tomb to properly anoint the Lord (Matthew 28:1–7; Mark 16:1–7; Luke 24:1–8; John 20:1–2). Further, amazingly, women were the first to announce his resurrection. We read this account in Luke 24:9–11 (see also Matthew 28:8–10; John 20:10–18): "When they came back from the tomb, they told all these things to the Eleven and to all the others. It was Mary Magdalene, Joanna, Mary the mother of James, and the others with them who told this to the apostles. But they did not believe the women, because their words seemed to them like nonsense."

However, note the response of the Eleven: "But they did not believe the women." Barger captures the pregnancy of this moment: "From this new beginning God continues the legacy of using women as instruments of grace. Instead of appearing to the powerful Pilate or the Sanhedrin, Jesus appears first to those of lowest status. Instead of calling a press conference, he sends discredited women as messengers into a culture that does not easily believe them. In this way Jesus continues to overturn the power paradigms of the world and establish his true justice."[20]

Jesus' choice of women to make the first resurrection announcement (not to mention his treatment of women throughout his time on earth) was nothing less than a repudiation of the sexism rampant in the cultures of the Greco-Roman world, in Judaism, too often in Christendom, and in the world today.

One Limitation

However, equality in being does not translate to sameness in role. Luke 6:12–16 records Jesus' choosing of the Twelve: "One of those days Jesus went out to a mountainside to pray, and spent the night praying to God. When morning came, he called his disciples to him and chose twelve of them, whom he also designated apostles: Simon (whom he named Peter), his brother Andrew, James, John, Philip, Bartholomew, Matthew, Thomas, James son of Alphaeus, Simon who was called the Zealot, Judas son of James, and Judas Iscariot, who became a traitor."

From among those who were his followers and disciples (both men and women), he chose twelve men to be his apostles. Why did he not choose any women?

This was no inadvertent lapse. He certainly could have done so. Jesus was a revolutionary. He would overturn the corrupt order that crushed women and restore the dignity of women. However, Jesus would not replace the sexist order with a feminist order. To the contrary, Jesus called for the restoration of the creation order, the Trinitarian order of complementarianism: men and women equal in being but with equally glorious and different functions. He would liberate women to be all that God intended them to be. He would call forth their giftings and their leadership. But he came to do this within the framework of the Trinitarian order. In the home and in the church, the loving, serving headship resides with the man.

This is underscored by the calling of the twelve apostles. With the Twelve, Jesus connects the past with the future. We see this connection reflected at the end of the transforming story in a remarkable way:

> [The angel] carried me away in the Spirit to a mountain great and high, and showed me the Holy City, Jerusalem, coming down out of heaven from God. It shone with the glory of God, and its brilliance was like that of a very precious jewel, like a jasper, clear as crystal. It had a great, high wall with twelve gates, and with twelve angels at the gates. On the gates were written the names of the twelve tribes of Israel. There were three gates on the east, three on the north, three on the south and three on the west. The wall of the city had twelve foundations, and on them were the names of the twelve apostles of the Lamb.
> —Revelation 21:10–14

In the mystery of God, the Holy City reflects the glory of God's order. The twelve gates of the city are each named with the twelve sons of Jacob, the twelve tribes of Israel. The wall of the city has twelve foundations. Each foundation is inscribed with the name of one of the twelve "apostles of the Lamb." Jesus overthrew the Jewish domination order rooted in baalism. He restored the creation order, reflected in the glorious City of God.

But this glorious city, with its identification with the twelve tribes and twelve apostles, has another identification. The city is identified as a woman:

"a bride beautifully dressed for her husband" (Revelation 21:2), "the wife of the Lamb" (Revelation 21:9).

We will learn more about this in the next chapter, as we move toward the consummation.

Notes

1. Alvin J. Schmidt, *Under the Influence: How Christianity Transformed Civilization* (Grand Rapids: Zondervan, 2001), 102.

2. J. C. Russell, *Late Ancient and Medieval Population,* published as vol. 48, pt. 3 of the *Transactions of the American Philosophical Society* (Philadelphia: American Philosophical Society, 1958); quoted in Rodney Stark, *The Rise of Christianity* (Princeton, NJ: Princeton University Press, 1996), 97.

3. Schmidt, *Under the Influence,* 99.

4. Stark, *The Rise of Christianity,* 102.

5. Loren Cunningham and David Joel Hamilton, *Why Not Women?* (Seattle: YWAM Publishing, 2000), 74.

6. Mary R. Lefkowitz and Maureen B. Fant, *Women's Life in Greece and Rome* (Baltimore: Johns Hopkins University Press, 1992), 23–24, in Mardi Keyes, "The Mystery of Gender" (paper delivered at L'Abri, Southborough, MA, July 20, 2001), 3.

7. Plato, *Timaeus,* in *Plato, Volume VII: Timaeus, Critias, Cleitophon, Menexenus, Epistles,* R. G. Bury, trans., Loeb Classical Library (Cambridge, MA: Harvard University Press, 1941); 91a-d, in Cunningham and Hamilton, *Why Not Women?,* 77.

8. Quoted from various works in Cunningham and Hamilton, *Why Not Women?,* 77.

9. Keyes, "The Mystery of Gender," 6.

10. J. P. V. D. Balsdon, *Roman Women: Their History and Habits* (New York: John Day, 1963), 272, in Schmidt, *Under the Influence,* 100.

11. Naphtali Lewis, *Life in Egypt under Roman Rule* (Oxford: Clarendon Press, 1985), 54, in Stark, *The Rise of Christianity,* 97–98.

12. Colin Brown, "Women, Mother, Virgin, Widow," in *The New International Dictionary of New Testament Theology,* Colin Brown, ed. (Grand Rapids: Zondervan, 1979), 1058.

13. Ibid.

14. Dorothy L. Sayers, *Are Women Human?* (Downers Grove, IL: InterVarsity, 1971), 47, in Phillip Yancey, *The Jesus I Never Knew* (Grand Rapids: Zondervan, 2002), 154.

15. Lilian Calles Barger, *Eve's Revenge* (Grand Rapids: Brazos Press, 2003), 153.

16. Ibid., 146.

17. Ibid., 154.

18. Sayers, *Are Women Human?,* 47, in Mardi Keyes, "Domestic Violence," (paper delivered at Gordon-Conwell Theological Seminary, South Hamilton, MA , March 2002), 90.

19. Mardi Keyes, "The Christian Family Collides with the 'Traditional' Family in the First Century and Today" (unpublished paper, October, 1993), 11.

20. Barger, *Eve's Revenge,* 175.

CHAPTER 15

The Bride of Christ

Since the Fall, male and female relationships have been broken and distorted. Sexism has crushed women. Radical feminism has called for women to become like men. In marriage, men have too often tyrannized their counterparts. And too often wives have either groveled in utter dependence before their husbands or become combative and sought to usurp their husband's authority. Thank God, the Bible shows us a better way. In the last chapter, we surveyed Jesus' radical treatment of women. We will explore what the rest of the New Testament says about women and marriage in this chapter.

Make no mistake: Women flocked to the early church because they were treated with dignity and were welcomed into kingdom life and ministry. They were treated as human beings with minds and gifts, not as property. The coming of Christ brought a new order. He began to restore, in the kingdom, what God intended from the beginning but which was lost in the Fall.

As Paul stated clearly: "You are all sons of God through faith in Christ Jesus, for all of you who were baptized into Christ have clothed yourselves with Christ. There is neither Jew nor Greek, slave nor free, male nor female, for you are all one in Christ Jesus. If you belong to Christ, then you are Abraham's seed, and heirs according to the promise" (Galatians 3:26–28).

We all come with the empty hands of faith to the foot of the cross. All human beings, female and male, are in the same boat. We are all sinners. And if we are saved, it is by grace alone, and there is no cause for boasting.

Outward Signs

The New Covenant broke down the old barriers between men and women. Whereas the sign of the Old Covenant was circumcision and was for males only (Genesis 17:9–14), the signs of the New Covenant are public confession (Romans 10:9) and baptism (Matthew 28:19–20; Acts 2:38–41), and both women and men alike are baptized. Gone is the pious Jewish man's prayer, "Thank you, God, for not making me a Gentile, a woman, or a slave." All the old divisions of age, race, class, and gender are obliterated.

Women had a very public role in the birth of the church. After Jesus' ascension, 120 believers, both men and women, gathered in continual prayer (Acts 1:12–15). Acts 2 records the coming of the Holy Spirit upon the assembled men and women on the day of Pentecost. When some onlookers accused the believers of being drunk, Peter explained:

> No, this is what was spoken by the prophet Joel:
> "In the last days, God says,
> I will pour out my Spirit on all people.
> Your *sons and daughters* will prophesy,
> your young men will see visions,
> your old men will dream dreams.
> Even on my servants, *both men and women*,
> I will pour out my Spirit in those days,
> and they will prophesy."
> —Acts 2:16–18 (emphasis added)

The Spirit and the gifts were given to men *and* women, and given publicly.

Ministry for All

The priesthood is now for all believers (1 Peter 2:4–5,9; Revelation 1:6; 5:10; 20:6). The birth of the church brought a sea change in attitudes toward women. Like Jesus, the early writers of the New Testament continued to advance the revolution. Matthew, Mark, and Luke refer to women in 112 distinct passages.[1]

In Romans, Paul sent personal greetings to fifteen women and eighteen men.[2] In Romans 16, he mentions seven women by name. He even named Priscilla before Aquila (16:3), something unheard of in that day. Paul positioned women as fellow saints and coworkers in a way that would have stunned and offended his fellow Jews. For instance, we see the significant part that women played in Paul's missionary journey into Macedonia and Achaia (Acts 16:13–15; 17:4,12,34; 18:2,18–19).

Women were identified as *diakonos* (ministers/servants, including the office of deaconess) and *sunergos* (coworkers).

- Dorcas was always helping the poor and widows through works of charity (Acts 9:36). Part of her work was making clothing for those in need (v. 39).
- Lydia, the first recorded believer from Europe, was at a place of prayer when Paul arrived. She responded to the message and, with her household, was baptized. She opened her home to the missionaries (Acts 16:13–15).
- Paul evidently sent Phoebe, a *diakonos* and a servant of the church in Cenchrea, on kingdom business to Rome (Romans 16:1–2). She was identified as a "succourer of many, and of myself also" (KJV). The Greek word here is *prostatis*, meaning "a woman set over others: a female guardian, protectress, patroness, caring for the affairs of others and aiding them with her resources."[3] Note also that although Paul was an apostle, Phoebe, had a certain "*prostatis* authority" over Paul.[4]
- Priscilla and her husband, Aquila, were Paul's coworkers (Acts 18:18). Twice Paul addressed them as "Priscilla and Aquila" (Romans 16:3; 2 Timothy 4:19), thus recognizing her fundamental equality with her husband.
- Philip, an evangelist in Caesarea, had four unmarried daughters who prophesied (Acts 21:8–9).

- Euodia and Syntyche "contended at [Paul's] side in the cause of the gospel" (Philippians 4:2–3). The root word for "contended" is *athlos*, from which we get the word "athlete."
- In Romans 16:7, Paul greets Andronicus and Junias. (Though NIV has "Junias," other translations use "Junia," likely the preferred reading. At any rate, Paul undoubtedly was referring to a woman.) Paul affirms Andronicus and Junias as "outstanding among the apostles." Some commentators argue this verse allows women to hold the office of apostle. Regardless of the answer to that question, evidently Junias was held in high esteem by church leaders.
- Paul acknowledges Chloe (1 Corinthians 1:11) and Nympha (Colossians 4:15). The indication is that their households hosted the meeting of the church.
- Paul speaks of the faith that Timothy's grandmother Lois and mother, Eunice, had and passed on to him (2 Timothy 1:5).
- Second John was addressed to a woman, "the chosen lady" (2 John 1:1). This label referred to an unnamed Christian woman in the province of Asia or was a symbolic designation of a church there.

Headship and Authority

Yes, the priesthood is for all believers—male and female. But it doesn't follow that every ministry is for every believer. Remember, at creation there is unity in being between men and women, but diversity in function. A significant part of that diversity in function has to do with authority. Adam was the head of his wife *before* the Fall. Authority is foundational, part of the pre-Fallen order of creation and is not evil in itself.

Authority is woven, not only into the very fabric of the universe, but, as we have seen, into the very triune nature of God. As Paul puts it in 1 Corinthians 11:3, "Now I want you to realize that the head of every man is Christ, and the head of the woman is man, and the head of Christ is God." Three times in this passage we find the word *head*. This is the Greek word *kephale*. It means "the head of men and often of animals . . . anything supreme, chief, prominent; of persons, master lord: of a husband in relation to his wife; of Christ: the Lord of the husband and of the Church; of things: the corner stone."[5]

Theologian and scholar Wayne Grudem has stated: "I once looked up over 2,300 examples of the word 'head' (*kephale*) in ancient Greek. In these texts, the word *kephale* is applied to many people in authority, but none without governing authority. *In the Greek-speaking world, to be the head of a group of people always meant to have authority over those people.*"[6]

God the Father is the head of Jesus the Son. Christ is the head of humanity, and in the same way, the man is the head of his wife. The cross did not abolish this authority structure, as if it were evil. The cross redeems it. This means that followers of Christ must be careful not to expand it beyond the boundaries established by Scripture. To defend against sexism, we must not add rules where God has given freedom. At the same time, to defend against radical feminism, we must not contradict this authority structure either.

It will help us greatly to again consider Jesus, the King of Kings and Lord of lords (Revelation 17:14; 19:16) who came to us as a servant (Mark 10:45). These roles are not in contradiction. They are both true. His leadership is defined by his service, his headship by his self-sacrifice. Remember that on the night of the Last Supper he took a towel, wrapped it around his waist, and washed his disciples' feet—a servant's task (John 13:1–17). This is godly leadership. Men, take note.

Four Spheres of Governance

How do we apply these authority structure in our daily lives, going no further than Scripture takes us? It helps if we understand that God has created four spheres for human beings to serve him as vice-regents of creation. These spheres are the individual, the family, the church, and civil society.

The first sphere of governance is individual self-government. Here, all human beings are free to govern their own lives. Each individual, woman or man, possesses common and unique giftings—internal property. These are gifts from God that are to be stewarded. Each person is to live before the face of God and must govern his or her life according to conscience.

In the family, Scripture designates the husband as the loving and serving head of his wife and family, according to the example of Christ. The wife is responsible to her own husband, but not to all men. She has received delegated authority to function as a servant-leader in the life of the family as the queen of the house, as the nurturer of her children, and as the succorer of her husband and the guests in her home. We will delve more deeply into marriage starting in the next section.

In the church, which is a priesthood of all believers, every Christian is called into *full-time ministry*.[7] Maleness is not a requirement for ministry in and through the church. Men and women are free to responsibly use all their natural and spiritual gifts to edify fellow Christians and to love and serve their community and the larger world.

There is only one limitation placed on many men and all women: the office of *episkope*, meaning "overseership, charge, the office of an elder; the overseer or presiding officers of a Christian church."[8] This one restriction has to do with *governance*—the exercise of authority *in the church* (not in the civil society). Just as God has chosen to delegate authority, under Christ, to men in the family, so men have governance of the church under the headship of the Chief Elder, Jesus Christ.

It is important to make the distinction between *ministry* and *office*. There are no restrictions on ministry. There are literally thousands of opportunities for women and men to serve, lead, and minister in and through the church. There is only one restriction, and that is in the office of *episkope*.

In civil society, there are no gender restrictions on work, service, and leadership. There is freedom for a woman to pursue being a servant-leader in any sphere of society.

The Pattern of Marriage

Marriage is a sacred, holy institution because it is God ordained. Marriage is not an invention of humanity or merely a social contract that we enter into lightly to gain favorable government treatment. Marriage is both a reflection of God's marriage to Israel and a metaphor of Christ's glorious marriage to the church.

In the first marriage, Adam represented Christ, and Eve represented his future bride, the church. Likewise in human marriages, the man is to represent Christ, and the woman is to represent the church. A godly marriage like this, so countercultural and so beautiful, can draw a watching world to Christ.

As we have seen in our study of Genesis 2, there is a mystery on the human level that partially reflects an eternal mystery. The Three-in-One God, the Trinity, creates the *imago Dei,* male and female, partially to express his mysterious nature. Genesis 2:24 recounts the wonder of *one flesh:* "For this reason a man will leave his father and mother and be united to his wife, and they will become one flesh." Just as God is *echad* ("united," "compound," or "bound together"), so the woman and man are *echad* in the sacred realm of marriage.

The mysteries are only beginning. Referring to husband and wife becoming one flesh, in Ephesians 5:31–32 Paul notes for us still another dimension of mystery: "'For this reason a man will leave his father and mother and be united to his wife, and the two will become one flesh.' This is a *profound mystery*—but I am talking about Christ and the church" (emphasis added). From this we see that the one-flesh state of husband and wife illustrates the profound mystery of Christ and the church.

Earthly marriage, derived from the heavenly marriage, provides an imperfect picture of the coming of Christ for his bride. But in verse 33 Paul also points out that the relationship between Christ and the church provides the pattern for husband and wife: "However, each one of you also must love his wife as he loves himself, and the wife must respect her husband." As Christ is the loving servant-head of the church, so the husband is to be the loving servant-head of his wife. As the church is the loving, respectful helper to Christ, so the wife is to be the loving, respectful helper to her husband.

Michael J. McClymond, associate professor of historical theology and apologetics at Westminster Seminary, writes of this profound mystery:

> Marriage is a tangible, concrete, earthly expression of an intangible, heavenly, and eternal reality, namely the loving relation between Christ and his people. Non-Christians may not know this, but Christians should. By their faithful, persevering, covenant love as husband and wife, Christian couples provide a tangible expression of a spiritual reality much greater than themselves. For this rea-

son, the two who are one, are also three, since they point beyond themselves to the Savior who draws people to himself in faithful love (John 12:32). What could possibly be more significant than that—my tiny and faulty little marriage relationship as a tangible sign of the everlasting and unfailing love of God?[9]

Here we find that the creation order of one man and one woman in marriage, in a profound and mysterious way, points to the glorious and eternal marriage of the Son of God to his bride. No one has captured this better than John Piper:

So marriage is like a metaphor or an image or a picture or a parable for something more than a man and a woman becoming one flesh. It stands for the relationship between Christ and the church. That's the deepest meaning of marriage. It's meant to be a living drama of how Christ and the church relate to each other. . . .

If you want to understand God's meaning for marriage you have to grasp that we are dealing with a copy and an original, a metaphor and a reality, [a] parable and a truth. And the original, the reality, the truth is God's marriage to his people, or Christ's marriage to the church. While the copy, the metaphor, the parable is a husband's marriage to his wife.[10]

The functional roles of husband and wife are to reflect the functional roles of Christ and the church. George W. Knight III writes in regard to this passage in Ephesians: "[T]he order Paul is speaking of here (submission and love) is not accidental or temporary or culturally determined: it is part of the *essence of marriage*, part of God's original plan for a perfect, sinless, harmonious marriage. This is a powerful argument for the fact that Christlike, loving headship and church-like, willing submission are rooted in creation and in God's eternal purposes, not just in the passing trends of culture."[11]

Elisabeth Elliot points out the absurdity of reversing the nouns in Ephesians 5:22–23: "Husbands, be subject to your wives as to the Lord. For the wife is the head of the husband just as the church is the head of Christ."[12]

The fatherly heart of God is reflected in manhood and husbanding. The motherly heart of God is reflected in womanhood and nurturing. These differences in function are part of God's design, not the Fall. C. S. Lewis calls masculine and feminine complementary. "We are dealing with male and female not merely as facts of nature but as the live and awful shadows of realities utterly beyond our control and largely beyond our direct knowledge."[13]

And yet, because of our sinful propensity to fall into sexist patterns, we need to keep reminding ourselves that although we are different in function, we are equal in being. Earlier in this same passage, Paul teaches our fundamental equality as brothers and sisters in Christ who, in the context of church life, practice mutual submission: "Submit to one another out of reverence for Christ" (Ephesians 5:21). We find a similar theme in Philippians 2:3–4: "Do nothing out of selfish ambition or vain conceit, but in humility consider others better than yourselves. Each of you should look not only to your own interests, but also to the interests of others."

Yet we also need to keep in mind that this mutual submission sets the tone for what follows about marriage. Mutual submission does not eliminate the distinctions between husbands and wives; it transforms the distorted, sexist crushing of women and the radical feminist disappearance of women into a profound mystery that reflects still deeper mysteries found in the divine being.

The Husband's Call: Loving Headship

Husbands, love your wives, just as Christ loved the church and gave himself up for her to make her holy, cleansing her by the washing with water through the word, and to present her to himself as a radiant church, without stain or wrinkle or any other blemish, but holy and blameless. In this same way, husbands ought to love their wives as their own bodies. He who loves his wife loves himself. After all, no one ever hated his own body, but he feeds and cares for it, just as Christ does the church—for we are members of his body.
—Ephesians 5:25–30

The pattern, as we have seen, is Christ and the church. Piper notes, "Headship is not a right to command and control. It's a responsibility to love like Christ: to lay down your life for your wife in servant leadership. . . . Headship is the divine calling of a husband to take primary responsibility for Christ-like servant leadership, protection and provision in the home."[14]

Note that this passage, speaking to husbands, *does not* say that the husband is the head of the wife. That word is spoken to the wives (v. 23). Indeed, the husband *is* the head of the wife. Note, as well, that the man is not the head of *all* women; he is the head of only one woman, his wife. But he does not need to hear *that* he is the head, but *how* he is to be the head. The husband is the head of his wife precisely as Christ is the head of the church. This is stated four times: "as Christ is" (v. 23), "just as Christ" (v. 25), "in this same way" (v. 28), "just as Christ does" (v. 29). While the word *head* implies a position of authority, the nature of that authority is defined by Christ's example, not sexism's.

The word *love* appears seven times in this passage. The word is not *eros*, or intimate, sexual love. Nor is it *phileo*, the love of friends. All seven times it is *agape* love—the love that sent Christ to the cross (John 3:16; 1 John 3:16). It is self-sacrificing love. This is God's love; it is the love that sacrifices oneself for another. It is the highest form of love. This self-sacrificing sets the standard of love that men are to have for their wives.

One final note for husbands. The man is not commanded to be head over his wife. The husband already *is* the head (v. 23), whether he or his wife believes it. God's order is built into the very fabric of our lives. The command to the husband is not to be head but to unconditionally love (vv. 25,28). Paul tells the husband to give himself up for her (v. 25), to sanctify her (v. 26–27), to feed and care for her (v. 29). Note the tender language. There is no place here for domineering, harshness, arrogance, and bossiness.

The man is to husband his wife, protecting her, providing for her safety, sheltering her, sacrificing himself for her, looking to her needs before his own. The apostle Peter speaks similarly in 1 Peter 3:7: "Husbands, in the same way be considerate as you live with your wives, and treat them with respect as the weaker partner and as heirs with you of the gracious gift of life, so that nothing will hinder your prayers."

The woman is the more vulnerable of the species. In what ways are women weaker than men? Mentally weaker? Self-evidently no. Morally weaker? Again, self-evidently no. Spiritually weaker? No. The woman is only weaker in one category: physically. She is generally weaker physically, which has led sinful men to treat her as an inferior, taking advantage of her vulnerability with violence, rape, and other forms of emotional, physical, and social abuse. Because she is the man's equal and counterpart, and because she is the "weaker partner," men should follow Christ's lead with the church and provide for, protect, and cherish women.

While the woman's task to respect and submit to her husband may be difficult, especially nowadays, the husband's task is far more difficult. He is called to sacrifice everything, including his life if necessary, for his wife. C. S. Lewis captured this so well in *The Four Loves*: "This headship, then, is most fully embodied not in the husband we should all wish to be but in him whose marriage is most like a crucifixion; whose wife receives most and gives least, is most unworthy of him, is—in her own mere nature—least loveable. For the church has no beauty but what the Bridegroom gives her; he does not find, but makes her, lovely."[15]

The Wife's Call: Loving and Respectful Helper

Wives, too, have a task. It is to follow the pattern as the church is to Christ and Israel was to be toward God.

> Wives, submit to your husbands as to the Lord. For the husband is the head of the wife as Christ is the head of the church, his body, of which he is the Savior. Now as the church submits to Christ, so also wives should submit to their husbands in everything.
> —Ephesians 5:22–24

Again, Piper notes: "Submission is not slavish or coerced or cowering. That's not the way Christ wants the church to respond to his leadership: he wants it to be free and willing and glad and refining and strengthening. . . . Submission is the divine calling of a wife to honor and affirm her husband's leadership and help carry it through according to her gifts."[16]

As we have examined earlier in this book, submission does not imply passivity or weakness, but instead an active strength. The Greek word for "submit," *hupotasso*, is a military term meaning "to arrange [troop divisions] in a military fashion under the command of a leader." In nonmilitary usages, it means "a voluntary attitude of giving in, cooperating, assuming responsibility, and carrying a burden."[17] While a wife is to be under her husband's authority, she is not in an inferior position. She submits to her equal as the body submits to its head.

The word *submit* is also found in other passages that speak of a woman's relationship to her husband (Colossians 3:18; Titus 2:4–5; 1 Peter 3:1). A number of versions translate it as "submit *yourselves,*" to reflect that this is an intentional, voluntary attitude. The husband is not to dominate; rather, the wife is to freely submit. Just as people are not forced to join a church, they are not to be forced into marriage. But once one makes that choice, there are obligations and responsibilities that accompany the choice. And just as the church surrenders her identity, her hope, her future, to her Bridegroom, so the wife submits herself to her husband.

There is symmetry here: the husband loves his wife as Christ loves the church, and the wife submits to her husband as the church submits to Christ. Note that she is to submit to her own husband (Ephesians 5:22). She is not told to submit to any other men. *Men are not the head of women.* A man is the head only of his own wife.

The wife, for her part, is to submit to her husband just as she would to Jesus Christ. This means that (1) she is motivated by Christ to submit and that (2) she is to submit to her husband the same way she submits to Christ.

And she is to submit to her earthly husband "in everything" (v. 24). The Greek word *pas* usually is translated "all" or "all things." Because there is a great potential for sexist men to abuse this directive, let me spell out what this does *not* mean:

- It does not require the wife to disobey God to obey her husband (Acts 4:18–20; 5:29).
- It does not preclude the wife from thinking and asking questions, as she is called to love the Lord with all her mind (Mark 12:30).
- It does not mean that the husband can lord it over his wife (2 Corinthians 1:24; 1 Peter 5:2–3), who is his equal.
- It does not mean that she is to be imprisoned in her home, "barefoot and pregnant" (see our earlier discussion of the Proverbs 31 wife).

Wives are also to respect their husbands (Ephesians 5:33). The Greek word is *phobeo*, meaning "to reverence, venerate, to treat with deference or reverential obedience."[18] This same word is found in Ephesians 5:21: "Submit to one another out of reverence [*phobeo*] for Christ." The same respect that women and men have for Christ is the respect that women are to have for their husbands. Respecting her spouse in this way is a challenging calling indeed.

Concluding Thoughts

The diverse functions of husbands and wives are complementary. Theologian Susan T. Foh writes: "God's commands concerning marriage involve self-denial for both husband and wife, but of different sorts. The wife's submission establishes the God-ordained headship of her husband, and the husband's love insures the wife's best interests, her treatment as a person. Each one's obedience helps the other to fulfill his or her duty."[19]

A husband may never be called upon to die for his wife, but he is called to sacrifice himself, his time, his work, his recreation, his wants, everything he has, to serve her. The wife may not be required to think as her husband does and do everything he wants right when he wants it. But she is called to remember that what he thinks matters and that she may be called to sacrifice her seeming self-interest for her husband's leadership and the unity of the family. Mardi Keyes states: "Marital oneness means that wherever I am, and whatever I'm doing, there's a mysterious sense in which my spouse is there too!"[20]

The commands given to the man to love his wife and the wife to respect her husband are not easily fulfilled, as they move contrary to our fallen nature. A man's fallen nature is to love himself. A woman's fallen nature is to rebel against authority. At the same time, a married woman's greatest need is for her husband to love her self-sacrificially. And the greatest need a husband has is for his wife to respect him. When a wife follows the call of Christ, she ministers to her husband at the point of his greatest need. When a husband follows the call of Christ, he ministers to his wife at the point of her greatest need.

Note that these commands are not built on reciprocity. A man may want to say that he will love his wife if she is lovely. And a woman may want to say that she will respect her husband if he is respectful toward her. But there is no such sense in Scripture. For his wife's sake and for his own, a man is to mimic Christ and Hosea: he is to love his wife even when she is unlovely. Likewise the wife, for Christ's sake, is to respect her husband even if he is not worthy of respect. These are our disciplines unto godliness. A godly, Christ-centered marriage has a way of drawing others into the light of God. May it be so in ours.

Notes

1. Loren Cunningham and David Joel Hamilton, *Why Not Women?* (Seattle: YWAM Publishing, 2000), 119.

2. Rodney Stark, *The Rise of Christianity* (Princeton, NJ: Princeton University Press, 1996), 98.

3. *Enhanced Strong's Lexicon*, s.v. "prostatis."

4. As we discussed in the last chapter, Jesus did not choose a woman as an apostle. Having said this, however, we should not conclude that all women are excluded from all ministry and all authority. Nor should we conclude that all men have authority over all women. Here is an example where a woman had authority in ministry. *Prostatis* is one of those specific places where you see women in "authority"—not as *episcope*, but as succorers. The Greek word *prostatis* [Strong's 4368] is the feminine of a derivative of *proistemi* [Strong's 4291]. *Proistemi* is derived from *pro* [Strong's 4353], "fore, in front of, prior" (figuratively meaning "superior to") and *histemi* [Strong's 2476], "to stand." Therefore, *proistemi* means "to stand before, i.e., in rank; to preside, be over, rule." But this is a different kind of authority than that of an *episcope*.

In this passage, Paul is commending Phoebe as "a servant." In the modern world, being a servant is equated with being menial. But in the kingdom of God being a servant is to manifest the heart of God. We must judge these things by biblical standards, not by worldly standards. Paul is in effect giving Phoebe a letter of reference for "any help she may need from you." Then Paul says that she has been a great helper of many and even a helper to Paul. Phoebe was a patroness, likely a woman of means who was set "over" others to care, succor, and protect. She was the patron of many, including Paul.

Paul was not a man after power as are many Christian sexists. He was a man who was able to recognize the dignity and integrity of one who had, in her patronage, been "over" Paul himself. Phoebe is the epitome of a servant-leader, and Paul honors her as such. This stands in contrast to sexists, on the one hand, who say there is no role for women in ministry and leadership in the church, and evangelical feminists, on the other hand, who blur distinctions and argue that this leadership implies *episcope* leadership.

5. Ibid., s.v. "kephale."

6. Wayne Grudem, "The Meaning of 'Head' in the Bible: A Simple Question No Egalitarian Can Answer," *CBMW News* 1:3 (June 1996): 8, in Alexander Strauch, *Men and Women, Equal yet Different: A Brief Study of the Biblical Passages on Gender* (Colorado Springs: Lewis & Roth Publishers, 1999), 56 (italics in the original).

7. For more on this subject, see my soon-to-be-published book, *Occupy Till I Come!*

8. *Enhanced Strong's Lexicon*, s.v. "episkope."

9. Michael J. McClymond, "Two Become One, Two Become Three: Pleasure and Procreation in Christian Understandings of Sex," *Modern Reformation*, November/December 2001, 21.

10. John Piper, "Husbands Who Love Like Christ and the Wives Who Submit to Them," sermon at Bethlehem Baptist Church, St. Paul, MN, June 11, 1989, http://www.desiringgod.org/ResourceLibrary/Sermons/ByDate/1989/683_Husbands_Who_Love_Like_Christ_and_the_Wives_Who_Submit_to_Them/.

11. George W. Knight III, "Husbands and Wives as Analogues of Christ and the Church," in *Recovering Biblical Manhood and Womanhood: A Response to Evangelical Feminism,* John Piper and Wayne Grudem, eds. (Wheaton: Crossway, 1991), 176 (italics in the original).

12. Elisabeth Elliot, *The Mark of a Man* (Old Tappan, NJ: Fleming H. Revell Company, 1981), 71.

13. C. S. Lewis, *God in the Dock* (Grand Rapids: Eerdmans, 1998), 39.

14. Piper, "Husbands Who Love Like Christ and the Wives Who Submit to Them."

15. C. S. Lewis, *The Four Loves* (New York: Harvest Books, 1971), 148.

16. Piper, "Husbands Who Love Like Christ and the Wives Who Submit to Them."

17. *Enhanced Strong's Lexicon*, s.v. "hupotasso."

18. Ibid., s.v. "phobeo."

19. Susan T. Foh, *Women and the Word of God: A Response to Biblical Feminism* (Phillipsburg, NJ: Presbyterian and Reformed Publishing Co., 1979), 208.

20. Mardi Keyes, "The Question of Women in Leadership II: The New Testament" (paper delivered at L'Abri, Southborough, MA, February 27, 1998), 7.

CHAPTER 16

The Wedding of the Lamb

We have examined the lies that enslave and crush women. We have looked at how God's people have alternately cooperated with these lies or stood against them. We have seen the Bible's estimation of women. Now we must catch a vision of the ultimate model for marriage. As mentioned previously, the Scriptures begin and end with the nuptial. In chapter 12 we studied the opening marriage, and here we will look at the consummating one. Our model, however, comes not from human figures such as Adam and Eve, Abraham and Sarah, or Priscilla and Aquila. Instead, it comes from the wedding of the Lamb, the union of Christ and his bride, the church. As we catch this vision, we will glimpse in a mirror darkly the glory of women.

History will be consummated in this wedding, foretold over the centuries in the Scriptures. History began, as we have seen, with the creation of the man and his *counterpart*. The end of history will come when the King of Kings and Lord of Lords marries his eternal *counterpart*. This future wedding, however, is not just for the sweet by-and-by. It shapes the context of our marriages and lives today.

Revelation 19:6–9 gives us a wonderful picture of the celebration:

> Then I heard what sounded like a great multitude, like the roar of rushing waters and like loud peals of thunder, shouting:

"Hallelujah!
For our Lord God Almighty reigns.
Let us rejoice and be glad
and give him glory!
For the wedding of the Lamb has come,
and his bride has made herself ready.
Fine linen, bright and clean,
was given her to wear."
(Fine linen stands for the righteous acts of the saints.)
Then the angel said to me, "Write: 'Blessed are those who are invited to the wedding supper of the Lamb!'" And he added, "These are the true words of God."

As beautiful as these words are, we need to ask ourselves what this means for how women are treated today. John Piper captures the significance:

The age-long preparation of the bride of Christ (the church!) is finally complete and he takes her arm, as it were, and leads her to the table. The marriage supper of the Lamb has come. He stands at the head of the table and a great silence falls over the millions of saints. And he says, "This, my beloved, was the meaning of marriage. This is what it all pointed toward. This is why I created you male and female and ordained the covenant of marriage. Henceforth there will be no more marriage and giving in marriage, for the final reality has come and the shadow can pass away."[1]

Moving on, the apostle John reports in Revelation 21:1–4:

Then I saw a new heaven and a new earth, for the first heaven and the first earth had passed away, and there was no longer any sea. I saw the Holy City, the new Jerusalem, coming down out of heaven from God, prepared as a bride beautifully dressed for her husband. And I heard a loud voice from the throne saying, "Now the dwelling of God is with men, and he will live with them. They will be his people, and God himself will be with them and be their God. He will wipe every tear from their eyes. There will be no more death or mourning or crying or pain, for the old order of things has passed away."

This is the beginning of a new heaven and a new earth. God will dwell with us permanently in the New Jerusalem, which is identified, in a mysterious way, with the bride. Revelation 21:2 notes: "I saw the Holy City, the new Jerusalem, coming down out of heaven from God, prepared *as a bride beautifully dressed for her husband*" (emphasis added).

Finally, Revelation 21:1–22:5 describes the celestial splendor of the New Jerusalem. Let's focus on 21:9–10 for just a moment. "One of the seven angels who had the seven bowls full of the seven last plagues came and said to me, 'Come, I will show you *the bride, the wife of the Lamb*.'" And he carried me away in the Spirit to a mountain great and high, and showed me *the Holy City, Jerusalem*, coming down out of heaven from God" (emphasis added).

The bride of Christ, the church, is now pictured as the New Jerusalem. While God is complete and whole in his mysterious Trinitarian nature, in another sense this heavenly union brings to perfection the plan he has been carrying out for the ages.

- Adam and Eve were the first couple.
- God and Israel were the prototype of God's intention for marriage (Isaiah 49:18; 62:5; Jeremiah 2:2).
- Christ and his bride represent the consummate union—*one flesh*—toward which all history moves.

Our Christian marriages today are to foreshadow, in some small way, the time when the Lord takes the church as his eternal bride. Will Christ beat his bride in order to establish his headship? No. Would Christ sell his future bride to the pornography industry or into prostitution? These are clearly acts that would be abhorrent to him. As the Lord of love, will Christ exercise the "right" to kill his bride to save his honor? Surely he already would have allowed the church to disintegrate since we have caused him much shame. Instead, the church still holds the role as his future bride. How then do we justify such actions today within our culture and those around the world? We need to redeem how unmarried women and women within the covenant of marriage are treated and treat them as Christ will treat his bride.

Gene Edwards captures the glorious moment of the wedding of Christ and his bride, near the end of *The Divine Romance*:

Every angel was now remembering that unforgettable moment

when, during the creation of Eve, the glory, the light, and the revelation of God overwhelmed all creation. It was a thing that, until now, they had never understood. Now they knew! When the Lord created Eve, He had been "seeing" *someone* else. He had fashioned Eve in the image of an exotically beautiful woman who belonged to some other dimension.

That woman now stood before them. There was no question, Eve was but the foreshadowing of *this one*. Before them stood a woman of incomparable glory and beauty, made up of unnumbered millions of portions of God's own being—portions of God chosen before the foundation of the ages, to be the composite of her being.

Here, at last, was the Mystery *who* had been hidden in God!

Angels hardly dared to look upon such terrible beauty, yet they dared not do otherwise.

Here was a woman, robed in the very brightness and glory of God, with a beauty defying their comprehension. She was like *him*, yet female! A loveliness so tender, a countenance so full of love, a being so pure that angelic eyes shone with awe and terror seeking to take it in. . . .

Her hair was black as ravens, her youth had once inspired a creating God to fashion springtime. Her features encompassed all the beauty of every race and tribe and kindred of womanhood from all ends of creation. . . .

Mercifully, the vision of the glorious woman began to recede. Once more there appeared before the angels the scene of the *All* of God. Exhausted, angels fell prostrate upon their faces.

"No suitors, no rivals, no enemies," one whispered.

"The mother of Eve," responded another.

"A new Jeru," declared yet another in soft delirium.

One of the angels stood, still half blinded by glory, and uttered, "A counterpart for our Lord."

"The bride of God."[2]

But until that glorious day we must once again ask: How are we to live our lives as men and women now? At the simplest level, our marriages can be pictures for a watching world of the coming, ultimate marriage. How can the world glimpse the mystery of Christ and his church save through the relationship of men and women in holy matrimony? We, in our marriages and in the way men treat women in general, can paint a powerful picture of Christ and his bride. No, it won't be perfect, because we are broken and sinful people living in a fallen world. But let us give our global neighbors a glimpse of the glory to come.

Notes

1. John Piper, "Male and Female He Created Them in the Image of God," sermon at Bethlehem Baptist Church, St. Paul, MN, May 14, 1989, http://www.desiringgod.org/ResourceLibrary/Sermons/ByDate/1989/679_Male_and_Female_He_Created_Them_in_the_Image_of_God/.
2. Gene Edwards, *The Divine Romance: The Most Beautiful Love Story Ever Told* (Carol Stream, IL: Tyndale, 1992), 190–91 (italics in the original).

CHAPTER 17

God's Design for Women: Nurturers of Nations

In *The Last Battle,* the final installment of *The Chronicles of Narnia* by C. S. Lewis, the Christ-figure Aslan invites Peter, Susan, Edmund, and Lucy to "Come further up! Come further in!"[1] As they follow Aslan into his Country, where they have never been, they sense greater and greater familiarity with their surroundings. Eventually they realize that Aslan's Country is England in all her glory, without any corruption or evil, the fulfillment of all their earthly longings.

We have sought to reclaim a biblical view of the dignity of women. Now as we draw to a close, we need to examine one major and specific role God has set aside for women. What will the outcome be when women embrace this role? Although even the best that earth has to offer women is imperfect, God's plan for women is immeasurably richer and more satisfying; but we must go "further up and further in" to experience it.

This plan has as a building block the truth that being a woman is glorious. A woman's nurturing nature is critical to building strong, healthy, and vibrant families and, ultimately, nations. Can we not call women and men to "come further up and further in" to their glory?

The Cultural Mandate

The call began in Genesis 1 and was for the *imago Dei*. Female and male are to work together as vice-regents to steward the earth, to create culture, and to build godly nations. As I mentioned earlier, it takes male and female to procreate and to take dominion. The family is at the start of this process, and women naturally nurture and teach in this setting. Both single women and mothers have this as part of their calling.

If the home is strong, the nation will become strong. If the home is dysfunctional, the nation will decline. The husband is the "king" of the home, the loving, serving head, providing structure and a hedge of protection around the family. The woman is the "queen" of the home and thus ultimately reigns as the nurturer of the nation. But for women to assume this exalted status, we must demolish the mental and spiritual strongholds of sexism and radical feminism that, in one way or another, have plagued us for centuries.

Author Nancy Wilson states: "Christian women need to have their perspective on mothering anchored in the Scriptures, not in modern culture. It is imperative that they know how the Bible defines mothering, for this protects them against the ungodly pressures to conform to the world. Christian women must learn to think like Christians about these things."[2]

We take as our model Jesus Christ, who challenged the stronghold of sexism not by feminism but by complementarianism, which is based on the Trinitarianism inherent in the biblical worldview. Taking on the sexism of his day, Jesus explained to religious allies and opponents God's heart for the dignity of women. Likewise, we too must take on misunderstandings in the church in our own day. We turn now to the twin challenges of feminism and its application in the church, careerism.

Careerism in the Church

In her book *The Way Home*, written in 1985, maternal feminist Mary Pride described how the church, despite its rhetoric, had largely become conformed to the world:

The sad truth is that the "traditional" role which feminists attacked in the fifties had already lost its scriptural fullness. Christian women were staying home out of habit, not out of *conviction* [emphasis added]. Women had been robbed of their role, even though they were "in their place." *And they were robbed by the church.*

The Christian churches in America had actually paved the way for feminism to succeed, even as preachers orated about the sanctity of motherhood! Denominations endorsed family planning and "therapeutic abortion." Church meetings were scheduled for every night of the week, giving out a clear message that family life was unimportant. Ministry was considered more worthwhile than motherhood. . . . Church life centered on the church building, not the home. . . .

At every turn Christian women found that their biological, economic, and social roles were considered worthless. *Men's* ministry, *men's* money, *men's* building and programs—*these* were the areas that mattered."[3]

In the midst of this male-focused emphasis, Christian feminists have naturally asked the question: *May a woman be a pastor?* But this may be the wrong question to ask. It is framed by the modern mindset, rooted in philosophic monism, radical feminism, egalitarianism, and, finally, careerism. And an egalitarian question will beg for an egalitarian answer: "Yes!"

When the goal of women is only one thing—to have the "right" to be a pastor—the issue is misshapen. If it is only the ability to be a pastor that establishes a woman's worth, then she clearly *must* be a pastor. But what happens then to all the men and women who are not pastors? Do they not have worth? Assuming that Christian women do not have worth unless they can be pastors is nonsensical. It zooms right past the biblical understanding that men and women are equal in worth but different in function. It forgets the fact that women have a glorious calling *as women.*

Again, Mary Pride observed: "Role obliteration is the coming thing in evangelical, and even in fundamentalist, circles. If women can't be women, by golly they will be men! All because two or more generations have grown up and married without even hearing that the Bible teaches a distinct role for women which is *different* from that of a man and *just as important.*"[4]

Yes, with the spirit of careerism pervading the church, it is hard to resist the notion that men and women must have the same vocations. Isn't God an equal-opportunity employer? And yet we seem to forget that men, of course, don't have the opportunity to be mothers. That opportunity is given only to women—and what a glorious calling. The following poem flowed from my pen as I pondered this calling:

> If I make a home
> If I conceive a child
>   carry a child
>   nurture a child
>   raise and educate a child
> This is "ministry work"
> These fundamental human activities are
>   ordained by God
>   valued by God
> And only a fool does not esteem them.

The War against Motherhood

Mothers set the spirit of the home, and it is the home where future citizens are nurtured. Too often the value placed on making money takes priority over making future citizen-leaders. Enola Aird, the founder of the Motherhood Project, notes: "There is a disconnect between the values of the marketplace and the values that make it possible to raise good children."[5]

Homemaking and nurturing children are not considered work. Ann Crittenden laments "how the hardest-working people on earth came to be defined as 'dependents' who 'don't work' and who have to be 'supported' by a spouse who is officially the only 'working' member of the household."[6] She states:

> The idea that time spent with one's child is time wasted is embedded in traditional economic thinking. People who are not formally employed may create human capital, but they themselves are said to suffer a deterioration of the stuff, as if they were so many pieces of equipment left out to rust. The extraordinary talents required to do the long-term work of building human character and instilling

in young children the ability and desire to learn have no place in the economists' calculations. Economic theory has nothing to say about the acquisition of skills by those who work with children; presumably there are none.[7]

Crittenden warns of a new egalitarian alliance that makes women become like men to run the markets of the world, calling women away from the absolutely critical work of making homes, nurturing children, and thus building the future of the nation. Crittenden writes of the bias she felt from her career-oriented peers when she became a mother:

> It was at a Washington, D.C., cocktail party, when someone asked, "What do you do?" I replied that I was a new mother, and they promptly vanished. I was the same person this stranger might have found worthwhile had I said I was a foreign correspondent for *Newsweek*, a financial reporter for the *New York Times*, or a Pulitzer Prize nominee, all of which had been true. But as a mother, I had shed status like skin off a snake. . . .
>
> But the moment of truth came a few years after I had resigned from the *New York Times*, in order to have more time for my infant son. I ran into someone who asked, "Didn't you used to be Ann Crittenden?"[8]

Ann Crittenden had been made to "disappear."

The Motherhood Project accurately states that "the work that we do as mothers is of paramount importance, but profoundly undervalued and demeaned. Our society treats mothers' work as less worthwhile and less valuable than the work of business. All too often, it subordinates the interests of children and families to commercial values and concerns. It relegates the work of caring for children to the margins of life and consistently gives short shrift to the work of nurturing and cultivating human relationships."[9]

As I noted in chapter 5, the ideologies of radical feminism and environmentalism have spawned organizations that promote the value of choosing not to have children. The message is that for women to be all that they can be they must be *child free*.

The death of motherhood leads very quickly to the death of nations. For a nation to survive, each woman needs to have an average of 2.1 babies. The average in Europe is far below this number. Some nations are hovering closer to one baby per woman: Germany and Austria, 1.3; Russia and Italy, 1.2; Spain, 1.1.

As a consequence of the war against motherhood, whole nations and cultures stand on the verge of extinction. Journalist Mark Steyn writes: "Much of what we loosely call the western world will not survive this century, and much of it will effectively disappear within our lifetimes, including many if not most western European countries. There'll probably still be a geographical area on the map marked as Italy or the Netherlands—*probably*. . . . Italy and the Netherlands will merely be designations for real estate."[10]

At the same time that historic Europeans' anti-maternal value system is leading to national suicide, the immigrant Muslim populations are traditionally having large families, each woman having four to six children. The handwriting is on the wall! Europe, as she has been known, is dying. Unless something dramatic changes, secular Europe will become Islamic in another generation.

A Christian Response

As we have seen, the trend in the secular world is influencing the church today. Amid the battle in the church over the role of women, several key Scripture passages have been largely forgotten. In order to uncover God's call for women, let's look at them now.

1 Timothy 5:9–10,14:

> No widow may be put on the list of widows unless she is over sixty, has been faithful to her husband, and is well known for her good deeds, such as bringing up children, showing hospitality, washing the feet of the saints, helping those in trouble and devoting herself to all kinds of good deeds. . . . So I counsel younger widows to marry, to have children, to manage their homes and to give the enemy no opportunity for slander.

Here are godly characteristics expected of an older widow:

• Known to be faithful to her late husband

- Well known for good deeds
  1. Bringing up children
  2. Showing hospitality
  3. Washing the feet of the saints
  4. Helping those in trouble
  5. Devoting herself to good deeds

Here are godly characteristics expected of a younger widow:

- Marry
- Have children
- Manage her home

It is important to take a moment and examine the phrase "manage their homes." This phrase is the translation of the Greek word *oikodespoteo*: "guide the house" (KJV); "to rule a household, manage family affairs." This word is related to *oikonomia*—"to steward the house"—from which we get the word *economics*. The importance of this task for nation building will become clear in a moment. Suffice it to say that this is the picture of the functions of a godly woman in Proverbs 31. The mother is the queen of the home!

While the verses in the proverb are worth pondering at length, which we did earlier, for the purposes of this discussion I will simply say that this woman is a model of many godly traits. Just as no Christian will possess all the spiritual gifts, so no woman will possess all the traits of Proverbs 31. She will, however, aspire not to be the slave of the house but the queen of the house, with incredible administrative responsibilities. The Proverbs 31 woman is the maker of a home environment conducive to the health of the family, especially the children, and the succorer of guests.

Titus 2:3–5:

> Teach the older women to be reverent in the way they live, not to be slanderers or addicted to much wine, but to teach what is good. Then they can train the younger women to love their husbands and children, to be self-controlled and pure, to be busy at home, to be kind, and to be subject to their husbands, so that no one will malign the word of God.

Older women are to mentor younger women to

- love their husbands
- love their children
- be self-controlled and pure
- be busy at home—"caring for the house, working at home";[11] implied in this is combining the creative (the arts) and the mind to make a beautiful and well-ordered home that will serve the family and become the founding order for a healthy society.
- be kind
- be subject to their own husbands

Note that these passages are addressed *to* women *for* women. Women are to minister to and teach other women about nurturing, succoring, motherhood, and homemaking. Let's look at these tasks.

The Roles

Motherhood

Motherhood is a reflection of God's maternal love, which he has manifested most fully in women. The concrete reality of the female body reveals, to all who will see, the transcendent nature of God's compassion, nurture, and protection. His compassion is revealed in a woman's womb, his nurturing nature in her breasts, and his protection through her "wings"—the maternal arms (1 Kings 3:20; 17:19).

Similar to God, a woman can conceive new life, bring that new life into existence, and nurture that new life. A woman who does this is simply and profoundly called *mother*. Of course, single women and women without children will not manifest this truth in their bodies, but they are able to manifest motherhood in their behavior, which reflects their transcendent nature.

Ann Crittenden summarizes motherhood well when she says it is simply "being there." She writes: "Mothers themselves often refer to the essence of childrearing as simply 'being there,' putting one's time at the disposal of another and signaling that the other's needs come ahead of one's own."[12]

Women, in the very fiber of their being, have been enabled to *nurture* and to *nurse*. *Nurturing* is the training and education of children, relating to the cultivation of mind and morals, as well as the training and care of the body. *Nursing* involves tending, suckling, cherishing, managing, and promoting growth. These concepts deal with the intimate relationship between mother and child. They include physical comfort, growth, and the reaching of potential. They also involve education, which deals with moral virtues as well as knowledge and wisdom.

Education is integral to nurturing and nursing. The mother plays perhaps the most critical role in the development of her children and thus the shaping of the nation. The words *nurse* and *nurture* speak of promoting growth, educating, instructing, and building virtue. The aim of education is *wisdom*, as Proverbs 1:7 indicates: "The fear of the LORD is the beginning of knowledge, but fools despise wisdom and discipline." Or as Proverbs 8:33–36 (emphasis added) says:

> Listen to my instruction and be wise;
> do not ignore it.
> Blessed is the man who listens to me,
> watching daily at my doors,
> waiting at my doorway.
> For whoever finds me finds *life*
> and receives favor from the LORD.
> But whoever fails to find me harms himself;
> *all who hate me love death.*

The reward of wisdom is life. Rejecting it is to "love death." The purpose of education is to create a nation that is wise, and in wisdom we find life. To give children a good education in manners, arts, and science is important. But to give them an education grounded in biblical principles is indispensable.

Succorer

Succoring is derived from the Greek word *prostasis*. Plutarch used *prostatis* to translate the Latin *patronus*: "a patron, someone who helps and defends a lower person, a protectress." According to Webster's 1828 dictionary, the word *succor* means "literally, to run to, or run to support; hence, to help or relieve when in difficulty, want or distress; to assist and deliver from suffering; as, to succor a besieged city; to succor prisoners."

Homemaker

A woman is the maker or creator of the home. She establishes the spirit that abides there.

She makes a home for herself, her husband, children, extended family, neighbors, friends, and even strangers. For a woman to create a home, she needs all the equipping she has as the *imago Dei*. Her calling requires all the artistic and intuitive reasoning powers God has given her.

Making and managing a home is not for the faint-hearted. It can include the following activities and more: communication, counseling, education and training, character development, gardening, interior decorating, investing, buying and selling, weaving and sewing, health care, evangelism and spiritual training, hospitality, charity and social welfare, cooking and baking, child-rearing and discipline, and household management and administration.

The caricature of lazy, stay-at-home mothers created by our money-focused culture does not match their incredible calling.

Maternal Feminists

The feminists of the second half of the nineteenth century and early twen-tieth century were focused on the home and child rearing. They understood that their children would someday inherit the world. They also understood that the home was the training ground of society. Maternal feminist Nellie McClung (1873–1951) states the creed of the movement: "A woman's place is in the home; and out of it whenever she is called to guard those she loves and to improve conditions for them."[13]

The mother has both a domestic focus and a public focus. Remember, the creation mandate was given to both the man and the woman. In their complementary relationship, they each had a place in the home and the public square.

Maternal feminists wanted to create a society that supports the family. They fought forces that undermined the family and threatened to destroy the nation. They opposed sweatshops and child labor and supported a family wage, temperance, and women's suffrage. The maternal feminists were very different from most current feminists. They were not fighting to get women into the workplace. They were fighting to get women *out of* the workplace and *into* the home, so that a woman was free to be a woman and do what she was made to do: nurture a nation.

In 1833, American poet and educator Lydia Sigourney published a book entitled *Letters to Young Ladies.* Her "letters" profoundly shaped an earlier generation of women and likewise shaped this chapter. She reminded women of their calling to nurture and educate future citizens and leaders. Sigourney reminded young women of the significance of this call. How might a young woman prepare herself for the high calling of the cultural mandate?

In the materially impoverished world there is little sense of nurturing a child for the future. And a selfish generation in the rich world thinks largely of personal fulfillment: *How might I have a child with the greatest of convenience, putting the child in daycare and getting back to "my career" as soon as possible?* These mindsets limit or demean the glory of female and motherhood and, in doing so, discount the motherly heart of God.

A mother, whether or not she is conscious of it, will pass on her values, virtues, and vices to the next generation. The questions are: *What ethic and knowledge will she pass on? Will she do so intentionally or "accidentally"? Will her family and children—or the marketplace and consumerism—be her priority?*

It is not only her children who inherit the results of her choices, but also the nation. Sigourney concludes: "If wisdom and utility have been the objects of her choice, society will surely reap the benefits. If folly and self-indulgence are her prevailing characteristics, posterity are in danger of inheriting the likeness."[14]

Will the mother invest her life in nurturing and educating her children both in wisdom and in practical knowledge? Will she put her children and family first, or will she be self-absorbed and put her own comfort and daily pleasure above all else? This choice will shape not only her children but, through them, the nation.

Nation Building

Such a concept is biblical. Examples of maternal influence on nation building abound in the Scriptures:

- Eve was "the mother of all the living" (Genesis 3:20).
- Sarah was "the mother of nations" (Genesis 17:15–16).
- Moses' mother (and nursemaid) sang him songs about the Hebrews' God and about Abraham, Isaac, and Jacob. While Moses was raised in Pharaoh's court as a prince of Egypt, the foundations for his life were laid by his mother.
- The unnamed mother of Lemuel taught him an oracle that shaped the young king's life (Proverbs 31:1–9).
- Mary, a faithful mother, raised our Savior to say, "My Father, . . . not as I will, but as you will" (Matthew 26:39).

A remarkable poem by American lawyer and poet William Ross Wallace (1819–1881) captures the profound influence that motherhood has on shaping the world. The title of the poem expresses the theme: "The Hand That Rocks the Cradle Is the Hand That Rules the World."[15]

Blessings on the hand of women!
Angels guard its strength and grace,
In the palace, cottage, hovel,
Oh, no matter where the place;
Would that never storms assailed it,
Rainbows ever gently curled;
For the hand that rocks the cradle
Is the hand that rules the world.

Infancy's the tender fountain,
Power may with beauty flow,
Mother's first to guide the streamlets,
From them souls unresting grow—
Grow on for the good or evil,
Sunshine streamed or evil hurled;
For the hand that rocks the cradle
Is the hand that rules the world.

Woman, how divine your mission
Here upon our natal sod!
Keep, oh, keep the young heart open
Always to the breath of God!

All true trophies of the ages
Are from mother-love impearled;
For the hand that rocks the cradle
Is the hand that rules the world.

Blessings on the hand of women!
Fathers, sons, and daughters cry,
And the sacred song is mingled
With the worship in the sky—
Mingles where no tempest darkens,
Rainbows evermore are hurled;
For the hand that rocks the cradle
Is the hand that rules the world.

Theodore Roosevelt, the twenty-sixth president of the United States, recognized the fundamental role that motherhood plays in the nation: "The good mother, the wise mother . . . is more important to the community than even the ablest man; her career is more worthy of honor and is more useful to the community than the career of any man, no matter how successful."[16]

Family: The Bedrock

The family is the bedrock of society. God gave the family the responsibility to create culture. Truth, beauty, and goodness are to be modeled and taught to children and (through children) to the larger society. The building blocks of kingdom culture are science, the arts, and ethics. One of the church's roles is to equip and support families for this task.

In a government of the people, by the people, and for the people, every citizen is important. At creation, God granted freedom. Free men and women must be inculcated in the principles and virtues of free societies. In a republic, society is governed, not by one person—a chief, king, or emperor—but by its self-governed citizens. A free nation will be shaped by the countless people whose names are not known by the society. Thus, each mother and child is critical to the nation's future.

Mothers are allies of legislators. The heart of the home will determine the heart of the nation. God's heart is passed to the heart of the mother and thence to the heart of the nation. Do the things that concern God concern the nation? The hand that rocks the cradle will make this determination.

Education and Character

The education provided by a mother is very significant. She will teach her child long before anyone else does. She shapes first impressions and sets the dreams that will be replayed in eternity. My good friend and colaborer Bob Moffitt often says that each child has been born to "write his or her signature on the universe." It is the mother who sets the child free to write on the universe. But what will the child write?

A mother is built to impart lessons to her child. As her milk gives nutrients for physical growth, so she also gives moral, spiritual, and intellectual instruction so her child may reach his or her God-given calling. What a contrast to a culture that puts a child into daycare so the mother may focus on her career. Who now will shape the dreams of her child? Who will "rock the cradle"?

The mind and character of the present generation will determine the mind and character of the next. Thus the natural human tendency to idleness and luxury must be fought. A young woman should order her life to receive the best education with its practical application; it is not merely about cramming facts for tests. The education must work toward wisdom, the godly application of the knowledge learned.

Why this care and preparation in motherhood? It is not merely about feeding children and plying them with toys and entertainment. No, we have here an immortal mind that will live for and shape eternity. These are ideas that shape the destiny of nations. Sigourney captures the indispensability of mothers in society: "While her partner toils for his stormy portion of that power or glory, from which it is her privilege to be sheltered, let her feel that in the recesses of domestick [sic] privacy, she still renders a noble service to the government that protects her, by sowing seeds of purity and peace in the hearts of those, who shall hereafter claim its honours, or control its destinies."[17]

While her husband toils to provide for his family, the woman is sheltered. She is protected, not for a life of ease, but for the critical task of nurturing the future citizens of the nation. While the government affords protection for her, she performs a noble service to the government. Her husband and the government create a protected space for her to fulfill her glorious calling. She is developing the character of future citizen-leaders, those who will "claim its honours or control its destinies."

God has brought forth the life of a child; now it is the mother's role to nurture that child's growth. She is to reign as a sovereign royal in the home and in the lives of her family. She has the significant responsibility to shape the destiny of her children and, through her children, the future of the nation. Historian, teacher, and writer Paula Giddings commemorates the impact of her mother on her life: "It was my mother who gave me voice. She did this, I know now, by clearing a space where my words could fall, grow, then find their way to others."[18]

Educator Dr. Elizabeth Youmans, who is a friend, raises an important question regarding the demise of nations: "So where would Satan come to destroy Christian civilization? He would come to assault the role of women, and he would say, 'Get out of the home, get the big job, put your children in childcare.'"[19]

Youmans continues: "The concept of [Career] Feminism has contributed to the destruction of healthy families and nations, because when women lose their sense of purpose as teachers of children and teachers of younger women, then by and large the next generation succumbs to a secular worldview and the goals of government education. Our rich Christian heritage and culture are lost, along with the divine identity of woman as primary teacher."[20]

Nations cannot survive and flourish without the virtue of motherhood. Their citizens will not have the requisite character, knowledge, and wisdom to govern a just and prosperous society. A well-ordered home will contribute to a well-ordered society. The role of the mother is to form character in her children. From the wellspring of character will come internal self-government. This will produce a well-ordered, just, and prosperous society.

In the Marketplace

As we have seen, the word "economics" is derived directly from the Greek word *oikonomia*, which means the management of the household for the larger good. The larger "house" is creation. The smaller house is the family home and property. God put us on this planet to manage his household through managing our own. The *imago Dei*, male and female, is thus "economic man."

We must make a distinction between *oikonomia* and *chrematistics*. *Oikonomia* is shaped by the biblical paradigm and is a *stewardship* economy based on nurturing human beings and natural resources to reach their fullest potential. It is a long-term process that seeks to benefit the entire community. On the other hand, *chrematistics* is shaped by the materialistic/secular paradigm and produces *consumer* or *money* economies. *Chrematistics* is self-centered rather than other centered. It seeks to manipulate people, property, and wealth so as to maximize short-term consumption for the individual.

These two types of economies will produce two very different results for the family and for the nation. It takes wisdom, long-term vision, commitment to community, and many other virtues to fulfill the economic mandate. Remember *oikodespoteo*—"to rule or manage the house"? A woman's management of the house is fundamental to the future and health of a nation.

Economists recognize three types of capital: natural, human, and manufactured. Experts estimate that 59 percent of the wealth in developed countries comes from human and social capital, only 25 percent comes from natural resources, and just 16 percent comes from manufactured capital. "This means that *in the wealthiest countries, human capital accounts for three-quarters of the producible forms of wealth.*"[21]

In other words, human capital is the primary resource, while natural resources are the secondary resources for a nation's health and development. Again, Ann Crittenden's perspective: "If most of our national prosperity reflects the productivity of our human capital, then the people who provide primary care to children are the single most important source of our most valuable economic assets. . . . Conscientious mothers are key players in the drama of economic growth, the stars who never receive top billing."[22]

Where is this human capital developed to its fullest? In the home! It comes from the hand that rocks the cradle.

Crittenden notes: "Without [a] conscientious mother, there would be no economic man. . . . Conscientious mothers, motivated by feelings of compassion and love, nurture, protect, and train children for adulthood. . . .

Conscientious mothers, in other words, are the contemporary practitioners of oikonomia: the building and preserving of long-term communal value that used to be the essence of economics."[23]

Mothers are the unsung heroes of healthy economies.

The Public Square

Nations will be ruled either by tyrants or by free women and men. Robert Winthrop (1809–1894), who was for a time the Speaker of the United States House of Representatives, understood that what happens in the home and other mediating institutions ultimately is played out in the larger society. In 1852, he wrote:

> All societies must be governed in some way or other. The less they have stringent State Government, the more they must have *individual self-government*. The less they rely on public law or physical force, the more they must rely on private moral restraint. Men, in a word, must necessarily be controlled either by a power within them or a power without them; either by the Word of God, or by the strong arm of man; either by the Bible or the bayonet. It may do for other countries and for other governments to talk about the State supporting religion. Here, under our free institutions, it is Religion which must support the state.[24]

Thus, freedom is God's gift to all men and women and is his calling for all nations. It was established in the garden of Eden (Genesis 2:15–17), reaffirmed in our salvation (Galatians 5:13–15), and is formed in us as we continue to abide in God's Word (John 8:31–32). Government of free women and men begins in the individual with the development of godly character. This self-government, then, is exercised in civil society. Lawyer, philosopher, and theologian Hugo Grotius (1583–1645) wrote:

> He knows not how to rule a kingdom, that cannot manage a Province; nor can he wield a Province, that cannot order a City; nor he order a City, that knows not how to regulate a Village; nor he a Village, that cannot guide a Family; nor can that man Govern well a Family that knows not how to Govern himself; neither can

any Govern himself unless his Reason be Lord, Will and Appetite her Vassals; nor can Reason rule unless herself be ruled by God and (wholly) be obedient to Him.[25]

British political philosopher Edmund Burke (1729–1797) observed: "Men are qualified for civil liberty in exact proportion to their disposition to put moral chains upon their own appetites. . . . Society cannot exist unless a controlling power be placed somewhere. . . . It is ordained in the eternal constitution of things, that men of intemperate minds cannot be free. Their passions forge their fetters."[26]

James Madison, the "Father of the Constitution" and the fourth president of the United States, pointed out: "We have staked the whole future of American civilization, not upon the power of government, far from it. We have staked the future of all of our political institutions upon the capacity of each and all of us to govern ourselves, to sustain ourselves according to the Ten Commandments of God."[27]

God has ordained four spheres of government. The most fundamental of these came before the Fall: the individual and the family, a collection of individuals brought together by blood and mutual commitment. Two more institutions were established after the Fall: the church and civil government. The order of these four spheres of governance is the individual → the family → the church (voluntary community) → civil government.

The health of all these institutions begins with the individual, not the state. It begins with internal self-government. Youmans writes: "The Christian principle of self-government is God ruling internally from the heart of the believer. In order to have true liberty, man must *willingly* (voluntarily) be governed *internally* by the Spirit and Word of God rather than by external forces. Government is first internal (causative), then extends outwardly (effect)."[28]

Where is the character of free men and women nurtured? In the home. Just as mothers nurture "economic man," so they nurture free societies. The home is the nursery both of the church and of free societies. Again, the hand that rocks the cradle is the hand that will shape the world.

Single Nurturers

What then is the role for single or childless women? What are the implications of motherhood for women who are not mothers? First, all women, by design and nature, reflect the motherly heart of God. Woman's maternal heart is God's gift of grace to each society.

Even though the ancient Hebrews exalted childbearing, Isaiah 54:1–3 speaks in expansive terms of the childless woman:

> "Sing, O barren woman,
> you who never bore a child;
> burst into song, shout for joy,
> you who were never in labor;
> because more are the children of the desolate woman
> than of her who has a husband,"
> says the LORD.

> "Enlarge the place of your tent,
> stretch your tent curtains wide,
> do not hold back;
> lengthen your cords,
> strengthen your stakes.
> For you will spread out to the right and to the left;
> your descendants will dispossess nations
> and settle in their desolate cities."

The barren woman may still shout for joy because she will have more children than biological mothers. In Hebrew culture, women would set up the tent. Here the woman is called to enlarge her tent, to expand her maternal influence to others who need nurturing and teaching. Those she influences will possess the nations that have been dispossessed.

A single woman's maternal heart may be expressed in:

- *The nuclear family.* She may be an older sister or an "aunt." My daughter, Mary Elizabeth, is a single medical student. But she is involved in her niece Breanna's life through going to tea and eating meals together, taking Breanna to her home to cook or bake together, and going on mini-vacations together.

- *The larger world.* She may be a godmother to a friend's child or a "big sister" to a child who does not have a mother, or she may adopt a child.
- *Friendships.* She may cultivate relationships with younger women to teach and model the transcendent maternal nature.

We also should remember that some women are called to a life of celibacy. They have a unique opportunity that married women do not have. Paul describes this in 1 Corinthians 7:34–35: "An unmarried woman or virgin is concerned about the Lord's affairs: Her aim is to be devoted to the Lord in both body and spirit. But a married woman is concerned about the affairs of this world—how she can please her husband. I am saying this for your own good, not to restrict you, but that you may live in a right way in undivided devotion to the Lord."

Being a wife and a mother takes time and is a sacred calling. But it is not the only calling. God calls some men and women to remain unmarried so that they may have "undivided devotion to the Lord." Let us also fully honor them.

What then are the God-ordained roles a women should hold in a world where she is treated as God intends? Men and women are inherently equal in their being. While their roles often differ, they are equal in value. Women have (and should have) expansive vistas. They are free to lead in the marketplace and the public square. They are free to lead in the family and the church, under the authority of their husbands or elders. By so doing, they bring the awesome (and desperately needed) feminine into the marketplace, the public square, the church, and the home. They provide servant-leadership that reflects the motherly heart of God.

Let us conclude with Lydia Sigourney's challenge to women to fulfill their highest calling:

> And now, Guardians of Education, whether parents, preceptors, or legislators—you who have so generously lavished on woman the means of knowledge—complete your bounty, by urging her to gather its treasure with a tireless hand. Demand of her, as a debt, the highest excellence which she is capable of attaining. Summon her to abandon selfish motives, and inglorious ease. Incite her to

those virtues, which promote the *permanence* and *health* of nations. Make her accountable for the character of the next generation. Give her solemn charge in the presence of men and of angels. Gird her with the whole armour of education and piety—and see if she be not faithful to her children, to her country, and to her God."[29]

Ultimately, we have seen that motherhood is a fundamental necessity for the health and development of nations. While the role of mothers is too often unseen and underappreciated, it is vital. Let us reverently encourage women to apply their maternal nature to nurture so that they may prepare the next generation.

It is time! Our challenge is to reclaim the dignity of women for the building and nurturing of nations. If we don't, heaven help both our homes and our nations.

I invite those who read this book to give constructive feedback that will help me grow and help to improve future editions of this book. We at the Disciple Nations Alliance also have a desire to get the book distributed wherever women are oppressed. If you find this book helpful, we welcome requests to translate, contextualize, and publish in other languages. See page 275 for Disciple Nations Alliance contact information.

Notes

1. C. S. Lewis, *The Last Battle* (reprint, New York: The Macmillan Company, 1967), 149.

2. Nancy Wilson, "The Woman as Mother," in *Family Practice: God's Prescription for a Healthy Home*, R. C. Sproul Jr., ed. (Phillipsburg, NJ: Presbyterian & Reformed Publishing, 2001), 55.

3. Mary Pride, *The Way Home: Beyond Feminism, Back to Reality* (Wheaton: Good News Publishers, 1985), xii–xiii.

4. Ibid., xxii (italics in the original).

5. Enola Aird, quoted in William Raspberry, "Mother Load," *Washington Post*, November 18, 2002; available at http://www.motherhoodproject.org/?p=58.

6. Ann Crittenden, *The Price of Motherhood* (New York: Henry Holt and Company, 2001), 45–46.

7. Ibid., 4.

8. Ibid., 11–12.

9. The Motherhood Project, "Call to a Motherhood Movement," October 29, 2002, http://www.motherhoodproject.org/?p=27.

10. Mark Steyn, "It's the Demography, Stupid: The Real Reason the West Is in Danger of Extinction," *The New Criterion* 24 (January 2006): 10 (italics in the original).

11. *Enhanced Strong's Lexicon*, s.v. "oikouros."

12. Crittenden, *The Price of Motherhood*, 72.

13. Nellie McClung, *In Times Like These*, 1915, http://timelinks.merlin.mb.ca/referenc/db0015.htm.

14. Quoted in Verna Hall, *The Christian History of the Constitution of the United States of America: Christian Self-Government* (San Francisco: Foundation for American Christian Education, 1983), 408.

15. William Ross Wallace, "The Hand That Rocks the Cradle Is the Hand That Rules the World," http://www.theotherpages.org/poems/wallace1.html (italics added).

16. Crittenden, *The Price of Motherhood*, 1.

17. Lydia Huntley Sigourney, *Letters to Young Ladies*, 4th ed. (New York: Harper & Brothers, 1837), 15; available at http://www.openlibrary.org/details/letterstoladies00sigouoft.

18. The Motherhood Project, "Celebrating and Honoring Mothers."

19. Elizabeth Youmans, personal communication, April 16, 2004.

20. Ibid.

21. World Bank, "Monitoring Environmental Progress," Washington, DC, 1995; quoted in Crittenden, *The Price of Motherhood,* 71 (italics in the original).

22. Ibid., 73–74.

23. Ibid., 68.

24. In Verna Hall, *The Christian History of the American Revolution: Consider and Ponder* (San Francisco: Foundation for American Christian Education, 1976), 20 (italics added).

25. Quoted in R.J. Slater, *Teaching and Learning America's Christian History* (San Francisco: Foundation for American Christian Education, 1960), 199, in Elizabeth Youmans, *The Christian Principle of Self-Government* (unpublished paper, 2005), 1.

26. In K. Fournier, *In Defense of Liberty*, vol. 2, no. 2 (Virginia Beach: Law and Justice), 5, in Youmans, *The Christian Principle of Self-Government*, 7.

27. In G. DeMar, *God and Government: A Biblical and Historical Study* (Atlanta: American Vision Press, 1982), 137–38, in Youmans, *The Christian Principle of Self-Government*, 7.

28. Youmans, *The Christian Principle of Self-Government*, 1 (emphasis in the original).

29. Sigourney, *Letters to Young Ladies*, 15–16 (italics added).

Glossary

American eugenics movement: A movement, beginning about 1890, espousing the genetic superiority of rich, white Americans over economically, socially, physically, or mentally challenged Americans and immigrants, leading to the involuntary sterilization of tens of thousands of American women in an attempt to protect American society.

androgyny: The sexual ideal established by philosophic monism. Since there is no transcendent distinction between male and female, individuals are free to determine their own sexual identity, including a fusion of masculine and feminine appearance, attitude, and behavior.

animism: A set of metaphysical assumptions that sees the world as ultimately spiritual and in which the physical world is animated by spirits or gods. In some cases the physical world may be considered an illusion. Man's highest good and ultimate goal is to return to spiritual oneness, while the physical is denigrated. Folk religions, Buddhism, and Hinduism are examples of highly animistic systems, but animistic beliefs can infect any worldview.

anthropomorphism: Attributing human characteristics, motivation, or behavior to inanimate objects, animals, or natural phenomena.

archetype: An original model or type after which other similar things are patterned.

atheism: Disbelief in or denial of the existence of God or gods.

atomism: The philosophy that "all is diverse!"; the belief that ultimate reality is a series of indivisible and indestructible particles. This is in contrast to philosophical monism. Atomism lays the foundation for sexism.

biblical complementarianism: The understanding that women and men, having been made in the image of the Trinitarian God, are equal in being, dignity, and value and are diverse in role and function. They were designed by God to correspond to or *complement* one another.

chauvinism: Activity indicative of belief in the superiority of men over women.

dowry: Money or property brought by a woman to her husband at marriage.

ecclesiology: The branch of theology that is concerned with the nature, constitution, and functions of the church.

egalitarianism: The belief in the moral equality of all human beings. When understood within the framework of monism, egalitarianism demands material equality in economic outcomes and the interchangeability of male and female.

Enlightenment, the: The Age of Reason. The period, following the Middle Ages, when intellectuals sought to free man from God's authority and established dogmas and free man for his own autonomy. One manifestation of this shift was the advent of deism, in which God was seen as transcendent but not immanent.

essentialism: The metaphysical theory that the essential properties of an object can be distinguished from those that are accidental to it. There is an essential nature to our sexuality, rooted in the transcendent nature of God.

evangelical feminist: Evangelical Christians who have either consciously or unconsciously adopted a modern feminist ideology.

exegesis: To bring *out of* biblical texts "the meaning the writers intended to convey and which their readers were expected to gather from it" (Walter A. Elwell, ed., *Evangelical Dictionary of Theology* [Grand Rapids: Baker, 2001], 611).

exposition: To make the meaning of the biblical text relevant to people today in their own cultural setting.

feticide: Destruction of a preborn baby in the uterus.

grammatical-historical approach: The approach to biblical interpretation that focuses on the *biblical texts* themselves. It uses disciplines such as linguistics, grammar, history, and archaeology and social, political, economic, and religious understandings in relationship to the specific text in order to answer the questions "What does the text say?" and "What does the text mean?" This was the framework of biblical understanding assumed by first-wave, or maternal, feminists.

hermeneutics: "The art of finding the meaning of an author's words and phrases, and of explaining it to others" (1828 Webster's Dictionary).

historical-critical method: The approach to biblical interpretation that focuses on the *authors* of the texts. "What were the authors thinking at the time they wrote the texts?" "What did what they wrote mean to *them?*" The presuppositions of modern secular skepticism were brought to a study of the Scriptures. This was the framework of biblical understanding assumed by second-wave, or modern, feminists.

imaging method: The approach to biblical interpretation that focuses on the *readers* of the texts and their perception of God. The question asked is, "What does this text mean to *me?*" This is the framework of biblical understanding assumed by current third-wave, or postmodern, feminists.

machismo: A culture that values male virility and male power and control over women.

maternal feminists: Active in the nineteenth and early twentieth centuries. Functioning from a biblical worldview or its memory, they were interested in *others*. Women were valued for both their being (fully human) and their function (nurturing nature and motherhood).

metanarrative: A comprehensive cultural narrative that orders and explains all of life and reality. It is a synonym for metastory or worldview.

metastory: A comprehensive cultural story that orders and explains all of life and reality. It is a synonym for metanarrative or worldview.

misogyny: The hatred or revulsion toward women.

modern feminists: Became active in the mid-twentieth century. Functioning from a secular, humanistic worldview, they were interested in *self*. Women were valued for their being but not for their function.

monism: The philosophy that "all is one!"; the belief in absolute unity, with no diversity. This is in contrast to philosophical atomism. Monism lays the foundation for sexual androgyny and ultimately sexual androgyny.

one-child policy: A law established in communist China in 1979 to control population growth, limiting all couples to one child. Fines, pressures to abort a pregnancy, and even forced sterilization accompanied second or subsequent pregnancies. This policy has been cited as one of the major causes of female infanticide in mainland China.

pantheism: Worship that admits or tolerates all gods; the doctrine or belief that God is the universe and its phenomena.

polytheism: Belief in many personal gods (who are ultimately impotent).

postmodern feminists: Became active in the late twentieth century. Functioning from a secular, humanistic perspective that believes there is no metanarrative, they are interested in overthrowing male and female distinctions. Their goal is interchangeability—androgyny.

postmodernism: A philosophic movement that is both postmodern era and post-Christian era. The basic assumption is that there is no metanarrative; rather, reality and meaning are personally defined.

radical feminism: A form of second- and third-wave feminism that seeks to redress the injustices of sexist oppression by diminishing or eliminating the uniqueness of men and women.

secularism: A belief system that sees the world as ultimately physical and limited, controlled by the blind operations of impersonal natural laws, time, and chance. Secularism renounces spiritual or transcendent reality. Also known as secular humanism, humanism, or naturalism, this is the increasingly prevalent worldview of the Western world.

sexism: Discrimination based on gender, especially discrimination against women.

sexist theology: Any theology, real or imagined, that purports that male is morally superior to female. Sexist theology seeks to justify emotional, spiritual, social, economic, political, and/or physical oppression of women.

shamanism: An animistic religion in which mediation between the visible world and the spirit world is effected by shamans.

teleology: From the Greek word *telos*. The study of design and ultimate purposes. Teleology asks such questions as "Why am I here?" "Where is history going?" "What is the purpose of my life?" "What was [a thing] designed for?"

teleonomy: The quality of purposefulness, in both structure and function, found in all living organisms.

theism: Belief in one God. This belief system sees the universe as ultimately personal.

tribalism: A strong feeling of identity with and loyalty to one's tribe or group.

Trinitarianism: One God, three persons of the Deity: Father, Son, and Holy Spirit.

tritheism: The belief that the Father, Son, and Holy Spirit are three separate and distinct gods, heretical from the perspective of orthodox Christianity.

unitarianism: A form of monotheism—belief in one God—that says there is a "single one" in the Godhead. This is the view of Islam and so-called Christian Unitarianism. This is in contrast to the Trinitarian form of monotheism that acknowledges the "combined one" of the Godhead.

Subject Index

abortion, 8, 27, 28, 29, 30, 57, 71, 73, 74, 76, 77, 243

absolute diversity, 12, 44, 46

absolute unity, 12, 44, 46, 80, 267

adultery, 31, 63, 182, 192, 206, 211, 212, 213, 214

AIDS, 22, 54

androgynous, 43, 75

androgyny, 12, 14, 75, 76, 81, 102

animism, 11, 41, 53, 190, 194

Aristotle, 41, 42, 44, 95, 102, 206

Ashtoreth, 192

atheism, 40

atomism, 12, 13, 41, 42, 43, 44, 45, 51, 102, 103

authority, 43, 44, 62, 79, 80, 88, 89, 98,105, 106, 107, 108, 113, 114, 115, 116, 117, 118, 119, 120, 178, 179, 180, 181, 219, 221, 222, 223, 224, 228, 230, 231, 260

Baal, 3, 171, 180,190, 191, 192, 193, 194, 199, 200, 201, 205, 208, 209

baalism, 213, 217

biblical theism, 43, 72, 74, 77

biblical worldview, 69, 71, 95, 208, 242, 275

Buddhism, 41, 42, 44, 53, 57, 58, 59

careerism, 242, 243

chauvinism, 13, 45, 81, 194

complementarian cultures, 47

complementarianism, 12, 40, 43, 44, 45, 88, 103, 217, 242

Confucianism, 62, 63

consummation, 161, 162, 163, 166, 168, 172, 187, 189, 204, 218

creation, x, 3, 43, 44, 76, 88, 94, 95, 96, 99, 100, 101, 107, 108, 113, 116, 118, 119, 120, 126, 127, 128, 130, 131, 132, 133, 134, 135, 150, 151,152, 153, 161, 162, 163, 164, 166, Chapter 12, 193, 197, 198, 204, 206, 208, 217, 222, 223, 226, 235, 238, 250, 253, 256

creation mandate, 125, 131, 133, 134, 174, 179, 250

dignity of women, 1, 2, 7, 12, 45, 71, 78, 79, 92, 98, 107, 168, 208, 217, 241, 242, 261

divorce, 23, 58, 76, 106, 194, 195, 213, 214

domestic violence, 21, 60

egalitarianism, 13, 45, 79, 101, 102, 119, 121, 131, 135, 243

environmentalism, 254

equality, 43, 46, 58, 75, 80, 99, 102, 103, 107, 109, 114, 116, 124,125, 131, 172, 216, 221, 227

essentialism, 128

Fall, the, 3, 91, 116, 133, 136, 171, 183, 185, 187, 189, 190, 219, 222, 227, 258

family, 4, 10, 13, 14, 16, 21, 30, 31, 32, 53, 56, 63, 71, 72, 74, 76, 78, 79, 96, 106, 107, 121, 129, 132, 134, 135, 168, 171, 181, 182, 195, 198, 199, 223, 224, 231, 242, 243, 247, 248, 250, 251, 253, 254, 255, 256, 257, 258, 259, 260

female genital mutilation, 28, 29, 43

feminism, 12, 45, 46,70, 71, 72, 77, 78, 81, 88, 103, 168, 172, 242, 243, 255
    evangelical feminist, 79, 80, 81, 106
    feminist cultures, 47,
    feminist movement, 72, 69,
    first-wave feminist,14, 71, 72
    modern feminism, 27, 75,
    postmodern feminism/feminist, 14, 74, 75
    postmodern feminist, 14, 74
    radical feminism/feminist, 2, 12, 40, 43, 44, 45, 52, 69, 70, 77, 78, 102, 106, 124, 139, 167, 168, 172, 178, 219, 223, 227, 242, 243, 245
    second-wave feminist, 14, 72, 73, 74
    secular feminism, 79, 80
    third-wave feminist, 14, 74, 79, 81
feticide, 29, 30, 57
Gnosticism, 95
Hinduism, 42, 44, 53, 55, 57, 58, 59, 95
homosexuality, 15, 43, 125, 168, 205
husband, 8, 10, 16, 21, 22, 26, 31, 32, 52, 55, 56, 57, 58, 59, 60, 61, 62, 63, 65, 71, 107, 119, 120, 121, 130, 132, 135, 136, 137, 141, 173, 177, 179, 180, 181, 182, 184, 187, 192, 193, 194, 195, 198, 199, 200, 201, 202, 203, 207, 208, 209, 218, 219, 221, 223, 224, 225, 226, 227, 228, 229, 230, 231, 232, 236, 237, 242, 246, 247, 248, 250, 254, 255, 259, 260
imago Dei, 15, 16, 17, 40, 43, 44, 46, 47, 50, 82, 88, 102, 103, 121, 125, 130, 173, 174, 175, 176, 180, 185, 193, 211, 225, 242, 250, 256
infanticide, 29,30, 55, 57, 205
infidelity, 184, 199, 205
ish, 16, 164, 173, 179, 193, 194, 201
ishshah, 16, 173, 179, 179, 202

Islam,28, 31, 41, 44, 53, 55, 59, 60, 61, 62, 96
Judaism, 41, 42, 96, 216
Kingdom culture, 63, 253
lust, 23, 58, 59, 187, 202, 213
machismo, x, 52, 53, 103, 124
marianismo, 52, 53
marriage, 7, 23, 31, 57, 58, 60, 62, 74, 76, 78, 106, 130, 136, 171, 179, 180, 181, 182, 183, 184, 190, 199, 200, 202, 204, 205, 213, 214, 219, 224, 225, 226, 227, 229, 230, 231, 232, 235, 236, 237, 238, 239
metanarrative, 3, 13, 50, 51, 90, 91, 95, 161, 162
metastory, 87, 92
misogyny, 2, 8, 13, 58, 69
monism, 12, 13, 42, 43, 44, 45, 51, 74, 79, 102, 103, 243
monotheism, 96
motherhood, 14, 70, 71, 73, 76, 77, 78, 243, 244, 245, 246, 248, 251, 252, 253, 254, 255, 259, 261
motherly love, 139, 143, 144
nation building, 247, 251
nurse, to, 148, 196, 248
nurture, 47, 125, 127, 128, 142, 143, 146, 210, 242, 244, 248, 249, 251, 255, 256, 258, 261
nurturing breasts, 143, 146, 148, 149
pagan humanism, 190, 194
Plato, 42, 44, 95, 102, 206
polygamy, 54
polytheism, 40, 41, 44, 96
pornography, 23, 24, 237
postmodern, 74, 75, 75, 77, 90, 127
poverty, 2, 26, 32, 49, 53, 73, 78, 163, 187
prostitution, 20, 23, 24, 25, 43, 72, 199, 205, 237

radical middle, 40, 41, 46, 88, 96

rape, 20, 21, 22, 31, 43, 119, 182, 184, 229

redemption ... 132, 133, 136, 161, 162, 163, 168, 172, 186, 187, 189, 200, 204, 205, 208

secular materialism, 75, 77

secularism, 11, 23, 72, 74, 90, 106

servant-leader(ship), 44, 108, 121, 180, 181, 224

servanthood, 112, 116, 119, 121

sex trade, 24, 59

sexism, 2, 3, 11, 12, 20, 40, 44, 45, 46, 52, 64, 69, 70, 71, 79, 80, 81, 88, 102, 107, 124, 139, 167, 168, 172, 178, 194, 201, 216, 219, 223, 228, 242

sexist, 11, 45, 47, 51, 65, 71, 81,102, 139, 140, 183, 205, 208, 217, 227, 230

sexist culture(s), 11, 45, 47, 205, 208

sterilization, 26, 27

submission, 3, 22, 107, 114, 115, 117, 118, 121, 137, 187, 226, 227, 229, 231

submit, 56, 101, 108, 120, 129, 132, 227, 229, 230, 231

subordination, 98, 107, 108, 111, 115, 116, 118, 206

theism, 11, 44

Trinitarian(ism), 3, 12, 13, 40, 41, 42, 43, 44, 45, 46, 51, 79, 96, 98, 102, 103, 114, 120, 131, 136, 166, 167, 172, 173, 182, 208, 217, 237, 242

Trinity, 2, 42, 46, 80, 93, 94, 95, 97, 98, 99, 100, 101, 102, 103, 106, 113, 114, 115, 116, 118, 119, 121, 129, 130, 150, 151, 167, 171, 176, 181, 225

tritheism, 96

Unitarianism, 41, 44, 96

unity, 2, 3, 4, 12, 16, 28, 42, 44, 45, 46, 80, 92, 93, 94, 95, 96, 98, 100, 101, 102, 103, 106, 124, 127, 129, 130, 131, 132, 135, 136, 176, 183, 222, 231

unity and diversity, 3, 12, 42, 44, 45, 46, 80, 94, 96, 98, 100, 101, 102, 103, 106, 127, 129, 130, 132

wife, 16, 19, 22, 24, 26, 32, 59, 62, 63, 71, 119, 120, 121, 132, 135, 136, 141, 150, 173, 178, 179, 180, 181, 182,183, 186, 187, 193, 194, 196, 197, 199, 200, 202, 206, 207, 211, 213, 214, 215, 218, 222, 223, 224, 225, 226, 227,228, 229, 230, 231, 232, 237, 260

worldview, 2, 7, 11, 13, 14, 15, 41, 42, 43, 45, 48, 50, 72, 77, 87, 90, 91, 92, 95, 124, 140, 150, 162, 255

Biblical Reference Index

Genesis

1:15, 43, 96, 97, 115,
  125, 129, 131,
  153, 166, 172,
  173, 174, 175,
  178, 187, 242
1-2:171
1-3:172, 189
2:7, 16, 115, 126, 133,
  135, 136, 166,
  174, 175, 176,
  177, 178, 179,
  180, 181, 182,
  183, 187, 202, 225
3:10, 43, 96, 97, 133,
  136, 163, 167,
  183, 184, 185,
  186, 187, 251
4:202
5:173
6:190
11:43
12:194
15-18:194
16:195
17:196, 220, 252
18:202
19:202
21:194
34:194
38:209

Exodus

19:142
19-24:179
20:179
20-23:179
21:193

22:193, 194
24:179
32:192
33-34:192

Leviticus

20:214

Numbers

11:196
14:192
22-25:209
25:193, 199
27:195
31:193
32:192

Deuteronomy

1:142
4:193
6:96, 183
22:214
24:193, 194, 214
31:202
32:142, 153
33:175
34:202

Joshua

2:209
22:193

Judges

2:192
4:196
19:193

Ruth

2:152

1 Samuel

1-2:194
2:209
25:196

2 Samuel

3:194
7:192
11:209
12:192

1 Kings

1:195
3:145, 248
11:194
14:192
16:193
17:196, 248
18:193

2 Kings

2:192
22:197

2 Chronicles

22:193
28:193

Job

31:145

Psalm

1:202
8:118
17:152
22:145
23:113
36:152
37:202
57:152

71:152
91:152
106:190, 193
115:175
121:175
139:145, 195

Proverbs
1:143, 198, 249
6:143
8:198, 249
9:198
31:78, 143, 197, 198, 230, 252

Ecclesiastes
3:119
5:193

Song of Solomon
1:203
2:203
4:203

Isaiah
1:193
42:142
44:96, 184, 195
46:142
48:202
49:142, 146, 237
52:111
54:179, 259
60:142
62:237
66:142, 143, 146, 148

Jeremiah
1:145
2:237

Ezekiel
16:162, 179

Hosea
1:200, 202

1 – 3:162, 179
2:193, 200, 201, 202
3:200
4:199
5:199
8:199
9:199, 193
10:199
11:179
13:199

Joel
2:196

Habakkuk
2:126, 184

Malachi
2:179, 195

Matthew
1:209
3:96, 97
5:213
11:115
12:212
13:212
15:213, 215
19:182, 194
20:115
23:142, 154
25:212
26:111, 115, 252
27:115, 215
28:97, 216, 220

Mark
1:96, 97
5:215
10:113, 214, 223
12:213, 230
14:115
15:215
16:216

Luke
1:209, 210, 215
2:153
3:96, 97
4:115, 212
6:216
7:212, 215
8:211, 214, 215
10:212, 215
13:142, 211, 212, 215
15:212
18:212
22:98
23:211, 215
24:216

John
1:88, 210
3:98, 111, 121, 115, 133, 151, 228
4:98, 115, 140, 211, 212, 214, 215
5:114, 115
6:114
8:114, 211, 212, 213
10:113
12:226
13:223
14:96, 98, 99, 114, 115
15:98, 115, 148
16:98, 99, 115
17: 98, 99, 108
19:215
20:216

Acts
1:220
2:133, 220
4:230
9:195, 221
16:221
17:133, 221
18:221

Romans

1:99, 184, 190
3:133
4:98
5:133, 136, 180, 185
8:115, 208
10:220
12:45, 81
16:221, 222

1 Corinthians

1:222
7:260
8:210
11:98, 115, 178, 180,
    181, 222
12:132, 133
13:95
15:98, 185

2 Corinthians

1:230
11:162
13:97

Galatians

1:145
3:11, 132, 133, 168,
    219
4:49, 148
5:133

Ephesians

1: 98
2:98
3:96
4:97
5:132, 136, 162, 179,
    180, 181, 182,
    202, 225, 226,
    227, 229, 230, 231

Philippians

2:108, 111, 115, 227
4:222

Colossians

1:210
2:49
3:230
4:222

1 Thessalonians

2:148

1 Timothy

2:133, 135, 136
3:180

2 Timothy

1:143, 222
2:180
4:221

Titus

1:180
2:230, 247
3:98

Hebrews

1:115, 210
13:180

1 Peter

2:220
3:137, 228, 230
5:108, 230

1 John

3:228
4:116

2 John

10:222

Revelation

1:220
5:220
13:113
17:223
19:162, 202, 223, 235
19-21:171
20:220

21:126, 142, 162, 217,
    218, 236, 237

About the Authors

Darrow L. Miller serves as vice president of Food for the Hungry International and cofounder of the Disciple Nations Alliance.

For over twenty-five years, Darrow has been a popular speaker at conferences and seminars on topics that include worldview and poverty, worldview and development, the Christian movement worldwide, Christianity and culture, Christian apologetics, and social issues. Before joining Food for the Hungry in 1981, Darrow spent three years working at L'Abri Fellowship in Switzerland, where he was discipled by Francis Schaeffer. He also served as a student pastor at Northern Arizona University and two years as a pastor at Sherman Street Fellowship in urban Denver, Colorado.

Two memorable experiences significantly shaped Darrow's vocational pursuits. The first occurred during a trip to Mexico, at age nineteen, when he first encountered poverty. The second happened while studying under Francis Schaeffer at L'Abri Fellowship in Switzerland, when he learned that Christianity is objectively true: it is reality, even if no one believes it. The combined effect of these two experiences has motivated Darrow to devote his life to serving the poor and hungry from a thoroughly Christian worldview.

In addition to earning a master's degree in higher adult education from Arizona State University, Darrow has pursued graduate studies in philosophy, theology, Christian apologetics, biblical studies, and missions in the United States, Israel, and Switzerland.

Darrow and his wife, Marilyn, reside in Blue Ridge, Arizona. They have four children and eight grandchildren.

Stan Guthrie is senior associate editor for *Christianity Today* magazine and author of the book *Missions in the Third Millennium: 21 Key Trends for the 21st Century* (Paternoster, 2005). He also worked with Darrow on the book *Discipling Nations*. Stan has been editor of *World Pulse* and managing editor of *Evangelical Missions Quarterly*. A guest on WMBI's *Mornings* and other radio programs, he blogs at stanguthrie.com. Stan and his wife, Christine, and their children live near Chicago.

About Disciple Nations Alliance

The Disciple Nations Alliance (DNA) is a global movement of individuals, churches, and organizations with a common vision: to see engaged, credible, high-impact local churches effecting real transformation in their communities and in sufficient mass to disciple their nations.

DNA was founded in 1997 through a partnership between Food for the Hungry and Harvest. Our mission is to envision churches with a biblical worldview and equip them to practice a holistic, incarnational ministry affecting all spheres of society. We provide simple tools that enable churches to begin the transformation process immediately with existing resources—no matter how materially poor they may be.

If you would like more information about the Disciple Nations Alliance or our teaching and training resources, please visit our website: www.disciplenations.org.

Disciple Nations Alliance
1220 E Washington Street
Phoenix, AZ 85034
www.disciplenations.org

FOUNDING PARTNERS
Food for the Hungry International
www.fhi.net

Harvest Foundation
www.harvestfoundation.org